EAT

THY NEIGHBOUR

A HISTORY OF
CANNIBALISM

MARK P. DONNELLY AND DANIEL DIEHL

SUTTON PUBLISHING

First published in the United Kingdom in 2006 by
Sutton Publishing Limited

This revised edition first published in 2008 by
Sutton Publishing, an imprint of The History Press
Cirencester Road · Chalford · Stroud · Gloucestershire · GL6 8PE

British Library Cataloguing in Publication Data
A catalogue record for this book is available from the British Library.

ISBN 978-0-7509-4373-4

Typeset in Photina MT.
Typesetting and origination by
The History Press.
Printed and bound in England.

Both DANIEL DIEHL and MARK P. DONNELLY are authors, screenwriters and historians. Over the last decade, they have collaborated to create nearly one hundred hours of documentary television programming and have co-authored ten books, including *Tales from the Tower of London*. Their next book, *The Big Book of Pain*, also to be published by Sutton, focuses on the history of torture and corporal punishment.

All spirits are enslaved that serve things evil.

Percy Bysshe Shelley

Contents

Acknowledgements

The authors would like to thank Christopher Feeney, our editor at Sutton Publishing, for his continued support of our work. A special thanks to Martin Smith, author of *River of Blood*, for helping us find some amazingly obscure dates and places. Thanks also to Matt Loughran for leading us to the Monty Python sketch, and to our photo researcher Peter Gethin.

 PART ONE

CULTURAL
CANNIBALISM

One

A Word of Warning: Cannibalism in Myth, Legend, Folklore and Fiction

Humanity's morbid fascination with cannibalism dates from well before the dawn of recorded history. Long before anthropologists and archaeologists found irrefutable evidence of early man's taste for human flesh the knowledge that human beings engaged in cannibalism was already embedded deep in our collective psyche. This inherent knowledge was incorporated into some of our earliest stories and handed down from generation to generation, probably as cautionary tales intended to warn listeners that there were some forms of behaviour that really must be avoided. But if cannibalism was too frightening and too alien for humans to contemplate, who then was it that might engage in such horrific behaviour and still escape the censure of law and social mores? It was, of course, the gods. Cruel, petty and pernicious, the ancient gods served not only as a source of awe and wonder, but provided a vast storehouse of cautionary tales meant to instruct mere mortals as to which behavioural patterns were best left to those who were ultimately above the law.

In the earliest Greek legends the god Cronos (better known as Saturn) was a member of an ancient race of violent and warlike giants called Titans: Cronos was, in fact, the son of Uranus (Heaven) and Gaea (Earth). Despite this enviable pedigree, Cronos was even more cruel and paranoid than the majority of his race. It was widely believed that he devoured five of his offspring in succession because he had been warned that one of them would eventually usurp his power. Obviously the story had a happy ending. Cronos' long-suffering wife (and sister) Rhea hid their sixth child – none other than Zeus – so that he could grow up in one piece and sort out his dad's little problem. Rather than simply kill Cronos, Zeus fed him an emetic that caused him to vomit up the rest of the kids who, amazingly, seemed none the worse for the experience.

A similarly gruesome Greek legend, and one with a far more cautionary element, tells the story of poor Pelops, who was murdered and cooked by his father, Tantalus, who thought he was such a clever fellow that he could serve human flesh to the gods and they would never know what it was. Obviously Tantalus was not as sharp as he thought he was, and the gods caught on to the ruse. Tantalus was properly punished and Pelops restored to life after his butchered body was returned to the cauldron in which it had been cooked. All a little silly, maybe, but even in the days of myth and legend cannibalism was seen to bring about serious repercussions. It also made a cracking good storyline, which was used again and again by classical Greek storytellers who had less interest in appeasing the gods than appeasing their audience. When the blind poet Homer wrote his immortal works, the *Iliad* and the *Odyssey* in the seventh century BC, he would have been hard pressed not to have included at least one story about someone who ate someone. In this case, a gigantic Cyclops named Polyphemus threatens Ulysses and his crew, devouring several of them before Ulysses outwits him, puts out his single eye and escapes.

Tragically, even in the civilised world of the classical Greeks, the phenomenon of cannibalism was not unknown in the real world. In the religious cult dedicated to the worship of the drunken, half-mad god Dionysus, the annual wine-fuelled revels frequently got far enough out of hand for crazed bands of female acolytes to attack young boys dressed as their god, tear them limb from limb and eat them raw. More than once the celebrants became completely demented and roamed the countryside, killing and eating any man who came within grabbing distance. To their credit, the Greeks were embarrassed by these unsavoury events, but stamping them out proved more than a little problematic. Still, cannibalism in general was seen as an awful thing and charges of consuming human flesh were often levelled against foreigners as an expedient way to make them look like barbarians. Such accusations were a device that would be used by successive societies for thousands of years to come.

At least one Greek, the historian Herodotus, was a little more understanding when describing the beliefs and practices among non-Greek societies. In the fifth century BC, Herodotus wrote his *Histories*, in which he described a variety of cultures, both real and imagined. In describing a people he called 'Issedones' who, he claimed, lived south of the Ural Mountains, Herodotus said, 'When a man's father dies, his kinsmen bring beasts of the flock to his house as a sacrificial offering. The sheep and the body of the father of their host are cut [up] and the two sorts of meat are mixed together, served and eaten.'

Herodotus tells a similar story about an Indo-European people known as 'Padaens' who had an even more direct approach to cannibalism, not waiting until the soon-to-be-dead had shuffled off the mortal coil before consigning them to the pot. He wrote, '. . . when a man falls sick, his closest companions kill him because, as they put it, their meat would be spoilt if he were allowed to waste away with disease. The invalid, in these circumstances, protests that there is nothing the matter with him – but to no purpose.' There seemed to have been a sexually specific aspect to this practice of the Padaens, because Herodotus insisted that if the sufferer was a woman it was her female friends who dispatched and devoured her and, likewise, males were eaten only by other males. While it all sounds a bit Monty Python, the Padaens were eventually identified as the Birhors, who did, indeed, kill and eat their dying. However, they insisted that it was only the immediate family who engaged in this peculiar rite because inviting non-family members to the memorial feast would have been sacrilegious in the extreme. This is a practice which is known to anthropologists as endocannibalism and is a concept which we will revisit in greater detail in chapter three.

Numerous other tribes, peoples and ethnic groups described in the *Histories* were credited with similar cannibalistic practices; virtually all concerned eating the dead in some form of memorial service rather than flesh-eating for its own sake. What is surprising – given the Greeks' xenophobia and insistence that cremation was the only respectful way to dispose of the deceased – is that Herodotus remained amazingly non-judgemental about the whole thing. He wrote, 'If it were proposed to all nations to choose which seemed the best of all customs, each, after examination was made, would place its own first.' A similarly lenient attitude was taken four centuries later by another Greek, Strabo, when he described the funereal customs of the Celts, who consigned their progenitors to the dinner table with the deepest dignity and reverence.

While the Greeks may not have devoured their dead, they did dispose of the body by cremation. This may seem entirely unrelated, but only if you do not firmly believe that the physical body must be preserved for a continued existence in an afterlife. This, however, was precisely the attitude of the ancient Egyptians and, in all likelihood, the beginnings of the Judaeo-Christian practice of burying the dead. Possibly through their centuries of contact with Egyptian culture, particularly during the reign of Pharaoh Akhenaton who is generally accepted as the first person to institute the concept of a single deity, the Hebrews came to believe that only the physical survival of the body could guarantee the person's eventual resurrection with the coming of the Messiah. Consequently, for the Jews, like modern Christians and followers of Islam, the bodies of the deceased were sacrosanct. To eat, or even to cremate, them could only be seen as the ultimate act of sacrilegious desecration. An early example of just how serious a matter cannibalism was to the Jews can be found in the Old Testament second Book of Kings, chapter 6, verses 24–30, which are excerpted and condensed, below.

> [24] And it came to pass . . . that [the] king of Syria . . . went up and besieged Samaria. [25] And there was a great famine in Samaria: and, behold, they besieged it until an ass's head was sold for four-score pieces of silver . . . [26] And as the king of Israel was passing by upon the wall, there cried a woman unto him saying, Help, my lord, O king. [27] . . . [28] And the king said unto her, What aileth thee? And she answered, This woman said unto me, Give thy son, that we may eat him today, and we will eat my son tomorrow. [29] So, we boiled my son, and did eat him: and I said unto her on the next day, Give thy son, that we may eat him: and she hath hid her son. [30] And it came to pass, when the king heard the words of the woman, that he rent his clothes . . .

Curiously, the act of cannibalism viewed with such obvious horror by the ancient Jews was, in a sense, incorporated into the most central tenet of the Christian religion, the Eucharist, or Holy Communion. Although the Eucharist will be dealt with again, in the next chapter, it is worth noting that in the Roman Catholic Church, the wine and bread used in the Communion are believed to literally transform themselves into Christ's body and blood in the mouth of the communicant through the miracle of transubstantiation. Instances of far more blatant acts of cannibalism also found their way into Christian legend. In the legend of St Nicholas, who became the patron saint of children and the progenitor of Santa Claus, the good saint is reputed to have resurrected two children after they were murdered, cut up and sold as meat by a pagan butcher.

No less an author than William Shakespeare also used cannibalism to intrigue his audiences in *Titus Andronicus*, and in Daniel Defoe's eighteenth-century classic *Robinson Crusoe*, the eponymous hero's friend, Friday, is introduced when he escapes from a band of fierce cannibals. In the 1960s, sci-fi author Rod Serling gave the subject a modern twist in his short story 'To Serve Man', wherein the true purpose behind a seemingly benign alien invasion is revealed when an alien book, whose title also served as the title of the story, proved to be a cookbook. Even children's literature is redolent with frightening characters who dine on humans, especially children. In *Jack and the Beanstalk*, Jack encounters a giant who bellows 'Fe, fi, fo, fum, I smell the blood of an Englishman. Be he alive or be he dead, I'll grind his bones to make my bread.' In *Hansel and Gretel* the abandoned children are lured into captivity by a wicked witch who puts Gretel to work sweeping and cleaning, while Hansel is kept in a cage where he is fattened up before being shoved into the oven. Even today the visage of the terrifying cannibal is never far from the best-sellers' list. In Thomas Harris's *Silence of the Lambs*, the character Dr Hannibal Lecter steals the show with the single line, 'A census taker once tried to test me. I ate his liver with some fava beans and a nice Chianti.'

A classic tale of cannibalism, based on numerous real-life sea disasters, came from the pen of Edgar Allen Poe. In Poe's 'Narrative of Gordon Pym' we read a fictionalised – and completely fantastic – account of a group of shipwrecked men who, after a series of disastrous adventures, are left to drift in a lifeboat without food or water. Nearing death, they agree to draw lots, the loser to be killed and eaten to ensure the survival of the remaining castaways. As we shall see in the next chapter of *Eat Thy Neighbour*, such nautical tragedies have happened more than once in real life.

If fictionalised tales of cannibalism have been employed to heighten the reader's sense of fear, the same device has been used in more than one instance of biting satire.

In 1728, Jonathan Swift, best remembered as the author of *Gulliver's Travels*, became incensed over the British Parliament's callous disregard for the plight of Irish peasant farmers. Due to increasing taxation, high rent and repeated crop failures, thousands of Irish were barely staving off starvation while others were actually starving to death. Rather than reduce rents to a level commensurate with a given year's harvest, the predominantly English landowners preferred to raise the taxes to compensate for the shortfall in crop sales. In a short tract generally known as *A Modest Proposal*, Swift wryly suggested a solution which he insisted would satisfy all concerned. If the Irish did not have enough money to feed their families, and the landlords were being deprived of their income because of their tenants' poverty, Swift suggested that the Irish sell their children to the landlords as a food source. In this way, he argued, the Irish tenant farmers would increase their income while simultaneously reducing the number of mouths to be fed. A small excerpt from *A Modest Proposal* will serve to illustrate Swift's vitriolic condemnation of British policy: 'I grant that this food will be somewhat dear [but not too much for the rich landlords] who, as they have already devoured most of the parents, seem to have the best title to the children. I believe no gentleman would repine to give ten shillings for the carcass of a good, fat child, which . . . will make four dishes of excellent nutritive meat.' Not surprisingly Swift was vilified by the British government. It would seem that starving the Irish was perfectly acceptable but even the suggestion of eating them was intolerable.

In a more recent context, the redoubtable team from the 1960s' *Monty Python's Flying Circus* took on the subject of cannibalism in a piece called the 'Undertaker Sketch'. In this sketch, a man brings his deceased mother – whose body has been stuffed into a large refuse sack – to a funeral home to make arrangements for her burial. Here is a portion of that sketch.

Undertaker:	Can I have a look? She looks quite young.
Man:	Yes, yes she was.
Undertaker:	Fred!
Fred's voice:	Yeah?
Undertaker:	I think we got an eater.
Man:	What?

Another Undertaker pokes his head around a door.

Fred:	Right, I'll get the oven on. (*Goes off*)
Man:	Er, excuse me, um, are you suggesting eating my mother?
Undertaker:	Er, yeah, not raw. Cooked.
Man:	What?
Undertaker:	Yes, roasted with a few French fries, broccoli, horseradish sauce.
Man:	Well, I do feel a bit peckish.
Voices from audience:	Disgraceful! Boo! (etc)
Undertaker:	Great!
Man:	I really don't think I should.
Undertaker:	Look, tell you what, we'll eat her, if you feel a bit guilty about it after, we can dig a grave and you can throw up in it.

A section of the audience rises up in revolt and invades the set, remonstrating with the performers and banging the counter, etc, breaking up the sketch.

What is interesting about this morbid bit of comedy is not that the Pythons would perform it; there was almost no subject they would not gleefully tackle. What is interesting is that even these brilliantly irreverent comics felt it necessary to ameliorate the effect of their own comedy by having the audience rise up in righteous anger and storm the set. Even here, the sense that there are bounds beyond which one must not tread is strictly adhered to.

Two

Ancient Origins:
Archaeological Evidence of
Cannibalism

lthough the earliest humanoid remains – found in Africa and dating from 3.5 million years ago – show how the human species originated and what our progenitors looked like, they are too few, and too scattered, to tell us much about the social structure in which proto-man lived. For such details we have to fast-forward three million years and travel to China. At a dig site known as Dragon Bone Hill, just south of Beijing, the plentiful remains of 500,000-year-old Peking Man show clear evidence that among the various food sources accessed by these early people were other humans; probably other members of their own genetic stock. This does not imply that human meat was a regular menu item, but when other animals were scarce, or the only available creatures were too fierce to tackle, members of less warlike clans may have been seen as easy prey. Cannibalism may not have been a practice of choice, but in times of need, any meat is better than none.

Evidence of cannibalism at Peking Man sites is similar in nature to that found at Gran Dolina in north-central Spain. Spain has proved the world's most fruitful site for the recovery of human remains between 1.5 million and 100,000 years old and a significant number of these sites have shown evidence of cannibalism. Other bones dating from 100,000 years ago, and providing nearly identical evidence, have been found in Krapina, Yugoslavia. Similarly, 12,000-year-old human remains found at campsites in Cheddar Gorge in Somerset show signs of cannibalism almost indistinguishable from those found in Yugoslavia, Spain and China. Nearly identical physical evidence has been found at innumerable campsites of Neanderthal man, but since there is wide controversy as to whether or not Neanderthal was actually a close relative of modern man or a dead-end offshoot of our family tree, his eating habits may not qualify in our argument. For our purposes, however, Neanderthal hardly matters because there is ample evidence that those who were unquestionably our direct ancestors did, indeed, eat each other. If this evidence is correct, it indicates that cannibalism was, to a greater or lesser extent, practised by human tribal groups in nearly every corner of the globe, over the course of hundreds of thousands of years. Of course, as many anthropologists argue, finding a heap of human bones – even when they are randomly mixed with the bones of game animals – is not viable evidence of cannibalism. The question now becomes: what proof do we have that ancient people were actually eating each other and not just rotting quietly away in a corner of their cave?

Among the first signs anthropologists look for when examining suspected sites of cannibalism are tool marks made when flint knives have been used to remove flesh from bone very shortly after death. While such marks may look like random scratches to the layman, to the trained eye they are as identifiable as a signature or fingerprints. Again, there are those who argue that defleshing is not proof of cannibalism. It may be that the flesh was removed from the bones of the dead and the skeletal remains reverently cleaned and buried or placed in an ossuary, or bone box. True again. There are many recorded societies that did exactly this and they were not cannibals, so we must look further for definitive proof of the practice.

The next piece in assembling our cannibalistic puzzle is determining exactly which types of bones are present in the spoil heap. In many cases, where the discarded bones are found at sites suspected of being field stops during a hunting expedition, it is only particular bones such as ribs, spine, hands and feet that have been discovered. The assumption here is that the meatier parts of the carcass were cut away and hauled home while the less savoury parts were left in the field. When it is the heavily fleshed long bones of the arms and legs that are discovered, they tend to be found at permanent campsites and randomly mixed with animal carcasses, all of which bear the marks of de-fleshing tools. In such cases these long bones often provide one more bit of telling evidence. The large knuckle ends of the bones have been crushed – as have corresponding bones of animal carcasses – in order to remove the protein-filled marrow. When these factors are combined they provide a preponderance of evidence that would surely stand up in any court of law. As a race, we are most certainly guilty of eating our neighbours. But if early man went around eating people indiscriminately, he would probably have eaten those closest to hand – the members of his own tribe – possibly beginning with those least able to defend themselves, the children and women. Had he done this, humanity would have died out in no time at all. In point of fact, there seems to be some evidence that Neanderthal was more than a little indiscriminate as to who he ate and we could conjecture that this might have been a contributing factor in his extinction. Obviously, if the human species was going to flourish, there had to be rules about who got spit-roasted and who did not.

One archaeologically substantiated instance of cannibalism, which has provided no clear-cut clues to the underlying cause, has left scholars scratching their heads in confusion and social activists shaking their fists in anger. It has only been a century and a half since the American Indian was the whipping boy for expansionist-minded white America, but in recent decades the Native American's past has been transformed into something sacrosanct. Now, the image of one of these supposedly peace-loving, spiritualistic tribes has been called into question by discoveries in Chaco Canyon, New Mexico, once the home of a people known as the Anasazi. The Anasazi flourished throughout the American south-west between AD 700 and 1300. During those six hundred years they developed a complex and advanced society that spread across Colorado, Arizona, New Mexico and Utah. Remnants of their culture can still be seen in the towering cliff dwellings at Mesa Verde and numerous other sites scattered across the Mojave Desert. The question of their disappearance has long troubled scholars and historians and, until recently, the accepted wisdom has been that a massive drought caused the Anasazi social structure to collapse. Certainly, there is ample evidence that as their population expanded they despoiled their land and hunted the game to near extinction. If this alone was not enough to raise the ire of those who believe the Anasazi were back-to-the-land-minded conservationists, recent evidence has caused one of the greatest social controversies since Charles Darwin proposed the theory of human evolution. Thanks to a mounting pile of physical evidence, many archaeologists and anthropologists have become convinced that the Anasazi practised cannibalism.

In 1994, the remains of seven dismembered bodies were found at an Anasazi site at Cowboy Wash, 40 miles east of Mesa Verde. All of these skeletal remains bore the distinct marks of defleshing and shattered bone ends described earlier as convincing evidence of cannibalism. Additionally, human blood residue was found inside fragments of cooking pots. Even more ominous were the human skulls that showed evidence of having been set on a fire to cook their original contents before being cracked open. While accusations of racism and political incorrectness were being thrown around, scientists continued to gather evidence; by the time they completed their research, similar remains had been gathered from no fewer than fifty Anasazi sites.

Most alarmed by these findings were members of the Hopi, Zuni and other Native American tribes who date their ancestry to the Anasazi. When a scientific symposium was held to discuss the Anasazi findings, the word cannibalism was excised from the conference's formal name. In a politically correct compromise, it was entitled 'Multidisciplinary Approaches to Social Violence in the Prehistoric American Southwest'. Dr David Wilcox, curator of the Museum of Northern Arizona, explained the problem succinctly when he said, 'Our understanding of the Anasazi is exactly parallel to what was thought about the Maya years ago – this advanced society, responsible for beautiful things, that now we realize was not a peaceful place.' Even Dr Wilcox, it seems, hesitated to use the 'C' word. There were those, however, who did not; among them were Christy Turner, professor of anthropology at Arizona State University and Richard Marler, a molecular biologist at the University of Colorado Health Services Center in Denver.

Turner not only followed all the established guidelines for proving cannibalism but added one of his own. 'Pot polish' is a term Turner uses to describe the shine given to bone fragments which have been continually stirred while being cooked in an earthenware vessel. Lo and behold, the human bones from the Anasazi sites bore the distinctive sheen of pot polish. For his part, Marler was asked to analyse a coprolite found among the remains of a cooking fire at one of the sites where human bones were discovered. 'Coprolite' is the technical term for preserved human faecal matter. According to Marler's tests, the Anasazi coprolites contained human myoglobin, a protein found only in muscle tissue. Although myoglobin is found in all animals, the myoglobin in each species of creature is unique and distinctive. In the coprolite Marler examined, not only was there human myoglobin, but there was a complete lack of myoglobin from any other species. In Marler's words, 'All we have found from the Cowboy Wash samples is human myoglobin – no other species. If you didn't eat human beings, this protein would not show up. This proves they put the meat in their mouths. They had a human meat meal.'

The burning question, of course, is WHY the Anasazi ate human flesh. Christy Turner believes the Anasazi were invaded by a group of Toltec Indians who were, indeed, cannibals. These invading Toltecs used torture, corpse mutilation and cannibalism to terrorise the Anasazi over a protracted enough period of time to destroy their civilisation. Others hold that simple starvation, brought on by a series of droughts and crop failures, along with the general depletion of game animals, may have led the Anasazi into cannibalism.

Whatever the reason, the controversy over Anasazi dining habits is sure to rage for years to come. Terry Knight, a Ute Mountain tribal leader who supervised the Cowboy Wash excavation, has a reasonable view on the matter: 'Like any other civilization, there were good, productive people, and there were bad people.' Southern Methodist University archaeologist Michael Adler puts it even more curtly when he says, 'This is not a happy past.'

What the Anasazi controversy makes clear is that most early societies, their geographic location and precise place along the time-line notwithstanding, were often unstable. When, for whatever reason, a society began to collapse, and the generally accepted rules of behaviour broke down, the prospect of cannibalism might become an appealing alternative to starvation or wandering aimlessly in the wilderness. Certainly, if drought or some other natural disaster killed off a succession of harvests, or the game died out or moved on, the neighbouring village, or the people next door, might start to look pretty inviting.

Three

Institutionalised Cannibalism:
Rituals, Religion and Magical Rites

I t was, in fact, the ancient Greeks – one specific ancient Greek – who first tackled the tricky job of identifying and classifying the phenomenon of cannibalism. In the fifth century BC, the Greek historian and chronicler Herodotus coined the word that is still generally accepted as the proper term for eating human flesh. The word is 'anthropophagy' and is a combination of the Greek words 'anthropos', meaning 'man', and 'phagein', meaning 'to eat'. Anthropophagy may not be as evocative as cannibalism but it is more technically correct and therefore the descriptive term of choice among historians, scientists and anthropologists. So, if anthropophagy is the proper, technical term for humanity eating its own kind, what then is the origin of the word cannibal?

That term was coined by the great explorer Christopher Columbus, no less, following his landfall in the West Indies island group known as the Lesser Antilles: what we now call the Caribbean Islands.

Among the tribes of the Lesser Antilles were a people who referred to themselves as 'cariba'. The Spanish explorers erroneously assumed this was their name for themselves when it was actually a descriptive noun meaning 'bold' or 'brave'. The Spanish had some trouble pronouncing cariba, and pronounced it 'caniba'. From caniba evolved 'cannibal' and once it was discovered that the 'cannibals' committed the ultimate sin of eating human flesh, the name of the islanders took on an entirely new, and more general, meaning. In the five centuries since Columbus' travels to the New World the term cannibal has been used to vilify nearly any culture seen as inferior, to describe those groups and individuals who consume, or have in the past consumed, human flesh, and to add titillating excitement to an endless litany of stories, both factual and fictitious.

But historians, scientists and anthropologists being, as they are, a precise lot, find that one term is not enough to cover the varying reasons for eating our own species. Under the general heading of anthropophagy there are the sub-classifications of 'endocannibalism' – eating dead friends or relatives as an act of respect – and 'exocannibalism' – the act of eating enemies slain in battle or killed as a sacrifice to some small and angry deity. It is worthy of note that in classifying the different types of anthropophagy, even science has fallen back on the common term 'cannibal'.

There are a variety of primary reasons why a society might practise cannibalism. It may be part of a ceremony meant to honour the dead; as a post-battle celebration in which the prowess of an enemy is absorbed by the victor; as a means of inflicting one final insult on a fallen enemy; as a desperate means of fending off starvation or to overcome a severe protein deficiency in the staple diet. Of course, there are also societies who eat people just because they like the taste. If a society eats flesh as a right of conquest (exocannibalism) or to revere the memory of the dead (endocannibalism) there is usually a religious aspect to the proceedings. Certainly there is an element of this concept in the Christian ceremony of Holy Communion particularly if, as those who follow the tenets of the Roman Catholic Church believe, the bread and wine used in the service quite literally turn into the blood and body of Christ through the miracle of transubstantiation.

In this chapter we will examine a number of first-hand accounts, provided by chroniclers, explorers and anthropologists, of exocannibalism, endocannibalism and just plain eating your neighbours; but all within social structures where cannibalism, in one form or another, is an accepted norm. Most of the societal groups we will encounter are, by most modern standards, primitive and warlike. In such societies, human flesh has often been considered little more than another form of booty to be shared out among the victorious. Because of the vast historical scope of these records and the number of instances and locales in which the phenomenon has been recorded, we cannot attempt an in-depth coverage of the subject. Rather we will present a few selective accounts, divided by geographic region.

One of the first verified accounts of martial cannibalism comes from the Roman historian and chronicler Tacitus. According to his *Annals* warriors of the Celtic tribes – particularly those in Britain – took the heads of their slain enemies and gave them to their priests, or Druids, who ate the brain believing that by so doing they would be imbued with the wisdom, knowledge and cleverness of the enemy. It is a pattern that we will find repeated with predictable regularity throughout the rest of this chapter.

The first contact of Europeans with cannibals in the New World came hand-in-hand with the discovery of the Western Hemisphere. Among the first people with whom Christopher Columbus' 1492 expedition came in contact were the Caribs mentioned earlier, and they routinely devoured their slain enemies. Another tribe of the same island group, the Arawak, who had not originally been cannibals, had taken up the practice as a means of revenging themselves on the Caribs. As the practice spread among the islanders, its battle-related significance dwindled. Where once it had been purely a victory right, it devolved into a simple shopping expedient. People were boiled, roasted, smoked, salted and eaten raw as an integral part of the Caribbean diet. The most popular way of preparing flesh was to roast it over a grill of green wood called a 'barbacoa', which has survived in the modern word barbecue. In essence, derivations of this term came to be used for both the grill and the meat that was cooked on it.

If the Spanish at first assumed the dining habits of the Caribbean people were a localised phenomenon, they revised their opinion after invading Mexico. In 1520–1 the Conquistador Hernan Cortez led a gold-hunting expedition of 550 heavily armed men into the land of the Aztec and encountered cannibalism on a mind-boggling scale. Because the Aztecs were wiped out by a combination of Spanish aggression and European diseases, most of what we know of them comes from contemporary accounts by priests travelling with the Spanish forces. Among the best of these accounts is that written by Fr Bernal Diaz, who was one of several dedicated priests who went to the new world in an attempt to convert the natives of Central and South America to Christianity.

Even as they entered Aztec territory, the Cortez expedition found half-devoured corpses scattered along the roadside and caged humans awaiting consumption. It is true that the majority of Aztec cannibalism was carried out in connection with ritual sacrifice, but the Aztecs were undoubtedly one of the most sacrifice-happy groups ever to inhabit the planet. In these ceremonies, the victim or, more often, multiple victims – frequently numbering in the hundreds or thousands – were paraded to the top of pyramid temples where their chests were cut open and their still-beating hearts ripped out. The bodies were then kicked over the edge of the pyramid to be divided among the people below according to social rank; the priest and noble class getting the revered internal organs, thighs going to the high council, and the commoners being left with the lesser chops and roasts. On particularly solemn occasions the king would eat a dish called 'man-corn' in which finely chopped flesh was mixed with maize meal and eaten during a religious ceremony. Sometimes the flayed skins of the victims were offered to the fertility goddess. Infants – who were obviously not prizes of battle – were offered to the rain god. There seemed no end to the number of reasons, and the number of gods to whom people were sacrificed, but the Aztecs always managed to gobble up the carcasses. The Spanish were told that in 1486 as many as 20,000 had been sacrificed and eaten over the course of a four-day religious orgiastic food-fest. When the Catholics challenged the fact that the natives sacrificed human beings to their gods, the Aztecs replied that yes, they did sacrifice their enemies to please and appease their god but – in a none too delicate reference to the Catholic communion rite – noted that the Spanish *ate* their god . . . and the Aztecs thought that practice barbaric. With mutual hatred now firmly established, the Spanish proceeded to declare all-out war on the Aztecs.

During a conquest nearly as bloody as the sacrifices practised by the Aztecs, Cortez saw many of his own men captured, sacrificed and devoured. Obviously, the result was a thorough demonisation of the Aztec and, by extension, nearly all the inhabitants of the New World. By 1530 many Europeans already had the sneaking suspicion that 'the only good Indian is a dead Indian'. It was a legacy that would follow the white man, and the Indian, into the colonization of what is now the USA and Canada.

Although the initial relationship between white settlers and Native North Americans was cordial enough, the continued mass incursion of whites into Indian Territory put a strain on public relations, particularly when the territory of the more aggressive, warlike tribes of the Great Plains started to be overrun. What most Europeans never understood was that the American Indian tribes had cultures as varied and diverse as the Europeans themselves. Some were peaceful farmers, traders and trappers while others were professional raiders, thieves and warriors. Although there were inevitably conflicts between white men and red men, only a few of the tribes routinely indulged in the cannibalism with which many of them were eventually charged.

Even before the Europeans encountered the really warlike tribes of the Midwest, there were encounters with tribes whose ferocity was almost beyond belief. The Iroquois were particularly aggressive and treated their prisoners with uncompromising cruelty. After extensive and highly creative tortures, prisoners were either beheaded and spit-roasted or simply roasted alive and eaten by the tribe at a celebratory dinner. The practices of the Iroquois were well recorded by a series of Jesuit priests who lived and worked with them over a number of years. The priests, presumably, managed to gain their trust. Other eastern tribes who practised cannibalism in one form or another were the Montaignes, the Algonquin and the Micmac.

Further west, the Dakota tribes were cannibals, but limited the practice to the bodies of fallen enemies who had performed particularly well in battle. Their hearts and livers – believed to be the seat of wisdom and courage respectively – were eaten by the victorious warriors who had engaged in the fight. The Dakota were very particular that only the bravest of their enemy made it to the table. To consume the body of a coward would have been disgusting. Along the north-west border of the USA, the Thingit, Tsinshuan and Heilsuk practised cannibalism, but only as a part of tribal magic. Other Native American tribes, particularly those in what is now Canada, often forced their prisoners to eat strips of their own flesh before being killed and butchered, as a means of inflicting one final humiliation.

The close association – for good or bad – of the white and native cultures brought about an inevitable degree of cultural cross-pollination. When the family of famous mountain man, Jeremiah Johnson, was wiped out by a Crow Indian war party, he went on a one-man revenge spree. Over several years, Johnson claimed to have killed 247 Crow and eaten every one of their livers. No matter how many braves and warriors were sent against him, Johnson killed them, leaving their liverless bodies as a calling card. Eventually, the Crow agreed to a truce. They would stop hunting Johnson if he would stop eating Crow.

If Europeans discovered numerous tribes of cannibals in the USA, their experiences in South America were equally disturbing; and because these encounters came hard on the heels of the discovery of Caribbean and Aztec societies, the belief that all Native Americans must eat each other disastrously influenced relations with more peaceful civilisations. A case in point is the encounter between Spanish Conquistador Francisco Pizarro and the Inca people of Peru in 1532–3, only twelve years after the conquest of the Aztecs by Cortez.

In a typically brutal and unnecessary attack, Pizarro and his soldiers destroyed the Inca capital, killed the cream of the imperial troops and took King Atahualpa captive. Atahualpa was told in no uncertain terms that he would bow to the power of Spain and adopt the religion of his conquerors. Despite being in obvious peril of his life, Atahualpa said he bowed to no man and told the Spanish exactly what he thought of their religion. His people, he said, only sacrificed their enemies to their gods and certainly did not eat people. The Spanish, on the other hand, killed their own God, drank his blood and baked his body into little biscuits which they sacrificed to themselves. He found the entire practice unspeakable. The Spanish were outraged and had Atahualpa publicly strangled on 15 August 1533.

The first objective account of South American cannibalism comes to us from a German sailor, Hans Staden, who was shipwrecked on the Brazilian coast only a few years after Pizarro's encounter with the Inca. According to Staden, the local tribe, the Tumpinamba, had taken a prisoner during a battle with a rival tribe. The prisoner was dragged into the village where he was subjected to the taunts and jeers of the local women, but was allowed to retaliate in kind, even being provided with overripe fruit and pottery to throw at his tormentors. Eventually, the tribal executioner appeared with a war-club and, after another exchange of insults, feints and parries, he proceeded to batter out the prisoner's brains, to the cheers of the crowd. The victim's blood was collected in ceremonial jars and immediately drunk by the old women and children of the tribe. According to Staden, 'Mothers would smear their nipples with the blood so that even babies could have a taste of it'. The body was then cut into quarters, roasted and eaten. Curiously, as barbaric as this sounds, it was purely ceremonial and only inflicted on a single representative of the enemy.

Although the example above took place nearly five centuries ago, the practice of cannibalism in South America, particularly along Brazil's Amazon basin, survived well into the twentieth century. The Cubeo tribe routinely made war for the specific purpose of eating captured enemies. In battles where more captives were taken than could be eaten at a single celebration, the excess meat was dried and saved for later. Those who were destined for immediate consumption were subject to a particularly horrible fate; their penis and scrotum were cut out, and worn over the genitals of the victorious warriors while they performed a celebratory dance. After the dance, as many enemy as were deemed appropriate to the size of the crowd were roasted and eaten. But it appears that not only the enemy found his way to the Cubeo table. When the mood struck them, they would dig up their own dead, who had been cremated before burial, grind up their bones, mix the powder with the local beer and drink it.

Other tribes along the Amazon who practised cannibalism but generally limited it to captive enemy warriors were the Tarianas, Tucanos, Tupi-Cuarani, Tupinamba, Panche and Paucura. The Paucura, who seemed to be gourmets, kept their prisoners caged for some time before consigning them to the pot or gridiron, fattening them up on fresh fruit and vegetables to improve the flavour of the meat. The Panche, who ate their enemies like the other tribes listed above, also ate their own firstborn in a gruesome fertility rite. Obviously, this kind of thing can get out of hand; the Tupi-Cuarani began practising cannibalism as a post-battle ritual, but decided they liked the taste of human meat so much that it became a routine affair. The same was true of the Cashibos who lived on the Brazilian/Peruvian border. They started eating their deceased parents as a sign of respect but eventually extended the practice to what can only be considered big game hunting. Cashibo hunting parties would lure hunters from other tribes into ambush by imitating the sound of birds and animals, turning the rival hunters into the hunted.

Some South American tribes were far more selective, and respectful, about who they ate. The Cocomas only ate their deceased relatives and friends, not only consuming their flesh but, like the Cubeo, grinding up their bones, mixing the powder with beer and drinking it. The Cocomas insisted it was a solemn gesture and that it was a far better fate to end up inside a warm friend than to be buried in the cold ground.

If images of fierce Amazonian tribes and bloodthirsty Aztecs have become an accepted part of history, the cannibalistic activities of certain African tribes have entered the realm of legend. Until relatively modern times, if you heard the word cannibal, the image your mind would most likely conjure up would not be Anthony Hopkins as the campy Hannibal Lecter, but a fierce, fat African chieftain watching gleefully while his henchmen tossed an English explorer – pith helmet and all – into a boiling cauldron. Like so much about cannibalism, it is an image based on half-truths twisted entirely out of shape.

Africa is a huge continent and vast areas of it have never experienced cannibalism, even though some Europeans bent on land acquisition and colonisation accused perfectly innocent tribes of the practice. Explorers such as Dr David Livingstone, and others equally famous, never once recorded an encounter with a cannibal. Those who did were probably exploring either the Congo or adjoining Cameroon, along Africa's western coast, both of which were hotbeds of man eating. Even those tribes that did indulge in the practice were often so particular as to the nature of their flesh eating that special cooking implements and pots were reserved for the purpose. Naturally, even those Africans who lived far from cannibalistic tribes were aware of the practice long before the white man set foot on their continent and this, like the encounter between Inca King Atahualpa and Francisco Pizarro, led to some awkward assumptions.

When Scottish explorer Mungo Park visited Africa between 1795 and 1797 it was almost inevitable that he encountered gangs of chained slaves awaiting shipment to the Americas. One of the things that struck him most was the slaves' firm belief that they were going to be eaten by their new masters in that faraway world. Park did his best to dissuade them of the idea, but discovered the reason for their fear was all too real. When slaves were sold to many West African tribes the cooking pot was, indeed, their ultimate destination.

Half a century later, French-American explorer Paul DuChaillu witnessed first-hand the reasons behind the queries that had been posed to Park. DuChaillu was in the territory of the Fang people in the Cameroon when, in his own words, 'I perceived some bloody remains which looked to me to be human, but I passed on, incredulous. Presently we passed a woman who solved all doubt. She carried with her a piece of the thigh of a human body, just as we would go to market and carry thence a roast or steak. In fact, symptoms of cannibalism stare me in the face wherever I go . . .' According to DuChaillu, when a Fang tribesman died, his or her body was simply sent to a nearby village to be chopped up and sold at the local market.

There seemed no ceremonial purpose to the practice beyond a convenient way to dispose of dead bodies. When there were not enough natural deaths to supply the demand for human flesh, slaves were purchased from outsiders and dispatched, like cattle, to the marketplace. The practice was so commonplace, and the locals so blasé about it, that when DuChaillu met the king of the Apingi people, his majesty presented him with a trussed-up slave, saying, 'Kill him for your evening meal; he is tender and fat, and you must be hungry.'

If the Cameroon was crawling with cannibals, its next-door neighbour, the Congo, was even more so. Even the most famous Congolese tribe, the Ubangi – once noted for their massive, ornamental lip plates – routinely ate the meat of slaves. We do not know which tribe, or tribes, in the Congo began the practice, but it seems that it was an idea whose time had come, and it quickly spread from one tribe to another, each giving it their own peculiar twist. Although no tribe claimed to eat raw flesh, some insisted that thigh steaks were best, others preferred arms, while some claimed that hands made the juiciest snacks.

German explorer Georg Schweinfurth toured the Congo and its environs almost constantly between 1869 and 1888 encountering, and recording, an endless stream of cannibalistic practices. Among the Azande the practice was so common that signs of it were everywhere. From trees hung shrivelled hands and feet, and skulls from past meals were displayed on stakes outside the huts. The Azande told Schweinfurth that almost no one was considered too good, or too bad, to be eaten, if the occasion arose. Enemies captured or killed in war inevitably went to the kitchen, as did any Azande who died unless their relatives went to extraordinary lengths to protect the body. On one occasion, Schweinfurth saw a one-day-old infant who had been left in the glaring African sun to die so it could be prepared for the evening meal. When Schweinfurth went off to explore the river Uele he encountered the Monbuttu tribe who, he insisted, were even more dedicated to devouring their neighbours than the Azande. Although the Monbuttu kept herds of cattle sufficient to supply their dietary needs, they still preferred human flesh, taking special pleasure in eating captured enemies. When an enemy warrior was taken in battle, Schweinfurth said, they were herded, 'without remorse, as butchers would drive sheep to the shambles . . . to fall victims, on a later day, to their horrible and sickening greediness'. King Munza of the Monbuttu made a notable concession to Schweinfurth's visit by insisting that no one should be seen eating human flesh in public as long as the white visitor was among them.

The Bambala, also of the Congo, preferred human flesh after it had been buried in the ground long enough to begin to putrefy. Another reported delicacy among the Bambala was a paste made from a mixture of human blood and flour.

Even the massive influx of Christian missionaries during the latter half of the nineteenth century could do little to stem the tide of cannibalism among the various Congolese tribes. The Revd Holman Bentley worked for the Baptist Missionary Society's outpost in the Congo for many years during the later decades of the Victorian era and reported numerous anecdotes concerning the local addiction to eating people. On one occasion, while Bentley and others were at dinner, they were interrupted by a young Boshongo chief, who asked to borrow a knife. To the horror of the missionaries, the man was later discovered to have used the knife to slit the throat of a slave girl and dismember her. When he was arrested, the chief had some of the girl's limbs, along with those of other victims, in a shoulder bag. It seems, however, that not all the local tribes went in for such a do-it-yourself approach to cannibalism. Some family groups, or perhaps several families, would pool their resources to buy a human haunch or even an entire, living slave who would be kept in a cage, fattened up and killed when he was judged ready for cooking. According to Bentley, 'The whole wide country seemed to be given up to cannibalism . . . They could not understand the objections raised to the practice. "You eat fowls and goats, and we eat men; why not? What is the difference?" The son of Matabwiki, chief of [the] Liboko, when asked whether he ever ate human flesh, said: "Ah! I wish I could eat everybody on earth!"' Bentley insisted on the veracity of these amazing occurrences when he wrote, 'This is no worked-up picture, it is the daily life of thousands of people at the present time in Darkest Africa.'

Towards the end of the Revd Bentley's African assignment, his assertions were upheld by Captain Sidney Hinde who served with the Congo Free State Force during much of the 1880s and 1890s. In his memoirs, Hinde wrote, 'What struck me most, during my expeditions throughout the country, was the number of cut-up bodies I found. Neither old nor young, women or children, are exempt from serving as food for their conquerors or neighbours.' It was a situation that would long outlast the easily shocked Victorian sensibilities.

As late as 1924, a Royal Society expedition to the Congo found conditions little changed from the previous century. According to their report, however, the tribes they encountered had a far more reverential motive behind their cannibalism than the ones discussed earlier. 'When a man died, the body was kept in the house until evening, when the relatives who had been summoned gathered for the mourning. When darkness set in, and it was felt safe to work without intrusion from inquisitive onlookers, a number of elderly women relatives of the dead man went to the place where the body lay, and cut it up, carrying back the pieces they wanted to the house of mourning, and leaving the remains to be devoured by wild animals. For the next three days, or sometimes four, the relatives mourned in the house in which the death had taken place, and there cooked and ate the flesh of the dead, destroying the bones by fire and leaving nothing.'

If this ritualistic approach to cannibalism seems much more purposeful than most of the examples cited above, it should also be noted that among the Doe tribe of Tanzania it was customary as late as 1900, when a chief died, that a stranger to the tribe was ritually killed and eaten in memory of the fallen chief. The unwitting parallel to Christian communion can hardly be missed.

Tragically, cannibalism for pure enjoyment survived in Africa until very recently. During the reign of Emperor Bokassa of the Central African Empire between 1976 and 1981, the imperial table was frequently graced with dishes made from the bodies of infants stolen from the families of Bokassa's political opposition. When Paul Bokassa was overthrown, his freezer was found to hold the bodies of dozens of field-dressed babies; whether Bokassa preferred baby meat or just saw it as one more way to terrorise his countrymen is a moot point. Almost simultaneous to Bokassa's reign, President Idi Amin kept Uganda in a constant state of terror with his continual 'ethnic cleansings' and political purges that reportedly took the lives of 300,000 to 500,000 of his own people. Like Bokassa, when Amin was overthrown in 1979, his presidential freezer was found to contain items more appropriate to a morgue than a food storage facility.

Continuing our anthropophagic safari eastwards, we move from Africa to the Far East. As we learned in chapter two, some of the earliest archaeological evidence of cannibalism has been unearthed at Dragon Bone Hill outside Beijing, China, but at half a million years of age Peking Man can scarcely be classified as Oriental and there are certainly no first-hand accounts of his dietary preferences. For that we must move to the north China kingdom of the Huns during the fourth century AD. There, during the reign of Shihu, dinner guests were served delicacies made from the most beautiful members of the king's harem. To demonstrate to his guests that he had not simply selected an ugly discard from among his many wives, Shihu had the girl's head displayed on the table during the festivities.

Half a millennium later, during the ninth and tenth centuries, Arab travellers returned from China with reports that human meat was routinely to be found in public marketplaces. The habit of cannibalism may have been fairly widespread among the tribes of China, because when Genghis Khan and his Mongols invaded Europe in 1242, they, too, were reported to be eaters of human flesh. Christian chronicler Ivo of Norbonne wrote that the Mongols ate their captives 'like so much bread'. Another chronicler reported that the Mongols ate nearly everyone captured in battle, male and female alike; the finest young women going to the officers' mess, lesser trophies going to the enlisted men. Evidently, the Mongols were not above eating each other when the necessity arose. John Pain del Carpine reported that when a Mongol army was under siege, one in ten of the enlisted men were sacrificed to feed the rest. Like the Arabs before him, Carpine also claimed that human flesh was a common dietary component throughout northern China during the Sung dynasty and that in the capital, Hankow, there were restaurants specialising in dishes prepared with human meat. Some of these reports must be taken with a pinch of salt, however. Most early travellers wildly exaggerated their experiences in foreign lands, and the fear of the Mongols was so great during their invasion of Eastern Europe that any claim – no matter how wild – would have been considered valid propaganda. Still, as recently as the 1890s, it was widely reported that Chinese soldiers fighting the French, in and around the Gulf of Tonkin, routinely ate French captives in the belief that it would stimulate their courage.

There must have been some validity in the reports of Chinese cannibalism because the practice is documented as having taken place on a fairly wide scale as recently as Mao Tse Tung's Cultural Revolution of the late 1960s. Anyone who had, or was suspected of having, any education at all was subjected to the most unspeakable torture and execution because they were 'enemies of the people'. After the hapless victim had met his grisly end, his liver was cut from his body and eaten raw by members of Mao's Red Guard as a public display of political correctness. Even as late as the 1990s, it was reported that physicians recommended that women having abortions, many of which were carried out in the seventh and eighth months of pregnancy under draconian one-family–one-child population control laws, should use the foetus as food for their families.

Some oriental cannibalism took place far from the vastness of China, cropping up in the isolated islands of the China Sea and the Pacific, so it seems only fitting that we now look at the dietary habits of the Pacific islanders who were among the most virulent cannibals in the world. From the reports of the earliest explorers we know that cannibalism was practised in the Solomon Islands, the Melanesians, New Guinea, New Caledonia, the New Hebrides, Guadalcanal, Bougainville and Fiji to such an extent that during the eighteenth and nineteenth centuries explorers simply referred to the area as the 'Cannibal Islands'. To understand the customs of the area it is only necessary to look at reports on the people of one island, Fiji.

It may be significant that, with the exception of ocean fish, the Fijians' diet was distinctly lacking in animal protein and this may have been a factor in the rise of cannibalism. It is equally true, however, that the Fijians ate their enemies out of revenge, their neighbours out of preference and were notoriously brutal to captives. Our earliest report, here, comes from the Revd David Cargill, a Methodist missionary working out of Rewa, Fiji. His diary entry for 31 October 1839 runs as follows:

This morning we witnessed a shocking spectacle. Twenty dead bodies of men, women and children were brought to Rewa [where] they were distributed among the people to be cooked and eaten. The children amused themselves by mutilating the body of a little girl. Mutilated limbs, heads, and trunks of bodies of human beings have all been floating about in every direction.

The following day, the Revd Cargill's entry said:

About 30 living children were hoisted up to the mastheads as flags of triumph. The motion of the canoes . . . soon killed the helpless creatures . . . Other children were taken, alive, to [the island of] Bau that the boys [there] might learn the art of Feegeean warfare by firing arrows at them and beating them with clubs. For days they have been tearing and devouring [the bodies] like wolves and hyenas.

Five years later, in 1844, another Methodist missionary named Jaggar made the following observation on the inhabitants of Bau who had so abused the young prisoners in the tale above. 'One of the servants of the king a few months ago ran away. She was soon, however, brought back to the king's house. There, at the request of the queen, her arm was cut off below the elbow and cooked for the king, who ate it in her presence.' Later, the Revd Jaggar recounted an equally horrible incident:

The men doomed to death were made to dig a hole in the earth for . . . an oven . . . to roast their own bodies. Sern, the Bau chief, then had their arms and legs cut off, cooked and eaten, some of the flesh being presented to [the prisoners]. He then ordered a fish-hook to be put into their tongues, which were then drawn out as far as possible before being cut off. These were roasted and eaten to the taunts of 'We are eating your tongues!' As life in the victims was still not extinct, an incision was made in the side of each man and his bowels taken out. This soon terminated their sufferings.

Numerous other stories of the Bau islanders could be added to these but, instead, we will move on to an account given by Alfred St John, an adventurer who visited Fiji in 1883. 'Such inordinate gluttons were some of these chiefs that they would reserve the whole . . . human body . . . for their own eating, having the flesh lightly cooked time after time to keep it from going putrid. So great was their craving for this strange flesh that when a man had been killed in one of their many bruits and quarrels, and his relations had buried his body, the Fijians frequently enacted the part of ghouls and, digging up his body . . . cooked it and feasted thereon.' It would seem, from St John's account, that the Fijians had a taboo against eating those who had died from natural causes, possibly as a precaution against whatever disease or bewitchment had killed the person.

In a rare epicurean insight, St John relates how the Fijians prepared human flesh for the table. 'The [body] was either baked whole in the ovens, or cut up and stewed in large earthenware pots. Certain herbs were nearly always cooked with the flesh . . . The cooks who prepared it and placed it in the ovens filled the inside of the body with hot stones so that it would be well cooked all through.' From St John's full accounts we gather that at least some victims were offered to the gods of battle, but this was not necessarily the case. In most instances people were just eaten because they were convenient. Still, whenever a special occasion arose, someone always seemed to be on the menu: 'No important business could be commenced without the slaying of one or two human beings as a fitting inauguration. Was a canoe to be built, then a man must be slain for the laying of its keel; if the man for whom the canoe was being built was a very great chief, then a fresh man was killed for every new timber that was added.' Inevitably, it seems, even St John had to comment on the goings-on at Bau. 'At Bau there used to be a regular display of slaughter, in a sort of open arena . . . In this space was a huge "braining stone", which was used thus: two strong natives seized the victim . . . and, lifting him from the ground, they ran with him head foremost – at their utmost speed – against the stone, bashing out his brains; which was fine sport for the spectators.'

As was true of Fiji, the people of Papua New Guinea were long known as dedicated cannibals. From as early as the 1500s we have an account from Portuguese sailor Jorge de Meneses, who discovered the island and named it Ilhas dos Papuas (Land of the Fuzzy-haired People), that something was not quite right here. But Papua New Guinea was so remote and inhospitable that it was not until the mid-1800s that white men established coastal communities and began pushing into the rugged interior.

Unlike many of their South Pacific neighbours, the Papuans seemed to have well-established rituals surrounding the consumption of human flesh. Enemies killed in battle were eaten to keep their spirits from returning and haunting those who had killed them, and also to absorb their fighting prowess. In some instances, the heads of slain enemies were hung above the door of the village 'spirit house' to drive away evil spirits and serve as a reminder to the womenfolk that they were not to enter the lads' clubhouse.

At the end of the nineteenth century, H.W. Walker, a Fellow of the Royal Geographical Society, wrote, 'The Papuans do not as a rule torture their prisoners for the mere idea of torture, though they have often been known to roast a man alive – for the reason that his meat is supposed to taste better thus.' After this enlightening culinary insight, Mr Walker went on to explain more of the Papuans' treatment of prisoners destined for the pot: 'In [battle] they always try to wound slightly, and capture a man alive, so that they can have fresh meat for many days. They keep the prisoners tied up . . . and cut out pieces of flesh just when they want them; we were told that, incredible as it seems, they sometimes manage to keep them alive for a week or more . . .'

In another account, the practices of a New Guinean tribe known as the Doboduras are described as follows: 'When they capture an enemy, they slowly torture him to death, practically eating him alive. When he is almost dead, they make a hole in the side of the head and scoop out his brains with a kind of wooden spoon. These brains, which are often warm and fresh, were regarded as a great delicacy.' A similarly grim account from the nineteenth century describes the funereal customs of an unnamed Papuan tribe: 'One of the tribes has the custom of taking out its grandparents, when they have become too old to be of any use to the tribe, and tying them loosely in the branches of a tree. The populace will then form a ring around the tree and indulge in an elaborate dance . . . As they dance, they cry out . . . "The fruit is ripe! The fruit is ripe!" Then . . . they close in on the tree and violently shake its branches, so that the old men and women come hurtling to the ground below, there to be seized and devoured by the younger members of the tribe.'

An equally bizarre custom was passed on to a western visitor by an old cannibal from the Purari Delta area. 'If I kill a man or a woman, someone else bites off his nose. We bite off the noses of people that others have killed. We bite them off, we do not cut them off. It is not our custom to eat a person we have killed ourselves,' he explained, saying that you could only eat someone who had been killed by another person. There seemed, however, to be a bizarre exception to this rule. 'If, after killing a man, you go and sit on a coconut, with also a coconut under each heel, and get your daughter to boil the man's heart, then you may drink the water in which the heart was boiled. You may eat a little of the heart also, but you must be sitting on the coconuts all the time.'

Cannibalism in New Guinea survived well into the twentieth century. In the 1950s, Tom Bozeman worked as a volunteer for a religious mission among the Papuans and reported a scene where one tribe paraded the body of a slain enemy in front of his friends and relatives, chanting 'We're going to eat him!'

which, to the shrieks and lamentations of the man's clan, they did. Another, similar report was given in 1956 by Jens Bjerre who noted that the Papuans were so protein-deprived that after burning the wild grass off a field, they would scurry around, snatching up the charred corpses of rats, mice, lizards and even smaller vermin, popping them into their mouths. As late as 1992 an ageing Papuan reminisced fondly about his days as a cannibal, insisting that human meat was 'better than pig or chicken . . . babies tasted like fish, the flesh was very soft'.

As the largest islands in the South Pacific, Australia and New Zealand seem to merit individual attention, particularly since the fierce Maori of New Zealand are among the best-known cannibal tribes in the world. The Maori seemed to have almost as many reasons to eat people as they had ways of preparing them. Dead relatives were consumed in solemn funereal rites and enemies were endlessly humiliated and tortured before being carved up, parboiled and consumed to ingest their fighting spirit and cunning. The first white man to take notice of the Maori was none other than that intrepid explorer Captain James Cook, who anchored his ship, the *Endeavour*, at Tasman Bay in 1769. In his log, Cook wrote, 'Soon after we landed we met with two or three of the natives who not long before must have been regaling themselves on human flesh for I got from one of them the bone of the forearm of a man or woman, which was quite fresh . . . which they told us they had eaten. They gave us to understand that but a few days before they had taken, killed and eat[en] a boat's crew of their enemies . . .'

In his log, Cook observed that the Maori did not practise cannibalism out of dietary necessity. 'In every part of New Zealand where I have been, fish was in such plenty, that the natives generally caught [enough to] serve both themselves and us. They also have plenty of dogs; nor is there a want of wild-fowl, which they know very well how to kill. So that neither this, nor the want of food of any kind, can in my opinion be the reason. But whatever it may be, I think it was but too evident that they have a great liking for this kind of food.' A century later, during the late Victorian era, an old Maori was equally sanguine about his people's eating habits. 'When you die, wouldn't you rather be eaten by your own kinsmen than by maggots?'

In nearby Australia, the Aboriginal natives had diverse and complex rules governing cannibalism that varied significantly from tribe to tribe. The most common and widespread practice was the consumption of enemy warriors, or those believed to be dangerous intruders, in a ceremony in which, as usual, it was believed that their prowess could be absorbed with their flesh. In 1933 an old chieftain from Yam Island remembered eating chopped human flesh mixed with crocodile meat which would, in his words, 'make heart come strong inside'. More savage were the Ngarigo who ate the hands and feet of slain enemies out of pure revenge.

To the tribes who inhabited the area surrounding what is now Queensland eating the flesh of one of your own tribesmen was an honour reserved for those of high status and may, again, have been seen to impart the power of the dead to his, or her, people. Similarly, among the Dieri people, the family portioned out small quantities of the deceased's body fat to close relatives. One Dieri tribesman explained, 'We eat him, because we knew him and were fond of him.' Sometimes, these funeral customs also had a more subtle purpose. In 1924, Australian Mounted Police Officers G. Horne and G. Aiston reported the case of an elderly, and rather stout, member of the Wonkonguru tribe who dropped dead of a heart attack during an emu-hunting expedition. Unexplained deaths among primitive people always carry the possibility of bewitchment, so the funeral dinner had a two-fold purpose. Those who knew and loved the man were celebrating his life by sharing his body, but should the person who put a curse on him partake of his flesh, they would die.

Officer Horne spoke to one of the deceased's elderly friends who insisted he had not really wanted to eat his friend's flesh, but felt he could not say no. In his words, 'Spose 'em me no eat 'em. 'Nother fella say, Him kill 'em. Me eat 'em, then all right.'

Among some Aboriginal tribes, the sacrificial killing and eating of newborn infants was a relatively common practice. Among the Kaura people it was purely a means of disposing of extra mouths during times of crop failure, drought or famine. Among the Wotjobaluk, however, it was only the second-born who was ritually killed, their flesh being reserved to feed the older child in the belief that this would make them stronger.

There is also evidence of less socially acceptable cannibalism in Australia: that which took place among the white population. During the days when Australia served as a vast prison for Great Britain, there was at least one case – which took place in 1822 – where a group of convicts escaped and remained alive in the Australian wastes by eating each other. The only one who survived to be recaptured was a man named Alexander Pearce who freely admitted his crime. No one believed him, so the next time he escaped, several years later, he took along another prisoner named Thomas Cox specifically to serve as provisions. On his final arrest, Pearce displayed a chunk of Cox to prove he had not been lying the first time. Pearce was hanged for his crime, as were the majority of people who have committed cannibalism in a society where it is not an acceptable part of the social milieu.

Four

Cannibalism in extremis:
Famine, Disaster and Warfare

T hus far we have examined cases where cannibalism was a cultural standard. That is to say, the members of a given society ate human flesh because it was an acceptable part of their culture. Let us now turn our attention to the other side of the coin. We will refer to this practice as cannibalism *in extremis*; eating flesh in extreme, or disastrous, circumstances for the purposes of survival, even if the culture of the individuals involved rejects cannibalism.

Not surprisingly, the majority of cannibalistic occurrences in modern times have come about as a result of desperate hunger. When there is no other food available and the difference between living and dying is determined by a person's ability to overcome the moral imprecations against consuming human flesh, morality usually flies out of the window. It may be that the thought of losing our thin veneer of civilisation frightens us as much as, if not more than, the act of cannibalism itself.

One of the earliest first-hand accounts of famine-induced cannibalism comes from medieval Egypt. In the years 1200–1, Egypt was stricken by a famine so massive that an observer named Abd Al-Latif – a physician living in Cairo – wrote that more than 500 people a day were dying in his city alone. Towns and villages everywhere were littered with the emaciated corpses of the dead. Eventually, driven mad by hunger, people were first reduced to eating the dead and later, to killing and eating each other, including their own children. Al-Latif wrote that he witnessed the bodies of children, gutted and dressed, hanging in public marketplaces, and claimed to have seen the roasted body of an infant being carried in a shopping basket. The authorities did their best to stem this wave of cannibalism; in the case of the roasted child, the parents were condemned to be burned. But when an individual is torn between the possibility of being caught and the certainty of starvation, the law holds little sway over their actions. Inevitably, when a society degenerates to this point, there are those who simply take advantage of the opportunity to indulge their perverse tastes regardless of need. Al-Latif claimed that even those who were rich enough to afford food often ate human flesh simply for the joy, or novelty, of it. In his account, Al-Latif recounts multiple instances where human heads and limbs were discovered simmering merrily away in some street-corner cauldron. Eventually, the practice of eating human flesh became so commonplace that some people continued even when the famine was over. As appalling as this seems, thirteenth-century Egypt was hardly an isolated case. At one point or another in the annals of recorded history, famine-induced cannibalism has been reliably documented in places as diverse as England, Ireland and Russia.

Worthy of note are famines that took place in the Ukraine in 1922 and in Russia between 1929 and 1931. Both were devastating on a scale impossible to imagine. Tens of thousands of peasants and townspeople went without food for months on end. Wallpaper was stripped from the walls and boiled for what nutritive value might be contained in the flour-based paste that held it to the walls. Even carpenters' glue was made into soup; anything to kill the pain of a stomach slowly digesting its own lining. The most tragic and psychologically damaging aspect of these famines is that they were both artificially created. The Ukraine had always been one of the most fertile farming regions in the Russian states, but when the Ukrainian people backed the White Russian government against the forces of communism, the Bolsheviks punished them by taking everything they could produce – including the seed grain for the following year's planting – to feed the Red Army. Similarly, the 1929–31 Russian famine was dictator Josef Stalin's way of punishing those peasants who resisted collectivised farming. The legacy of this political terror has resulted in a continuing blasé attitude towards cannibalism that haunts the remnants of the Soviet Union to this day. We will look at this tragic phenomenon in greater depth in the final chapter of this book.

It could be argued that cannibalism takes place during times of famine because of the nature of famine itself. Generally speaking, the food supply dwindles slowly, disease weakens the population, theft and violence become rife and the general fabric of society slowly unravels. But what happens when a few individuals are suddenly trapped in an extreme situation, deprived of food and, possibly, of water? Will the group's shared social structure and the threat of peer condemnation hold the brute instinct in check despite the threat of starvation, or will they, too, resort to cannibalism? The best-known examples of this type of survival cannibalism have been recorded in connection with disasters at sea and, in at least some well-documented cases, the strong will, indeed, resort to eating the weak in order to survive.

Among the best-known cases of cannibalism on the high seas is that of the French frigate *Medusa*, which foundered and sank in 1816 while on its way to Senegal. More than 150 survivors clung desperately to an intact section of the vessel's hull for days, slowly dying from their wounds, starvation and thirst. Inevitably, order broke down and the survivors began fighting among themselves. Some were murdered, their blood and raw flesh then being devoured by their attackers. When the raft was finally picked up only fifteen remained alive.

While not wanting to belabour the point of sea-related tragedies, there is one other shipwreck which, because of its legal ramifications, bears examination. In 1884 the 32-foot, English-registered sailing yacht *Mignonette* was being delivered to new owners in Australia by a skeleton crew of four. As the craft passed around the Cape of Good Hope, it foundered in a terrible storm and the crewmen were forced to abandon ship and take refuge in the lifeboat. Without food or water, and tossed wildly on stormy water, it was all Captain Tom Dudley could do to keep his three crewmen from panicking.

By the fifth day the teenage cabin boy, Richard Parker, was near death. A novice sailor, he had drunk sea water before anyone could stop him and was suffering severe dehydration, stomach cramps and diarrhoea as a result. Ten days later, the boy still clung to life but the rest of the crew were in nearly as bad a shape as he was. The other men discussed the possibility of killing the boy and devouring his blood and flesh to keep themselves alive. Taking the responsibility on himself, Captain Dudley stabbed the boy in the neck, collected the blood and passed it around. His heart and liver were cut out and eaten immediately and the rest of the meat was eaten over the course of four days, after which his carcass was thrown overboard. After twenty-four days adrift, the three survivors were picked up by a German schooner and returned to England.

During the voyage home, Captain Dudley wrote an accurate and detailed account of the experiences in the lifeboat, accepting any and all responsibility for his crew's actions. The arrest of the three men on charges of murder was not a surprise; legal form must be followed no matter what the circumstances. Certainly there was complete understanding among the general populace of Falmouth, where they landed and were being held, that what they had done to Richard Parker was not a matter of choice, but of simple survival. A legal defence fund was even established to help defray their court costs and they had the good wishes of the local press. But the law took its course, the men were prosecuted, and the national press turned the whole thing into a circus, ladling out great dollops of macabre sensationalism for which the British press has become infamous.

The defence took the position that the laws governing civilised society, in this case the injunction against murder, were not always applicable in extreme situations. They also argued that after going so long without food and water the men were obviously not thinking clearly and could not be held responsible for their actions. And even if they were responsible, it was an accepted truism that the needs of the many outweighed the needs of the individual. It was a well-planned, well-presented argument with much legal precedence to back it up. The jury, however, thought otherwise.

In a part of their guilty verdict, the jury stated, 'A man who, in order to escape death from hunger, kills another for the purpose of eating his flesh, is guilty of murder although at the time of the act he is in such circumstances that he believes, and has reasonable grounds for believing, that it affords him the only chance of saving his life.' We can only assume that no one on the jury had ever been in similar circumstances. The judge was so distressed by the verdict that he appealed to the Crown to commute the sentence and Queen Victoria, in her wisdom, complied. After serving six months in prison the three men were released.

The sea is a vast and unpredictable place as, until relatively recently, was much of the earth's land area. Before the advent of railways and reliable roads, a person could become hopelessly lost only miles from home; and if you were hundreds – or thousands – of miles from home the situation could become desperate in a very short time. In 1846 a group of settlers, led by George Donner, set out from Utah towards the fertile hills of California. Included in the group were twenty-six men, fourteen women and forty-four children. Everything went well until mid-

October when a severe blizzard trapped the group in a pass high in the Sierra Nevada mountains. Some of the group decided to make do where they were, converting their wagons into makeshift cabins, while another contingent determined to press on, eventually reaching an abandoned cabin 5 miles further along the trail. It was more than two months later when two members of the Donner party slogged their way to civilisation, obtained help, and returned for their stranded companions. Of the original eighty-four pioneers there were only seven survivors in addition to the two who went for the rescue party. Amazingly, although the Donner party had been divided by 5 miles of heavy snow, and suffered almost identical deprivation, both groups had ultimately resorted to eating their dead companions in an attempt to stay alive.

With the passing of the age of sail there are now few tragedies at sea and, with the exception of vast national parklands, modernised countries retain few areas sufficiently remote to be considered a wilderness. Does this mean that cannibalism *in extremis* has become a thing of the distant past? It would seem not.

On 13 October 1972 a Uruguayan Air Force plane, chartered by an amateur rugby team from Stella Maris College in Montevideo, Uruguay, crashed in the Andes mountains while on its way to Santiago, Chile. On board were fifteen team members and twenty-five friends and relatives. Although only ten people died in the crash itself, many of the survivors were wounded, some seriously. While there was the random selection of snacks and drinks you would expect to find on board, there was nothing like the amount of food needed to sustain thirty people for an indefinite period of time.

Despite intensive air searches no trace of the plane could be found and the survivors began to fear they would not live long enough for help to reach them. The details of their horrific experience have been well detailed and are not of primary importance here, but the moral dilemmas they had to overcome to justify the consumption of their dead companions are of specific interest. All the survivors were staunch Roman Catholics and nearly all of them flatly refused even to contemplate cannibalism. Roberto Canessa, a medical student, argued that the dead were no longer human beings, that their souls were with God and what was left behind was just the same as any other meat. He also pointed out that it was the survivors' duty to their families, to God and to themselves to remain alive until they were rescued. Some agreed, but no one was willing to take the first step across the boundary into savagery. Finally, Canessa himself led the way. One of those who only reluctantly joined in the consumption of human flesh was Pedro Algorta, who justified what he was doing by comparing the act with Holy Communion, saying that Christ had sacrificed himself so that mankind could be saved and, in effect, their deceased companions were making a similar sacrifice. On 21 December, after seventy days stranded without food, the survivors were rescued by helicopter. No charges or public recriminations were ever levelled against the survivors.

The specific instances of cannibalism detailed above have all been concerned with societies or small groups of people trapped in an extreme and unusual situation in which they were forced to choose between eating human flesh or starving. Unlike the primitive, warlike societies encountered in the previous chapter, where violent conflict was an accepted part of the social structure and human flesh was just so much plundered booty, modern warfare can produce similar acts, but for entirely different reasons. The breakdown of acceptable behaviour, death and famine that visits war-torn countries can completely undermine social structures and, sometimes, lead people who normally abhor cannibalism to embrace flesh eating as either the only alternative to starvation, or out of an otherwise helpless desire to avenge themselves on a hated enemy. Obviously, when starvation was at the root of the phenomenon, it mattered little who was eaten. If, on the other hand, the motive was vengeance, it was the uniform, as much as the man inside it, that became the meal of choice.

An enlightening vengeful account comes from ninth-century Spain. When an invading army of North-African Moslems defeated a Spanish army at Elvira, near Granada, in the year 890, the Arab commander ordered the massacre of nearly 12,000 Spanish prisoners. Later, as so often happens in war, the Moorish commander was himself killed in a Spanish counter-attack. When his body was hauled into Elvira, the furious widows and orphans of the town tore it limb from limb and devoured it.

During the First Crusade (1095–9) the combined armies of Christian Europe invaded the Holy Land in an attempt to wrest control of Jerusalem from the Moslems. An auxiliary contingent of European cannibals, led by a Norman nobleman, was attached to the Crusaders and used primarily to terrorise the Moslems, who believed that their bodies must remain intact after death if they were to reach heaven. In this instance, we might say that cannibalism was a means of humiliating the enemy even before they were defeated.

As late as the sixteenth century, the Uscochi tribe of the Balkans routinely ate their defeated Turkish enemies, steadfastly insisting it was only done to insult them. Similar claims have been made on behalf of Walachian Prince Vlad, or Dracula (best known as the inspiration for the mythical blood-drinking count), who lived in the same area and at the same time as the Uscochi. Even Sioux war-chief Rain-in-the-Face claimed to have cut out Colonel George Custer's liver after the Battle of Little Big Horn and eaten a slice of it, again insisting it was not done as an offering to the spirits; he just hated Custer.

The scant amount of historical evidence for cannibalism in Japan is hardly surprising; Japan was closed to outsiders until

1864 and what we know of Japanese culture prior to that period is still pretty much what the Japanese want us to know. There is, however, ample evidence of semi-institutionalised cannibalism among the Japanese military during the Second World War. Whether this behaviour was brought about because the Japanese still believed all non-Japanese were less than human, or simply a result of the appalling conditions under which Imperial Japanese troops were forced to live and fight is unclear. Some of the tales that follow, however, offer a disturbing glimpse of the possible answer.

The first documented evidence of cannibalistic behaviour among Japanese troops came hard on the heels of their invasion of New Guinea in January 1942. At Temple's Cross and Buna-Gona beach, Allied soldiers repeatedly found bodies of their fallen comrades scattered around Japanese campsites, their arms and legs missing and the charred remains of human flesh and bone scattered around the fire.

In 1945, Havildar Chandgi Ram, of the British Indian Army, testified that he had witnessed the Japanese downing of an American plane on 12 November 1944. According to Ram's testimony, 'About half an hour from the time of the forced landing, the [Japanese] beheaded the pilot . . . some of the Japanese cut flesh from his arms, legs, hips and buttocks and carried it off to their quarters . . . They cut it in small pieces and fried it.'

As the Japanese forces were steadily driven back from one island to another by Allied forces, they were cut off from their supply lines and frequently resorted to cannibalising their enemies, and each other, to stay alive. Still, there is ample evidence that the practice was carried out when there was no necessity. One Japanese soldier who surrendered to Australian forces early in 1945 claimed that he deserted after being ordered by his superior officer to report to the cookhouse to be slaughtered.

Another, incontestable instance of cannibalism came to light when an official order was discovered at an abandoned Japanese campsite. Here is the text of that order:

Order Regarding Eating Flesh of American Flyers
I.   The battalion wants to eat the flesh of the American aviator, Lieutenant (Junior Grade) Hall.
II. First Lieutenant Kanamuri will see to rationing the flesh.
III. Cadet Sakabe (Medical Corps) will attend the execution and have the liver and gall bladder removed.

Signed: Battalion Commander Major Matoba,
9am, March 9, 1945.

Major Matoba was later captured by Allied troops and admitted to the incident, adding this titbit of information: 'I ordered Surgeon Teraki to hurry up and remove the liver because I wanted to take it to the admiral's head-quarters . . . I had it sliced and dried . . . later on we all ate the liver at a party.'

*   *   *

It seems obvious, by now, that there are a vast variety of reasons why individuals and societies engage in the practice of cannibalism and in many of these instances there are stringent rules as to who may be eaten and for what reasons. To the person being consumed, the reasons are probably irrelevant, but to the consumer, they may be all-important.

In the first instance we examined acts of cannibalism in our ancient, prehistoric past as evidenced in the archaeological record. We cannot be entirely certain of the motivations for these acts, though we can conjecture that protein deficiencies, famine or religious ritual practices may have been at work. From there we examined cases of cannibalism which were part of a cultural norm. When one is a member of a culture where cannibalism lies at the centre of social or religious practices, all of that society are expected to eat people – but only those approved for consumption. Next we addressed the idea of cannibalism for survival, where flesh eating has been practised by individuals from cultures that normally condemn cannibalism, and yet their actions are understandable, forgivable or carried out under such extreme situations as to place them beyond the normal social restraints.

In all these cases we find situations – be they cultural, religious or desperate in nature – whereby we in the 'civilised' western world find the action of eating one's neighbours understandable, if not acceptable. The remainder of this book, however, deals with a different sort of cannibalism. This is an aberrant cannibalism performed by individuals who are members of societies which flatly condemn the practice. These are not cases of desperation, or of an acceptable ideological or religious belief. These are the acts of sociopaths, psychopaths and diseased minds . . . and these deviants will be our close companions for the remainder of this book.

 PART TWO

CASE STUDIES OF TABOO BREAKERS

Five

Keeping it in the Family:
Sawney Beane (c. 1400–35)

Life in Scotland has always been hard. Its climate is bleak, windswept and cold in the winter and its infertile soil too often results in crop failure. Throughout the Middle Ages life for the Scots was frequently worsened by the military adventures of the English who burned farms and villages and dispersed the people in an endless attempt to subjugate them. The overall result of such a harsh life inevitably led to an unstable society where violence and suspicion were endemic at the best of times; at the worst times murder – both random and institutionalised – and, on occasion, even cannibalism, were accepted as simply another of life's grim realities.

If Scotland was poor in most respects its people developed a rich tradition of storytelling. Scottish legends are still among the greatest folkloric treasures in the English language. One of the most famous of these stories is that of Sawney Beane (also spelled Sawny Bean) and his cannibal clan.

Most historians dispute the existence of Beane and his tribe, and it must be admitted that no records have ever been found to support the story. A part of the problem lies in the fact that, although the general story remains the same, its place in time has shifted from the early fifteenth century (during the reign of James I) to the end of the sixteenth century under James VI, who later became James I of England.

There is little doubt, however, that from time to time there were cases of cannibalism in the more desolate and remote reaches of Scotland. In his *Chronicles of England, Scotland and Ireland*, first published in 1570, Raphael Holinshed tells of a cannibal named Tristicloke who, according to the chronicler, 'spared not to steal children, and to kill women, on whose flesh he fed'. Although he gave no specific location for the tale, Holinshed dated Tristicloke's story to 1341. Later in the same decade as Holinshed published his *Chronicles*, Robert Lindsay of Pitscottie published a *History and Chronicles of Scotland*, telling a similar story of flesh eating, but dating his incident to 1460.

The first confirmed, written version of the story of Sawney Beane dates from Captain Charles Johnson's book *A General and True History of the Lives and Sections of the Most Famous Highwaymen, Murderers, Street-Robbers, &c.*, which appeared in 1734, but this too is probably based on a similar story which appeared thirty years earlier. The most popular, and generally accepted, version of Beane's tale is found in John Nicholson's *Historical and Traditional Tales Connected with the South of Scotland* which first appeared in 1834.

Today, many historians insist that the Beane tale was conjured up by the English as a means of demonising the Scots at the time of the Jacobite uprisings under Bonnie Prince Charlie. Certainly the accusation of cannibalism has often been used by a superior power looking for an excuse to subjugate a weaker society; in this case, however, the theory does not hold much water. When Captain Johnson first published his story, the Jacobite troubles were still in their infancy and, if his story was based on one three decades older, then the connection becomes even more tenuous. Add to this the fact that the majority of evildoers in Johnson's book are English, and the Scottish connection falls apart entirely.

It is our belief that, in a sense, the Beane story is true. There may never have been an individual named Sawney Beane, but his story is probably based on several similar tales, which appear to be factual. Over decades of retelling, the stories of man-eating hermits melded together in much the same way that the legends of Robin Hood and King Arthur were compilations of much earlier, fact-based tales, blended together to form a new, and more potent, story.

With this in mind, we have chosen the earliest possible date for the version of the Sawney Beane tale that follows. Not only does this roughly correspond with the time period of Holinshed and Lindsay's accounts, both of which more or less agree with the only hard date given in any version of the legends, that being Bean's supposed execution in 1435, but it is also likely that if the incident had taken place at the end of the sixteenth century the miscreants would have had a much harder time escaping detection and their deeds would almost certainly appear in the historical record. With these limitations in mind, here is the tale of Sawney Beane as we have pieced it together.

*   *   *

Sawney Beane was born in the county of East Lothian, 8 or 9 miles east of the city of Edinburgh, sometime between 1385 and 1390. He was christened Alexander, after his father, but like many of his countrymen he was gifted with a hefty thatch of red hair and people soon began referring to him simply as Sawney – the old Scots term for Sandy.

Although Alexander senior was a hard-working peasant who eked out a living as a hedge layer and ditch digger, from his earliest years Sawney exhibited a wild unruliness. At his best, the boy was bone idle; at his worst he bordered on dangerously violent. Eventually, Sawney took up with a girl who had a disposition very similar to his own, and together they were far worse than either of them had been on their own. Their brawling, stealing and half-savage ways ensured that they were constantly in trouble with both their neighbours and the law. In exasperation, Sawney's parents turned him out when he reached his late teens, assuming that he was old enough, and tough enough, to fend for himself. In no time, the other villagers followed suit and drove Beane and his girlfriend out of town, threatening dire consequences if they ever returned.

Now on the run, and possibly declared outlaws by the king's local agent, they robbed their way across the country, always only days, or hours, ahead of the forces of justice. Eventually they came to Galloway (now in south Ayrshire) on the south-west coast. It seemed an ideal place for them. Lonely and desolate, the landscape lent itself to furtive movements and provided dozens of hiding places where the law could never find them. Here, among the windswept dunes and rugged coastline, they decided to make their home, hiding by day and venturing out in the evening and early morning to prey on whatever unsuspecting travellers they could find wandering along the lonely tracks and roads that connected the isolated villages along the coast. Galloway was just the kind of place where people could disappear without anyone taking much notice.

Eventually, the Beanes discovered a cave located about half-way between the tiny villages of Lindalfoot and Ballantree near an outcrop of land known as Bennane Head. Situated at the foot of a steep cliff, the cave wound for nearly a mile inside Bennane Head, leading off into one dark, dead end after another and peppered with numerous rooms where they could make a home that was equally safe from prying eyes and the long arm of the law. Best of all, when the tide came in, the crashing surf surged into the mouth of the cave for nearly two hundred yards. No one would ever suspect that members of the human race could survive in such a place.

Their new home may have been safe and sound, but being confined to one spot presented certain problems to their livelihood as thieves. They might become known in the locality. To avoid being recognised and followed back to their lair, they could simply kill all their victims, but this still left them with the problem of disposal – not of their victims, but of the spoils. They could not take the money, weapons and valuables they stole to any nearby town to sell or trade for food and goods. This was a very small and isolated world. Not only were all strangers suspect, but someone would inevitably recognise the plunder as belonging to a friend or relative who had disappeared. But if the Beanes never went into a town or village, how would they get food? They could always steal cattle; cattle rustling was one of the most common occupations for Scottish outlaws, but it was also impossibly dangerous. A captured cattle thief was guaranteed to die on the end of a rope and this did not appeal to Sawney in the least.

The Beanes may have been morally deficient, and possibly even mentally under par, but they were not lacking in a degree of animal cunning and soon the solution to their problems became clear. They would no longer waylay and murder people for their possessions; they would simply use their victims as a source of food and thereby eliminate the need to dispose of their valuables. The first few dismemberings may have been a little distasteful even to Sawney Beane; but after a while it became routine.

Assuming that an average adult human being would render up about 60lb of edible meat, the Beanes could survive on a single kill for a month or more. But the speed at which flesh rots presented another problem. This time it was Mrs Beane who stepped in. To prove she was a good and thrifty homemaker she began to salt down the body parts with salt from the tidal basin, like any other meat being put up for the winter. Eventually, some parts were soaked in ocean brine and other tasty morsels hung over the fire to be smoked like a fine bacon or ham. Now, when Sawney had a particularly good day and brought home more than one victim, nothing would go to waste. And if pickings got slim out on the highway, there would always be enough food in the larder to see them through the lean times.

With life in the cave safe and secure, and assured of a plentiful supply of food, Sawney and his partner-in-crime settled down to produce a new crop of Beanes. And produce they did. Over the years – while busying himself with depopulating the countryside – Sawney and his mate propagated no fewer than fourteen children. In the fullness of time, these provided them with a collection of eighteen grandsons and fourteen granddaughters, presumably through conjugal combinations best left uncontemplated.

As the children grew up they naturally came to accept that anyone outside their own barbarous clan was to be considered as nothing more than a legitimate food source. What little education they received would have centred on the skills of the hunter-killer and, when they were old enough, they joined their dad in bringing home enough victims to supply the expanding number of mouths lurking inside the cave.

Undoubtedly, the populace around Lindalfoot and Ballantree were now wary enough of the lonely stretches of road between their towns that fewer and fewer travellers dared travel alone. This meant that the Beanes had to range farther and farther afield on their hunting expeditions and lugging home the kills required the help of the younger and stronger members of the clan. To make the most of their forays across Galloway the tribe began organising its attacks with military precision. Guards were concealed on hillocks and behind dunes to alert other members of the clan when likely prospects were coming their way, or when there were signs of trouble lurking over the next rise.

There were also rules of engagement. So long as there were enough Beanes in the hunting party, they could attack groups of travellers as large as four or five if they were on foot, but never more than two if they were on horseback. When the unwary passer-by came within range, the ferocious, feral Beanes would rush out of hiding, swarm over their victim, slit their throat and drag the carcass back to the cave, leaving little or no evidence of their passing.

It would seem likely that, over the years, someone would have seen this half-naked tribe scurrying across the landscape and assume these were the creatures responsible for the disappearance of so many innocent people. Undoubtedly this did happen. The only reason they did not report their findings is because they, too, became victims of the Beanes. For more than two decades Sawney Beane and his clan carried out their lonely, vicious guerrilla war against the people of the Galloway coast undetected and unsuspected.

Inevitably, as long as the Beanes remained at large, the populace lived in mortal terror. Fewer and fewer people travelled the roads, businesses that relied on outside trade began to collapse and people moved away. Each time a person failed to return home their grieving family reported their disappearance to the local authorities, who duly reported it to the King's Magistrates and from time to time soldiers came looking for the miscreants who were terrorising the area around Ballantree Bay. Sometimes they made an arrest. Strangers who still dared to come to the area were frequently arrested and taken in for questioning. If they failed to present a legitimate reason for their presence in the area, they were hanged, but still the disappearances continued. The occasional lynching by a fearful and paranoid mob brought no better results. Eventually, in utter frustration, the magistrates decided that the perpetrator had to be someone who lived in the area. The most likely suspects would seem to be the landlords of inns, who might follow any of their overnight guests on their travels, waylay them and dispose of the bodies. Consequently, a few of the more disreputable innkeepers in the area were taken into custody, questioned and executed, but it did nothing to quell the rash of missing travellers.

With so many mouths to feed, the Beanes' biggest problem now became not how to procure food, but how to dispose of the waste. The bones were piling up and threatened to fill the cave. To solve the problem the Beanes began to make bone disposal forays under cover of darkness, tossing the remains into the receding waves to be carried out to sea. Naturally, some of the body parts washed back on to shore when the tide returned. It did not take long for local people to realise they were dealing with far more than murder and robbery. The embedded smell of brine combined with the obvious marks of knives and teeth led to the inescapable conclusion that a tribe of cannibals had been operating along the coast for years.

The Beanes' first – and apparently only – mistake came one day in the spring or summer of 1435 when they waylaid a young couple returning along the coast road from a village fair some distance away. The man and his wife were sharing a horse, probably the only one they owned. The man rode in front, his wife behind, her arms around his waist. As they passed the point where the Beanes lay in wait, the clan jumped out, whooping and screaming, and dragged the woman from the horse before her shocked husband could react.

As she fell to the ground struggling, some of the clan members slit her throat, lapping at the blood as it gushed from her jugular vein, while others slit open her belly, pulling out her entrails as though they were field-dressing a dead animal. While the poor woman lay on the road, thrashing out her life, the stronger members of the Beane clan tried to pull the man from his horse. In terror, he jerked back on the reins, using the horse's hooves as weapons, scattering the Beanes and wounding some of them horribly in the process. In the confusion the man managed to draw his sword, slashing to the left and right, driving back his attackers. Eventually, the man would have succumbed or escaped but, as it happened, while the struggle still raged, another group of fair-goers – more than twenty in number – came along the road, causing the Beanes to scurry in all directions.

Shaken and terrified, the man babbled out his incredible tale, taking his rescuers to the spot near the edge of the road where the horribly torn remains of his wife lay in a pool of blood. Having no doubt that they had witnessed an encounter with the Galloway cannibals, the group escorted the sobbing man to Glasgow where he repeated his story to the local magistrates, his companions attesting to the truth of his statements.

The incredulous Chief Magistrate immediately sent a courier to the king at Edinburgh who, in turn, assembled a guard of 400 soldiers and set out for Glasgow. Four days later, King James I and his men arrived to hear the tale of murder and mayhem repeated yet again and asked the man to lead them to the spot of the attack.

For days on end the king, his soldiers and a pack of tracker dogs scoured the roads and lanes between Lindalfoot and Ballantree and all through the surrounding area, but to no avail. Finally, as they were tramping up and down the beach running along the base of Bennane Head cliff, some of the dogs made a dash for a narrow opening in the rock face and set up an unholy, howling racket. Seeing how narrow the opening was, and how far the water ran into the cave, the guards tried to drag the dogs back to the beach, but they refused to budge.

Finally, King James called for torches and ordered some of the men to investigate the entrance of the cave – at least as far as they could. Through the twists and turns of the cavern the men wandered, peering into one dark hole after another until they came upon a stench-filled room piled high with human bones. Some of the remains were obviously old, but others were fresh enough for bits of flesh still to be clinging to them.

Sending a runner back to the mouth of the cave, as many of the party as could scrambled inside, swords and halberds at the ready.

Room after room now yielded up their terrible secrets. In some were piles of half-rotted clothes, in others were stacks of swords, purses of money and other trinkets while in still others were human arms, legs and trunks hung from the ceilings and pickling in casks. It looked like a butcher's warehouse.

Once the horrified men composed themselves, they made their way deeper and deeper into the dank darkness until they encountered the Beane clan – shrieking and growling like trapped animals. The struggle was short and brutal, but the king's men eventually dragged twenty-seven savage men and twenty-one women out of the cave where they were securely chained for their return to Edinburgh.

While the prisoners were held under heavy guard, the soldiers removed the bones and body parts, burying them in a pit above the tide line where they were given as near to a Christian burial as was possible under the circumstances. Finally, with the small treasures culled from the piles of debris in the cave securely crated up, the party began working its way back to the capital.

The news of what had happened spread before them, and all along the way crowds of people, some fiercely angry, others gawping with curiosity, gathered to stare in wonder at the Galloway cannibals as they were hauled to justice.

Justice, when it came, was swift and merciless. Because their guilt was so obvious there seemed no need for the expense and delay of a trial. Certainly the nature and extent of their crimes had been witnessed by the king himself and as all justice was meted out by the king, a trial would have been superfluous.

After spending a single night in the Edinburgh Tollbooth, the Beanes were taken to Leith, now the site of Edinburgh's Leith docks. There, while the women were forced to watch, the men had their arms and legs struck off with axes and were left to bleed to death. The women were then chained, in groups, to three great stakes and burned alive like common witches. To the very end the half-savage Beanes expressed no sign of remorse for their crimes; rather they died shrieking curses at those who had finally brought an end to their horrible, twenty-five-year reign of terror.

Some versions of the story report that one of the grandchildren, a girl who was only one year old, was spared the flames to be fostered out to a home where she was brought up without any knowledge of her horrible beginnings. But medieval justice was harsh and unforgiving. When the girl reached the age of eighteen she was arrested, informed of who she was and where she had come from before she, too, was consigned to the flames.

No one knows how many men, women and children fell victim to the Beanes over the two and a half decades they roamed Galloway, if, indeed, they ever did, but the number stated in the legends is always 1,000. Considering the number of people in the clan, and the length of time they were active, the figure is not at all out of line.

Dreadful as this tale is, the legend of the Sawney Beanes has remained alive and still finds as many new and innovative ways of being adapted as it did while it was evolving into the story related above. In 1969 the tale was turned into a stage play, *Sawney Bean*, by Robert Nye and in 1977 horror-meister Wes Craven adapted Sawney's legend into the low-budget cult-classic film *The Hills Have Eyes*. There is currently a rock band using Sawney's name and the Scottish tourist industry busily markets the site of the Beane cave. According to the Ayrshire Tourist Board, if you travel along the A77 for 2½ miles south from Lindalfoot, you will come to a parking area. There you will find a sign leading down a steep trail to the half-submerged seaside haunt of the Beane clan.

There is also a traditional Scottish poem entitled 'The Ballad of Sawney Bean', which does a masterful job of preserving the legend. It is printed here in its entirety.

> Go ye not by Gallowa
> Come bide a while, my frein
> I'll tell ye o' the dangers there –
> Beware o' Sawney Bean.
> There's naebody kens that he bides there
> For his face is seldom seen
> But tae meet his eye is tae meet your fate
> At the hands o' Sawney Bean.
> For Sawney he has taen a wife
> And he's hungry bairns tae wean
> And he's raised them up on the flesh o' men
> In the cave of Sawney Bean.
> And Sawney has been well endowed
> Wi' daughters young and lean
> And they a hae taen their faither's seed
> In the cave o' Sawney Bean.
> An Sawney's sons are young an' strong
> And their blades are sharp and keen
> Tae spill the blood o' travellers
> Wha meet wi' Sawney Bean.
> So if you ride frae there tae here
> Be ye wary in between
> Lest they catch your horse and spill your blood
> In the cave o' Sawney Bean.
> They'll hing ye ap an' cut yer throat
> An' they'll pick yer carcass clean
> An' they'll yase yer banes tae quiet the weans
> In the cave o' Sawney Bean.
> But fear ye not, oor Captain rides
> On an errand o' the Queen

And he carries the writ of fire and sword
For the head o' Sawney Bean.
They've hung them high in Edinburgh toon
An likewise a their kin
An the wind blaws cauld on a their banes
An tae hell they a hae gaen.

Six

The Proof of the Pudding is in the Tasting: Margery Lovett and Sweeney Todd (1789–1801)

Occasionally a mythical character becomes so ingrained in the collective consciousness that we simply accept at least the possibility that they were real people: King Arthur, Robin Hood and, to some lesser extent, Sherlock Holmes all fall into this category. It is a rare thing, however, for flesh and blood people to become so mythologised and distorted by subsequent retellings of their lives, that the public at large assumes they had never been more than creations of fictional literature. But this is precisely what has happened in the case of Mrs Margery Lovett and her homicidal lover Sweeney Todd. How this reversal of reality took place is unclear, but maybe it has something to do with the fact that there was just a little too much 'flesh and blood' involved in their flesh and blood existence for them to remain comfortably among the habitués of reality.

Late eighteenth-century London was a hard place to get ahead in. The city's population had doubled and redoubled over the course of the century as industrialisation drove workers off the farms and sent them swarming into filthy, disease-ridden slums in search of work. To escape the horror of their lives, tens of thousands turned to drink – mostly gin – which was so cheap it was advertised as making you 'drunk for a penny, dead drunk for two'. With rampant poverty and alcoholism inevitably comes rampant crime and, again, London was the criminal's ideal haunt. Greasy smoke from factory chimneys and cooking fires combined with the mists rising from the Thames to blanket the city in a fog so dense that between early November and late March even a passing glimpse of the sky was considered a minor miracle. Thieves, robbers, cutpurses and murderers could ply their trade at will, slip around a corner and simply disappear under the heavy grey blanket of foetid air. Those criminals who were caught were dispatched with almost medieval brutality. In 1785 alone nearly 100 offenders were sent to the gallows at London's Newgate prison, most of them for such heinous crimes as stealing a loaf of bread or a piece of meat; lifted to keep themselves and their families from starving.

Among the budding denizens of this blighted underworld of crime and depravity was a youth with the unlikely name of Sweeney Todd. During the late 1770s, while still in his middle teens, Todd had already done time as a youthful offender in Newgate prison. Here he was assigned to serve as an apprentice to the prison barber in the hope that learning a useful trade would keep him off the streets and allow him to earn an honest living. Eventually the plan would work . . . at least in part.

Barbering during the eighteenth century consisted of far more than knowing how to give a man a shave and a haircut. Haircutting, in fact, was the least of the trade because most men simply cut their hair short and wore a powdered wig. Integral to the trade, however, were a variety of surgical procedures. Pulling teeth, 'bleeding' patients as a curative for a wide variety of minor ailments, as well as an array of lesser surgical procedures, which licensed physicians still thought to be beneath their dignity, were all in the purview of the barber-surgeon. To advertise their surgical abilities, barbers of the period displayed a pole with alternating red and white stripes;

the red representing blood, the white the bandages used to dress wounds. If this diverse bag of talents meant nothing else to Sweeney Todd, it provided him with both the knowledge of how to use a surgical knife and the perfect cover for his future occupation as homicidal maniac. A barber seen wearing a blood-spattered apron would not attract the least amount of public attention.

By 1785, Todd was out of prison and busily establishing himself in his dual occupation of barber and murderer. It was probably in this same year that he opened up his shop at 186 Fleet Street. The shop was located immediately east of St Dunstan's church; a short walk from St Bartholomew's hospital and only a few dozen yards from the Royal Courts of Justice. The courts were located at the point where Fleet Street changes its name to The Strand at the junction where it crossed a tiny alley known as Bell Yard. As was true of so much of London during this era, the area around the royal courts was a mixed bag comprised of regal splendour and abject squalor. The Strand, where the courts stood, was the home of the best and finest legal minds which London society had to offer. Less than 100 feet away, in Bell Yard and on Fleet Street, crime was so rampant that it was a heavy competitor with disease and rats as the most effective means of population control.

It was in this claustrophobic mixture of haves and have-nots that Sweeney Todd made a name for himself. His name, in fact, was painted over the door of his shop at 186 Fleet Street and beneath it were the words 'Easy shaving for a penny – as good as you will find any'. Almost as soon as the shop door first opened, Todd began practising his homicidal skills, but initially he did so off the premises. The first murder ascribed to him was committed at nearby Hyde Park Corner and the second, which took place on 13 April 1785, was boldly carried out on the pavement in front of his shop. An article in the next day's *Daily Courant* ran as follows:

A Cut-Throat Barber

A horrid murder has been committed in Fleet Street on the person of a young gentleman from the country on a visit to relatives in London.

During the course of a walk through the city he chanced to stop to admire the striking clock of St Dunstan's Church and there fell into conversation with a man in the clothing of a barber.

The two men came to an argument and of a sudden the barber took from his clothing a razor and slit the throat of the young man, thereafter disappearing into the alleyway of Hen and Chicken Court and was seen no more.

Since this entire grisly episode took place immediately in front of Todd's shop, one can only wonder why the constabulary of the time – the Bow Street Runners – failed to grill Todd, especially since he already had a criminal record and had served time in prison. Whatever the reason, it seems he was never questioned about the matter. Although Todd skated away from his first two murders, he must have sensed that if he continued his homicidal activities in public, sooner or later someone would see him and report it to the authorities. A change of venue, and tactics, was obviously called for.

How Todd came to discover that his shop stood over the old crypts of St Dunstan's church, the fact that the crypts and vaults were connected to a series of old catacombs and how he came to invent his notorious revolving barber's chair, are all matters open entirely to conjecture. What we do know is that before the end of 1785 he had installed the mechanism which would eventually make him infamous. Into the floor of his shop Todd fitted a trap-door, arranged so it would revolve on a centrally located pivot. The swinging section of floor was held in place by an iron bar that slid back and forth beneath the floor. When a lever in the back room of the shop was pulled, the bar withdrew, allowing the trap-door to fall open. On to this revolving floor panel Todd fixed two wooden barber's chairs – one on each surface – so that when the trap was sprung, one chair would fall backwards, heading downwards towards the basement vaults, while its twin would swing upwards to take its place.

The first customer known to have test-piloted Todd's chair was Thomas Shadwell. Shadwell was a local beadle, or watchman, employed by St Bartholomew's hospital. He was well known, well liked and well respected; he also had a particularly expensive watch and made the mistake of showing it to Todd. Had Shadwell been a regular at Todd's shop, or had it been a sunny day with lots of people milling around outside in Fleet Street, he might have had his shave and wandered off to work as he did every other day. Sadly, it was late evening, it was raining, a heavy fog blanketed the area and since Shadwell had never been to Todd's before, it was unlikely that anyone would ever connect him with the place. After settling his customer in the chair and complimenting him profusely on his fine watch, Todd excused himself, walked into the next room and pulled the lever attached to the bar beneath the floor.

Thomas Shadwell must have been more than a little surprised when the floor in front of him suddenly tilted upwards . . . his head and shoulders flew violently back, pitching him towards the floor. But of course the floor was no longer there. Shadwell – as would so many others over the years to come – fell backwards into the darkness of a subterranean crypt, landed on his head and broke his neck. Just in case a victim survived the fall, which about one in three did, Todd raced to the basement and slit their throat with his razor.

Initially, Todd stashed the carcasses of his victims in a series of vaults which led off the crypt beneath his shop, once he had removed their valuables, clothes and wigs, but this soon presented a problem. The bodies were beginning to pile up. A better method of disposing of them had to be found. Enter Mrs Margery Lovett.

Although no records exist to confirm the facts in the case, it is probable that Margery Lovett was born and bred in the same London 'stews' that created her associate, Sweeney Todd. What separated her from most members of the underclass of her day seems to have been her charm and determination to rise above her surroundings. Physical descriptions of her vary considerably; some reports say she was already plump, greying and middle-aged by the time of her arrest, while others say she was tall and slender with a mass of dark, curly hair and a fine, pale complexion. Whatever the case, it is beyond argument that she possessed charm and was more than ready to cash in on it to improve her social condition.

While still in her teens she had married a baker named Joe Lovett and learned his trade, which included making meat pies. When Lovett died unexpectedly a few years later, she took up with a 'Major' Barnet who dumped her when he fled London with the law nipping at his heels. Later, she became the mistress of a rich merchant who rented a house for her in the fashionable Covent Garden area. Sometime between 1786 and 1787 she took up with Todd who had already become rich on the booty left behind by the victims of his revolving barber's chair. Quick to recognise a golden opportunity when he saw one, Todd realised that Margery Lovett's talent as a pie maker could add more money to his already growing pile of cash while simultaneously providing an efficient means of disposing of his victims.

Todd invested some of his ill-gotten loot in a property located in Bell Yard directly across the street from the east front of the Royal Courts of Justice, and installed Margery as proprietor. In the basement of the shop he built a large furnace designed to supply heat for several baker's ovens with a capacity great enough to turn out batches of 100 or more pies at a time.

Accomplished in her trade, Mrs Lovett's veal and pork pies quickly became the rage of the neighbourhood and attracted a large luncheon crowd drawn mostly from among the judges, solicitors, barristers and clerks who worked at the courts across the street. Lovett dutifully churned out pies of all sizes from small individual-sized pies which sold for a penny to large, family-sized pies which patrons could take home with them to share with their loved ones as an evening meal.

At what point Todd suggested the use of his victims as a substitute filling for the pies, or whether it had been the plan from the day the shop was opened, is unknown, but obviously his partner in crime agreed to the abominable suggestion.

To facilitate moving the 'meat' from the basement of his shop to the basement of hers, Todd extended a tunnel from one of the westernmost crypts of St Dunstan's so that it crossed beneath Chancery Lane and ended in the subterranean bakery of the pie shop. Each time he dispatched one of his customers, Todd hurried to the cellars beneath the shop, stripped the victim of their clothes and valuables and carved them up like a side of beef. Amid the flowing fountain of blood, he lopped off the head and removed the entrails. He then skinned the carcass, removed the limbs and carved the 'meat' from the bones, all by the dim light of a candle or a small oil lamp.

The offal, heads and bones were carted to one of the crypts where they were heaped among the ancient coffins while the boxes of meat, along with the edible organs such as heart, liver and kidneys, were hauled along the dark, blood-spattered floor of the tunnel to a secret entrance at the back of the bakery. Here, Lovett carved the flesh into small pieces and boiled it until it was tender and ready to be mixed with animal meat where it became an invisible ingredient in the succulent pie filling. The fame of Mrs Lovett's cannibal pies is attested to by one of the earliest authors of the Sweeney Todd tale, Thomas Peckett Prest, who worked in Fleet Street at the time of the events and would have been familiar with the people and places involved. According to Prest's 1841 account:

> On the left side of Bell Yard, going down from Carey Street, was, at the time we write of, one of the most celebrated shops for the sale of veal and pork pies that ever London produced. High and low, rich and poor, resorted to it; its fame had spread far and wide; and at twelve o'clock every day when the first batch of pies was sold there was a tremendous rush to obtain them.
>
> Their fame had spread great distances, some even carried them into the country as treats for friends. Oh, those delicious pies! There was about them a flavour never surpassed and rarely equalled; the paste was of the most delicate construction, and impregnated with the aroma of delicious gravy that defied description; the fat and the lean meat were also artistically mixed.

As the popularity of the pie shop continued to grow, Margery Lovett was forced to hire assistants; a young girl helped wait on the customers who crowded around the horseshoe-shaped counter and a baker's helper was put to work in the kitchens below. While it is entirely possible that an assistant baker would be unable to tell human flesh from that of an animal, it has been suggested that if an employee became suspicious they soon joined the pile of hapless victims destined to become pie filling. One is forced to wonder, though, if there *was* a kitchen helper at the time of Mrs Lovett's arrest, why they were not called as a witness at Todd's trial.

For more than a decade and a half, Lovett and Todd grew rich in their unspeakable enterprise, throughout which they were apparently also lovers. Amazingly, there is no record of the two of them ever being seen together in public. The answer may lie in the tunnels and crypts beneath their respective shops. To keep their connection a secret, Todd only visited Lovett clandestinely; slopping his way through the bloody mud to her pie shop where they would retire to her lavishly appointed upstairs apartment and make love.

Their scheme began to unravel during the summer of 1800 when an unspeakable stench started to permeate the sanctuary of St Dunstan's church next door to Todd's barber's shop. Failing to find the source of the smell, the vicar, the Revd Joseph Stillingport, and the sexton called in the local beadle, Mr Otton. Although Otton was as mystified by the smell as the vicar and the sexton, he duly reported the incident to his superior, Sir Richard Blunt, head of the Bow Street Runners. In his report, Otton said the smell reminded him of rotting corpses, but the vicar had assured him that none of the crypts beneath the church had been used in decades. Blunt, however, decided to investigate for himself.

Accompanied by Otton, Blunt descended into the crypts beneath St Dunstan's. Although the crypt doors were sealed and intact, and there was no evidence that the sewers had backed up into the vaults, the rotten smell was so overpowering that the men had to cover their noses and mouths with cloths soaked in vinegar to keep from retching. Blunt retired from St Dunstan's none the wiser than when he had entered.

A few weeks later Blunt heard a strange report from another of his men who told him that a number of customers had been reported as having gone into a barber's shop at 186 Fleet Street and apparently failed to reappear. When Blunt located Todd's shop on a city map, he saw immediately that it was next to St Dunstan's church. What connection, if any, there might be between the stench in St Dunstan's and the supposed disappearance of Todd's customers, Blunt could not imagine – but he decided to post a team of constables in an upstairs room opposite Todd's shop to keep an eye on the place. Over the next three months at least three customers who went into the shop failed to reappear on the street. With this evidence – and a mounting pile of dark suspicions – in hand, Blunt decided to take another team of men and re-examine the vaults beneath St Dunstan's.

Prising open the long-sealed doors of one crypt after another, Blunt and his men were confronted by scenes of unimaginable horror. Piled around and on top of one coffin after another were mountains of bones, skulls and decaying entrails. Some had obviously been there for years while others still had relatively fresh flesh clinging to them. By the light of their candles, Blunt and his men followed a blood-soaked path from the crypt and found that it led in two directions. To the right, it came out beneath Todd's shop and to the left it wound its way beneath Chancery Lane and into the basement bakehouse of Margery Lovett's pie shop. The horrible, unthinkable truth dawned on Blunt and his men: Sweeney Todd was murdering his clients and sending their bodies to Mrs Lovett to be made into pies.

If further proof were needed, Blunt assigned one of his men to break into Todd's house when the barber was away and see what he could find, but cautioned him not to remove anything that might be used as evidence. When the constable reported back several days later, he read the names of a number of missing persons whose names he had taken from the inside of watch cases and the sweatbands of hats found stashed in Todd's closets. A furious Blunt immediately prepared to close in on Todd and Lovett.

A group of constables was rushed to Bell Yard with a warrant for the arrest of Mrs Margery Lovett and the seizure of the contents of her pie shop as evidence. When the men burst into the shop and read the warrant, customers at the counter, as well as a few curious passers-by who were drawn by the commotion, were first stunned beyond words and then thrown into confusion that quickly turned to rage. As the crowd grew, constables were afraid the swelling mob would grab Lovett and string her up to the nearest lamp post. Hustling their suspect out of the back door, they hailed a passing coach and sped her off to Newgate prison.

Inside the coach, wedged between two guards, Lovett broke down and began mumbling a nearly incoherent confession. Once safely inside Newgate, she asked to see the governor and said she wanted to make a statement. In the presence of the governor, a recording clerk and witnesses, she claimed that the real criminal was Sweeney Todd and that she was only his accomplice and had no intention of hanging alone. Although the original confession has been lost, a creditable version was later printed in the *London Chronicle* and runs, in part, as follows:

> Believing that I am on the edge of the grave, I Margery Lovett, make this statement.
>
> Sweeney Todd first conceived the idea of that mutual guilt which we have both since carried out. He bought the house in Bell Yard . . . and . . . excavated an underground connection between the two, mining right under St Dunstan's Church, and through the vault of that building.
>
> When he had completed all his arrangements he came to me and made his offer . . . I was willing.
>
> The plan he proposed was that the pie-shop should be opened for the sole purpose of getting rid of the bodies of people whom he might think proper to murder in his shop . . . He murdered many. The business went on and prospered and we both grew rich. This is how we fell to our present state.

The only question she posed to the governor was to ask if her confession could be used as evidence against Todd himself. The governor assured her that it could, and would, be so used.

While the distraught Mrs Lovett was stumbling through her confession, Sir Richard Blunt and his Bow Street Runners were preparing for their raid on Todd's barber's shop. Covering both the main and rear doors, Blunt and several constables burst into the shop and read out the warrant for Todd's arrest. Although he tried to bluff his way out of the mess, Todd was arrested, shackled and hustled into a coach, which was waiting to bear him to Newgate prison.

The frenzy that gripped London after the pair's arrest threw the city into turmoil and virtually destroyed the meat pie market for months to come. Sensationalised newspaper accounts – dubbing Todd 'The Demon Barber of Fleet Street' and inventing 'facts' where none had been released – made an already horrific situation even worse. Meanwhile, Blunt and his men stolidly began building a watertight case against the felonious pair. Although Blunt pressed for as early a trial as possible, his efforts in bringing the cannibal-pie-maker to justice would prove to be a case of too little, too late. A few days before Christmas 1801, Sir Richard was brought the news that despite her stated desire to turn King's Evidence against Todd, Margery Lovett had committed suicide in her cell.

How she obtained the poison with which she ended her life is not known, but it is likely that she had sent word to one of her servants to bring her a change of clothes, or some other necessity, and secreted among them was a small vial of poison. When the guards brought her breakfast at eight o'clock the following morning they found her dead. Not only had she escaped justice, but also left unanswered the nagging question of why she had agreed to be a part of the monstrous scheme in the first place.

In spite of the loss of one of his prime suspects, and the most creditable witness against Todd, Blunt forged ahead with the case. A full search of the barber's shop and the crypts below yielded up sufficient clothing, jewellery and skeletal remains to account for somewhere in the neighbourhood of 160 victims. Although nearly everyone in the city was well aware of the general facts in the case long before Todd's trial began, the recounting of the mountain of physical evidence brought repeated gasps and 'Ohhhs' from visitors and jury alike. It seems that at the height of his murderous rampage, Todd was committing an average of one murder a month, and may have worked at this frenetic pace for as long as five years. When all the evidence was in, and the time came for the jury to deliberate, it took them scarcely more than five minutes to find Sweeney Todd guilty of murder.

On 25 January 1802, only days after the verdict was handed down, Sweeney Todd, the 46-year-old 'Demon Barber of Fleet Street' was taken to the gallows at Newgate prison where, according to newspaper accounts, he 'died hard' – kicking and choking away his last moments of life.

After his execution, according to common practice of the day, Todd's body was handed over to the Royal College of Surgeons where it would be dissected by medical students. In the end, Todd himself wound up in the same dismembered condition as had so many dozens of his victims. Today, more than two centuries after their demise, Sweeney Todd still holds claim to being the greatest mass murderer in English history and, together with his cannibalistic cohort, Margery Lovett, inspired one of the most successful musical plays of all time.

A Hunger for Adventure: Alfred Packer (1874)

In the nineteenth century most of the American West was inhospitable at the best of times. In addition to its endemic lawlessness and the threat of attack from angry Indians and white outlaws, it was blessed by a climate that ranged from blistering heat and drought to freezing cold. It was the kind of place that brought out the best, and worst, in those brave enough to challenge its perils, often turning otherwise ordinary men and women into legendary figures. One of those apparently ordinary people whose story turned out more grotesque than most was Alfred Packer.

Like most of the individuals who populated the Old West, Alfred Packer was born in the eastern USA, in his case Allegheny County, Pennsylvania, in January 1842. As a teenager he was apprenticed to a shoemaker but, as with most young men, Alf was too full of energy to be tied to one job for long. He wanted to go to important places and see big things.

In 1862, with the American Civil War at its height, the twenty-year-old Packer joined the Union Army where he served for only nine months before being discharged because of a mild case of epilepsy. Six months later he tried to re-enlist, but again he was discharged on the same medical grounds. So far as we know, the only notable event during his time in the military was the evening when he, along with some of his buddies, decided to get a tattoo. The tattoo artist, either because he was only semi-literate, or drunk, or both, misspelled his client's name. There, for all time, was the word 'Alferd' etched into the boy's flesh. Making light of the sloppy mistake, throughout his life Packer joked about the misspelling, often referring to himself as 'Alferd' Packer.

Discouraged by two discharges in less than eighteen months, Packer returned to shoemaking until 1871 (or 1872 depending upon the source material) when the itch to travel became too much for him to bear. He headed west to the gold fields of Utah and Colorado where he alternated between prospecting and returning to the cobbler's last long enough to grubstake himself for another turn at the sluice box. If nothing else, Alf Packer certainly looked the part of a rugged westerner; he was above average in height, had piercing, deep-set grey eyes, a massive head of flowing, dark wavy hair, a large moustache and a goatee. All in all, Alf cut an imposing figure.

The summer of 1873 found Packer in Provo, Utah, again prospecting for gold. As the weather turned cold, he drifted towards Bingham where he fell into conversation with a group of men who were anxious to find a guide to lead them south to the new goldfields at Breckenridge, Colorado. With no immediate prospects in sight, Packer told them he knew the territory well, even claiming that he had driven an ore-wagon in several mining camps in the general area of Colorado Territory. Whether this was true or not remains uncertain, but the men believed him and within a few days a group of twenty-one prospectors had agreed to share the expense of hiring 'Alferd' as their guide. By now it was mid-November and any sane man knows that the dead of winter is not the time to trek across the Rocky Mountains – but this fact never seemed to dawn on anyone in the group, including Packer.

For three months the expedition trudged through ever-deepening snow and gale-force winds. With their food supply already running low, when they lost several crates of supplies while crossing a half-frozen river on a raft, the situation became desperate. But for the moment, luck seemed to be with them. On 21 January 1874 the half-frozen, starving crew stumbled into a camp of Ute Indians near present-day Montrose, Colorado. Shaking his head at the stupidity of the white men, the chief, Ouray, took the men in, fed them and urged them to remain with his people until springtime. Sixteen of the party took Ouray's advice, thanked the chief for his hospitality, and settled in for the winter. Packer himself was more than happy to stay where he was, but five of the men were determined to press on and offered to pay Packer a hefty bonus if he would guide them over the treacherous, wintry heights of the mountains and on to Breckenridge.

The men, Israel Swan, Shannon Bell, George Noon, Frank 'the Butcher' Miller and James Humphrey, wheedled and cajoled until, exasperated and anxious for the extra money, Alf agreed. On 9 February, during the harshest days of winter, the six men left Chief Ouray's camp and set out into the mountains. Only days later the worst blizzard of the year descended on the Rockies, trapping Packer and the others on a trail somewhere near the site of what is today Lake City, Colorado.

Nine weeks later, on 6 April, Alfred Packer stumbled into the Los Pintos Indian Reservation near Gunnison, babbling incoherently about how he and the others had been trapped in the storm, and while he tried to set up a camp, the others went off in search of firewood and food. He didn't know if Bell, Swan, Noon, Miller and Humphrey had deserted him, or become lost in the blizzard and died. All he knew was that he was alone and had survived two months of lonely hell out there in the wilderness. Among those who heard Packer's tale of woe was Chief Ouray, who had brought his people to Los Pintos with the spring thaw. He, along with the others, listened to the tragic tale with awe and wonder. As Packer turned to leave the office of local Indian Agent General Charles Adams, Ouray is reported to have muttered, 'You too damn fat'. Whether the chief actually said this is almost irrelevant. The fact was that other than suffering from prolonged exposure to the cold, Packer was as sleek as a beaver.

After a few days spent getting warm, Packer left Los Pintos for the nearby town of Saguache, where he seemed to have an excess of cash to throw around in the local saloon. While whooping it up one evening, Packer was confronted by several men who had been among the original party that had elected to remain at the Ute camp for the winter. Packer told the same story to them as he had told on his arrival at Los Pintos, but some of the men noticed he was carrying the skinning knife and rifle of other members of the tiny group that had disappeared into the wilderness.

The men voiced their suspicions to General Adams, who subsequently called Packer into the Los Pintos Agency to make a formal statement. In this, the first of two confessions, Packer abruptly changed his story. On 5 May 1874, he made the following statement:

Old man Swan died first and was eaten by the other five persons, about ten days out from camp; four or five days afterwards Humphrey died and was also eaten; he had about a hundred and thirty dollars [on him]. I found the pocket-book and took the money. Some time afterwards while I was carrying wood, the Butcher was killed, as the other two told me, accidentally, and he was eaten. Bell shot 'California' [Noon] with Swan's gun, and I killed Bell; shot him – covered up the remains. Bell wanted to kill me, struck at me with his rifle, struck a tree and broke his gun. I took a large piece of meat along. Then I travelled fourteen days into the 'Agency'.

The confession was sworn to and witnessed by the local Justice of the Peace, James Downer.

Packer was arrested and taken back to Saguache where he was jailed, pending formal charges. There he languished until 8 August. That day, the remains of the all-too-dead Packer party were found in a valley known as Slumgullion Pass. The discovery was made by John Randolph, a writer for *Harper's Weekly*, and his Indian guide. As a journalist, Randolph was already familiar with the story as well as Packer's conflicting claims. The grisly campsite was almost exactly where Packer claimed it would be, but contrary to Packer's statement, the carcasses were not scattered out along miles of trail. They were clustered together at a single site – and there was evidence of terrible violence. Most of the men's heads had been split open with a hatchet and large chunks of flesh had been carved from the bodies, particularly in the upper chest and thigh areas.

That same evening, before word of the discovery was brought back to Saguache, Packer managed to escape from his cell. He made it all the way to Arkansas where, for the next nine years, he lived under the name of John Schwartze. His movements and activity during this time remain clouded in mystery but it is certain that by March 1883 he was staying in Wyoming. Here again, exactly where in Wyoming seems to be in dispute. Some sources say Douglas, others insist it was Fort Fetterman and still others claim Cheyenne. What is not in dispute is what happened to him while he was drinking in the local saloon on the evening of 11 March.

By yet another odd twist of fate, Frenchy Carbazon, a member of the original party of twenty-one miners, happened to be in the same watering hole and recognised Packer's laugh. Hours later, Packer was arrested and hauled to Denver where he was confronted by General Adams for a third time. Again, Packer made a confession and, again, it conflicted with his previous statements. The only details that seemed to remain the same were the claims that whatever he had done was in self-defence and that he had taken money and a rifle from the dead men's bodies.

The new confession, dated 16 March 1883, runs, in part, as follows:

> When we left Ouray's camp we had about seven days of food for [each] man . . .
>
> When I came back to camp after being gone nearly all day I found the redheaded man [Bell], who [had] acted crazy in the morning, sitting near the fire roasting a piece of meat which he had cut out of the leg of the German butcher [Miller], the latter's body was lying the furthest off from the fire, down the stream, his skull was crushed in with the hatchet. The other three men were lying near the fire, they were cut in the forehead with the hatchet, some had two, some three cuts – I came within a rod of the fire, when the man [Bell] saw me, he got up with his hatchet [came] towards me when I shot him sideways through the belly, he fell on his face, the hatchet fell forwards. I grabbed it and hit him in the top of the head . . .
>
> I tried to get away that very day but could not, so I lived off the flesh of these men the better part of the 60 days I was out.
>
> I cooked some of the flesh and carried it with me for food.

The confession also explained just how he managed to escape from the Saguache jail. 'When I was at the Sheriff's in Saguache I was passed a key made out of a pen-knife blade . . .' The name of the friend who smuggled him this key was never divulged.

If there had been some original doubt as to what, if anything, Packer would be charged with, it had long since disappeared. The horrific find at the campsite nine years earlier, along with Packer's constantly shifting confession, led the authorities to charge him with the single murder of Israel Swan, presumed to have been the first of the party to be killed. Packer was clapped in irons and hauled back to Lake City to await trial for first-degree murder.

The courtroom of Judge Melville Gerry – Hinsdale District Court, Lake City, Colorado – was packed on the morning of 6 April when case number 1883DC379, the case of the 'Colorado Cannibal', went to trial. The trial lasted a week, but when the jury returned from deliberation on the afternoon of the 13th, the verdict was no surprise. Alfred Packer had been found guilty of murder.

In his sentencing of Packer, Judge Gerry said, in part: 'A jury of twelve honest citizens . . . have set judgement on your case, and upon their oaths they find you guilty of wilful and premeditated murder . . . to the other sickening details of your crime I will not refer . . . On the 19th day of May 1883, you will be taken to a place of execution . . . and you, then and there . . . [will] be hung by the neck until you are dead, dead, dead, and may God have mercy upon your soul.'

The vast and furious mob that had gathered outside the courthouse had no intention of waiting until mid-May. What if Packer escaped again? Rowdy and fuelled by booze, they surged towards the courthouse doors and were only held back by the Sheriff and his deputies, who threatened to shoot the first man who tried to touch Packer. A terrified Alf was bundled through the crowd, shoved into a waiting police wagon and hurtled through the gathering dusk on a wild ride to Gunnison where, rather than having his neck stretched a few weeks later, he remained in jail for the next three years.

Following his conviction, Packer's lawyers immediately filed an appeal on the grounds that the alleged crime, and the laws governing them, had taken place while Colorado was still a territory. The trial, however, had taken place after it had become a state and certain laws had been changed in the process of statehood, those pertaining to the charges against Packer being a case in point. The appeal was heard in the Colorado Supreme

Court and the conviction overturned in October 1885. If the state still wanted Alf Packer, they would have to try him again – so they did.

Packer's second trial took place in Gunnison, where he was still being held prisoner. Although he was exonerated of premeditated murder, he was found guilty on five counts of manslaughter. Given a minimum sentence of eight years per charge, Packer was sent to the Colorado State Penitentiary at Cañon City where, considering he was already forty-four years old, he would undoubtedly spend the rest of his life.

Years passed and tales of 'Alfred Packer the Colorado Cannibal' had long since ceased to make the news, much less the headlines. But in 1897 Packer wrote yet another version of the horrific events that had taken place in Slumgullion Pass, during the winter of 1874. This new, much longer and improved version of his story was penned at the request of editor D.C. Hatch of the *Rocky Mountain News* out of Denver, who hoped to get a little mileage out of an old story. This time, Packer's statement ran to more than 3,000 words. He obviously worked hard to generate as much sympathy for himself as possible, as the two-sentence extract below makes clear.

> Can you imagine my situation – my companions dead and I left alone, surrounded by the midnight horrors of starvation as well as those of utter isolation? My body weak, my mind acted upon in such an awful manner that the greatest wonder is that I ever returned to a rational condition.

When Packer's account was published it generated the interest Hatch had hoped for, not only among the general public, but also on the part of a woman who went by the most unlikely name of Polly Pry and worked as a journalist for the *Rocky Mountain News*'s major competition, the *Denver Post*.

Today Ms Pry would be labelled a 'politically correct' scandalmonger; at the end of the nineteenth century she was called a 'sob sister' and a 'muck raker'. The terms may have changed over the past hundred years, but the meaning remains the same.

Polly Pry, whose real name was Leonel Campbell, was the sort of journalist who took up causes simply because they were there to be taken up. In her world, there were no bad people, only victims who needed to be cuddled and coddled. To her credit, many of the causes she championed over the years were both worthy and noble. She supported miners and other underpaid workers in their struggle to have their unions recognised. She must have raised a lot of ire over the course of her career, because on at least one occasion an attempt was made to assassinate her in her own home.

In late 1899 Pry, along with the *Denver Post*'s legal eagle, one William 'Plug Hat' Anderson, was assigned by the *Post*'s co-publishers and editors, Frederick Bonfils and H.H. Tammen, to get the Packer case reopened and wring as much news out of it as possible. It was a job for which the pair were ideally suited. Polly was a Pollyanna if ever there was one, and 'Plug Hat' was the epitome of every nasty lawyer joke ever told.

With Pry taking the lead, they went on the theory that if murderers and rapists could regularly be let out on parole, then a man convicted of five counts of manslaughter was due no less. The fact that he may, or may not, have slain his victims to eat them was, technically, of no legal consequence.

Meanwhile, 'Plug Hat' Anderson tried to find a precedent that would stand up in court. The angle he hit on was both ingenious and workable. According to Anderson's brief, the alleged murders had taken place within the boundaries of the Los Pintos Indian Reservation and therefore, Packer's case should have been tried in federal court, not in a state or territorial court.

By now, the Colorado legal system had no real interest in Alf Packer; he had already been tried twice and taken up the time of the State Supreme Court with his bothersome appeal. The best thing to do was simply to get rid of him. Consequently, and probably with much frustration, in January 1901, Colorado Governor Charles Thomas consented to parole Packer on medical grounds. According to the wording of the original parole document, dated 7 January, Packer was being released because the prison physician had certified that he suffered from 'hydrocele and Bright's Disease'. Hydrocele is defined by *Webster's Collegiate Dictionary* as 'an accumulation of dangerous fluids in a bodily cavity'. Bright's Disease is described as 'an archaic term describing a generalized, chronic kidney complaint'.

After being incarcerated for almost seventeen years Packer was overjoyed. Polly Pry was happy because she had done something 'good'. 'Plug Hat' Anderson was happy because he would get paid and the *Denver Post*'s publisher/editors were happy too. In the last case, Bonfils and Tammen were happy not because they had done what they thought was right, or even because Pry's story had sold a lot of newspapers; they were happy because they were going to make a lot of money out of Alf Packer. It seems that Bonfils and Tammen not only owned the *Denver Post*, but also the Sells Floto Circus, and they had offered to take up Packer's case on condition that he join their travelling troupe as a sideshow freak. Evidently they thought there would be a big appeal in advertising 'Alf Packer the Colorado Cannibal' all across America.

So everyone was happy. At least they were happy until Governor Thomas attached a single condition to Packer's parole. Possibly because 1900 was an election year and Thomas wanted to avoid being accused of turning America's only convicted cannibal loose on the country at large, or maybe it was just to ensure Alf's good behaviour, he stipulated that Packer had to remain in the Denver area for a period of not less than six years and nine months after his release. Although Packer described the condition as 'arrogant and vicious' he accepted the offer. Bonfils and Tammen were less sanguine about the restriction.

What happened next is unclear, but conjecture allows us to assume that because Packer's movements were restricted he became useless as an attraction in a travelling circus. It is also possible that Bonfils and Tammen then refused to pay 'Plug Hat' Anderson because the case had not turned out to their complete satisfaction. Whatever the reason, Anderson and his employers got into a terrible row and in the finest tradition of the Wild West, the lawyer shot both Tammen and Bonfils. What eventually happened to Anderson is unclear, but both Bonfils and Tammen recovered from their wounds and apparently held no animosity against Packer for the incident.

Once free, Alfred Packer moved into a small house in Littleton, Colorado, where, reportedly, he became a model citizen, was liked by his neighbours and spent the rest of his life as a vegetarian. In truth, he was probably looked on as a curious relic of America's fast disappearing Old West. He died on 23 April 1907, one day after his sixty-fifth birthday, and was buried in Littleton's Prince Avenue Cemetery. Because he had served in the Union Army during the Civil War, he was accorded full military honours at the interment. His grave was, and still is, visited by thousands of tourists every year.

Nothing else of much note happened in Alf's life – or death – until 1989 when a forensic expedition exhumed the bones of his victims, who had been buried near the campsite at Slumgullion Pass. Having remained in surprisingly good condition, the evidence of their murders was clearly shown by the hatchet marks in their skulls. Forensic examination also showed that certain portions of their flesh had been cut from the bone with a skinning knife. Most noteworthy, however, was a bullet hole in one of the pelvises. To check this evidence against Packer's testimony that he had shot Bell when the man attacked him with the hatchet, lead scrapings from the wound were compared with bullets still resting in the revolver which had been confiscated from Packer at the time of his first arrest, and was now housed in the collection of the Museum of Western Colorado. Amazingly, the metal samples matched perfectly, supporting Packer's claim that Bell had murdered the other men and that he, Packer, had only killed Bell in self-defence. 'Alferd' Packer may have been a cannibal, but it seems likely that he was not, after all, a murderer.

Throughout the century since his death, Alf's weird tale has, somehow, continued to gnaw at the bones of America's popular imagination. From time to time Alfred Packer fan clubs have been formed, allowing his legend to grow large enough for folk singer Phil Ochs to write a song in the early 1960s entitled 'The Legend of Alfred Packer'. A few years later, in 1968, students at the University of Colorado, at Boulder, named their new cafeteria the Alfred E. Packer Grill and fourteen years after that, in 1968, a statue of Packer was erected on the campus. The following year James E. Banks wrote *Alferd Packer's Wilderness Cookbook*, published by Filter Press.

With his fame now spread far and wide, two movies were made about Alf's life. The first, *The Legend of Alfred Packer*, came out in 1980, and in 1996 Trey Parker and Matt Stone, creators of the animated *South Park* television series, wrote, directed, produced and starred in *Cannibal: The Musical*, a bizarre, over-the-top, song-filled rendition of Packer's life.

Those who find themselves hungry for souvenirs of the Old West's only convicted cannibal should visit his online store at www.everythingalferd.com. (note the alternative spelling of his name) where you can buy everything from the movies mentioned above to mugs, tee-shirts and Christmas cards.

Eight

This Little Piggy Went to Market: Karl Denke and Georg Grossman (1921–4)

War, and the inevitable economic hardships that follow in its awful wake, can rip even the most stable societies to shreds. When Germany lost the First World War in 1918 the resultant chaos was unequalled in modern history. The governments of the triumphant allied powers – France, Great Britain, Italy and the United States – demanded that Germany reimburse them for every penny they had spent on the war. Faced with this clearly impossible demand, the German economy went into free-fall. Inflation spiralled so far out of control that it became cheaper to burn money than to buy wood or coal. A life's savings could be wiped out in a matter of days. As factories and businesses collapsed and banks failed, unemployment soared to epic proportions.

The disaster was compounded by a severe food shortage linked directly to the economic implosion. Farmers simply could no longer afford to raise and sell their products. A piglet that may have cost a few marks to buy in 1920 suddenly cost millions of marks to keep. Even if a cow or pig was slaughtered and taken to market, trying to sell it at anything less than a dead loss would have made it too expensive for people to buy, even if they had any money, which most of them did not. The German depression was a recipe for social and political disaster. Eventually its effects would cause the worldwide depression of the late 1920s and early '30s and be the prime factor in the rise of Adolf Hitler and the Nazis, but in the early and mid-1920s, its effects remained more localised; that is not to imply they were any less horrific for the people involved. In the frantic, paranoid atmosphere of a poverty and famine-stricken nation, only those who were emotionally and physically strong could hope to survive. The morally debased and emotionally unstable, like the men we are about to meet, as well as Hitler and his circle of cronies, often became social predators, while those least able to defend themselves became their victims. Although not all of these social predators were cannibals, it is interesting to note that there were more of this ilk than the subjects of this chapter, notable among them being the notorious child murderer and cannibal, Fritz Haarmann.

Karl Denke was born on 12 August 1870, just outside the tiny mining village of Oberkunzendorf, Germany, located in the north-eastern province of Silesia near the Polish border. He came from a family of prosperous and respected farmers and seems to have had as much going for him as a young person in that place and time could reasonably expect, but he always had trouble keeping up at school. Undoubtedly there were recurring family arguments about his academic performance because, at the age of twelve, he ran away from home and took a job as an apprentice gardener.

What he did and where he lived over the next dozen years is almost entirely unknown, but he must have remained on relatively good terms with his family. When he was twenty-five his father died, leaving the farm to Karl's older brother but willing enough money to Karl for him to buy a small farm of his own outside Oberkunzendorf. It would seem that farming was simply not Karl Denke's forte because the land failed to make a profit and he eventually sold it, using the money to buy a two-storey house in the nearby town of Münsterberg, now Ziebice, Poland.

Next door to his new home Denke rented a small shop where he sold food and daily necessities to the people of his neighbourhood. Over the years he became well liked and respected among the town's 8,000 occupants. A pillar of his local Evangelical church, he dutifully pumped the bellows of the old church organ every Sunday morning and was cross-bearer in the funeral cortège when one of his fellow parishioners passed on to their final reward. He neither drank nor chased women. He liked children and was kind to friends and strangers alike. When a homeless person passed through Münsterberg, Denke was among the first to offer them a hand-out, occasionally allowing one of them to stay in his house long enough to receive a few hot meals, a clean bed and a hot bath. As he aged people began referring to him simply as 'Papa Denke', as though he was everyone's favourite uncle. He may never have become rich or famous but he had good friends and there was always enough food on his table. To all appearances it seemed that Karl Denke was the type of person we would all like to have living next door to us.

Eventually, like nearly everyone else in the German Empire, Denke's life was shattered by the aftermath of the First World War. His shop failed in the depression and in 1921 he was forced to sell his house, which the new owners divided into a number of small apartments. The income from the sale allowed Karl to rent a two-room flat on the ground floor of his former home. In an effort to keep some money coming in Denke applied to the local police for a street vendor's licence. Not surprisingly, they issued it at once.

During the week Karl went from door to door selling shoelaces, trouser braces, belts, homemade soap and other trinkets, and once a week he took his small stock of goods to the nearby town of Breslauer where he set up shop in the municipal market. Soon he added home-packed jars of pickled pork to his inventory. Due to the food shortage caused by so many farm failures, the meat turned out to be one of his biggest selling items. Eventually, he applied to the Butchers' Guild in Warsaw, Poland, for a licence to sell his canned meat there. The licence was granted and Denke's small circle of customers slowly expanded beyond his local community. Although at the age of fifty-two it was unlikely that he would ever find a real job, at least it looked as though he would not starve.

Even in such dire economic straits, Denke remained as kind and charitable as ever. When a straggler from the army of displaced people who were now wandering across the German landscape passed through Münsterberg, they were always welcomed at Papa Denke's flat. Undoubtedly, these lost and friendless folk were grateful for even this small act of Christian charity.

The first sign of trouble came on 21 December 1924, when a young, itinerant man by the name of Vincenz Olivier came staggering out of Denke's apartment bleeding profusely from a head wound and screaming his lungs out. Alerted by the commotion, Denke's upstairs neighbour, a cab driver named Gabriel, came running out to see what was going on. As Gabriel emerged from his rooms, a young man covered in blood slumped into his arms jabbering that the old man in the ground-floor flat had just tried to murder him with an axe. Incredulous, but concerned for the injured boy, Gabriel gently led him to the local police station where the police hurriedly summoned a doctor to tend Olivier's wounds.

After staunching the bleeding and suturing the wound, the doctor explained to the police that the boy had, indeed, been attacked. After taking Olivier's confused and disjointed statement, the officer-in-charge dutifully dispatched two constables to pick up Karl Denke for questioning. No one quite believed the young man's incredible story, but there was obviously something very odd going on and it was the police's job to find out what it was.

When Denke was interrogated he explained that, as was his custom, he had offered Vincenz Olivier a place to stay for a few days. The young man had attacked him during an attempted robbery and he, Denke, had simply defended himself with the first thing he could grab. Obviously the police would have to carry out a thorough investigation of the conflicting stories and Denke would have to be placed in a holding cell for a day or two until all the facts were known. Around 11.30 that evening, the night officer, Sergeant Palke, wandered into the cell block to see if Denke needed anything. To his horror, he discovered the lifeless body of 54-year-old Papa Denke dangling from the bars of his cell. He had hanged himself with the oversized pocket-handkerchief he always carried. For the moment, this terrible turn of events seemed both tragic and inexplicable. In retrospect Denke's death has also denied us any hope of understanding what motivated him to carry out the atrocities the police would later unearth at his apartment.

The following day, Denke's relatives were notified of the suicide and the body was turned over to the local mortician for burial. Because of the unusual circumstances of the old man's death, and the still outstanding accusations of Olivier, Denke's apartment was declared off limits to everyone but the police until a thorough investigation had been carried out.

On Christmas Eve, a police detail went to Denke's home to search for any pertinent evidence before releasing the remainder of his belongings to the family. On entering the tiny flat they were assailed by the acrid smell of vinegar, but in a nation where pickled meat and sauerkraut were dietary mainstays this was hardly surprising, particularly since everybody knew that Denke made most of his money from packing and selling boneless pork. The smell came from two large pickling crocks, filled with meat and brine, standing in a corner of the kitchen. Nearby, a set of shelves were stocked with jars of the finished product waiting to be taken to market. Some sources claim there was also a quantity of fresh pork in the icebox, presumably for Denke's own use and possibly to be shared with those unfortunates who occasionally stayed with him. There were also chemicals and equipment both for soap making and tanning leather as well as leather-working tools that Karl used to make the belts and braces he sold. It may have been the pile of bones that gave the investigating officers their first indication that something here was not quite right. They were obviously not pig bones; they were human. When one of the policemen found the dish containing 240 human teeth their confusion quickly turned to revulsion. When they moved into Denke's bedroom, the nightmare got a whole lot worse.

On the wall hung dozens of pairs of braces and an equal number of belts made, as it turned out, not from pigskin but from human leather. The closet was filled with blood-stained clothing. Every little detail seemed to cry out the truth of what Karl Denke had been doing. Even the shoelaces were made either from human leather or braided from human hair. If anyone needed more proof, it was lying on the windowsill and the table in the corner of the bedroom. There, in neat piles, were Denke's records, carefully recorded from 1921 to the present. Three years of murder and cannibalism. In his ledger were the recorded details of thirty-one victims; their names, the dates he had murdered them and how many pounds of meat he had taken from each body. There were also the documents and identification papers he had taken from twelve of his victims, and newspaper cuttings listing the names of individuals who had recently been released from nearby prisons and hospitals. To verify the obvious, a jar of Papa Denke's popular pickled pork was sent to a police lab in Warsaw for testing. When the results came back, they were no surprise to anybody.

No story can be kept out of the press for long, and when this one broke in the local paper – with the improbably coincidental name of *Journal Frankenstein* – it was as salacious and grim as possible. 'Murder', 'cannibal' and 'peddler of human flesh' screamed out at every horrified reader in Münsterberg. By the time the tri-weekly *Münsterberger Zeitung* newspaper came out, the tests on the pickled 'pork' had come back from the lab and the panic started all over again. Not surprisingly, although pork is the traditional New Year's dinner throughout Germany, that year no one in Münsterberg could bear to look at it.

Police examination of the articles taken from Denke's apartment positively identified twenty of his victims – about two-thirds of the names listed in his ledger. Although the final count may never be known, estimates of Denke's victims run anywhere from his own thirty-one to as high as forty.

In 1999 the tiny museum in Ziebice, located in one room of the town hall, held a display of the knives, vats, jars and other paraphernalia used by Denke during his grisly days as the chief purveyor of pickled people in Münsterberg. The display, named 'An ancient iconography of Ziebice', proved so popular with locals and tourists alike that it still remains in place.

If the grim facts of Karl Denke's crimes came as an unbelievable shock to the good people of Münsterberg, it was only one small part of a much larger pattern that was taking shape all over Germany. Three years earlier and more than 300 miles to the west, in Berlin, an incident had occurred that was so similar in its details to those of the Denke case that it makes the mind reel. Sadly, if the morbid details in Karl Denke's story are rather limited, they appear positively abundant in comparison to the information available on Georg Grossman. This may, in part, be due to the massive amount of information destroyed when Berlin was repeatedly bombed during 1944 and 1945.

Georg Grossman was born in 1863 in the town of Neuruppen, Germany, and spent most of his working life as a peddler of used clothes, but sometimes worked in the better paying butcher's trade where he specialised in sausage making. Sullen and anti-social, Grossman was a great bear of a man who neither cultivated nor wanted friends; but few people wanted to make friends with a surly rag merchant anyway, and that suited Georg Grossman perfectly.

Like many of his countrymen, in the wake of the First World War Grossman lost his business premises and was reduced to selling his second-hand clothes from a handcart on the streets of Berlin. Although he could not find work in a legitimate butcher's shop, Grossman supplemented his income by making, and selling, sausages on the black market. Because meat was tightly rationed and could only be purchased with government-issued coupons, unlicensed meat was in constant demand. Eventually, Grossman found that his most profitable market was to be found at the main railway station where he not only sold bulk sausages but offered sausage sandwiches to hungry travellers. Those few people who could still afford to travel could, presumably, also afford a few marks for a sausage sandwich. With the ensuing food shortage, Georg was forced to make his sausages from whatever meat he could scrounge: often horse, mule or even dog meat. As the quality and quantity of available meat continued to drop, so did Grossman's income.

Some sources insist that Grossman had served three prison sentences for molesting children and that the charges may have included accusations of sadism and bestiality, but there is little hard evidence to support anything beyond the heinous crime of child molesting. What we do know is that once he began selling his sausages at the railway terminal, Grossman made a habit of picking up itinerant and homeless women who had been reduced to prostitution by the economic crisis and used Berlin's central railway station as their base of operations.

With an almost animal cunning, Georg Grossman decided he could, quite literally, kill more than one bird with a single stone. From his sausage cart at the railway station he would spot women who appealed to him sexually and make the appropriate advances. When they had settled on a fee for the woman's service, Grossman would take her back to his tenement, have sex with her, murder her and grind up her flesh, using it as the main ingredient in his tasty sausages. Georg's sexual appetite had been satisfied, he did not have to pay for his victim's service, he had a steady supply of free meat and was guaranteed to turn a profit and get rid of the evidence all in one fell swoop.

How long Grossman carried on this grim pattern is unknown, but unless it began before Germany's economic collapse, it cannot have been more than two years. In August 1921, neighbours in Grossman's tenement were alarmed to hear the piercing screams of a woman coming from Grossman's flat. Dutifully, someone notified the landlord who, in turn, rang the police. If, indeed, Grossman was already on the list of known sex offenders, the police's response would have been all the quicker. In either case, when constables kicked in the door of Grossman's apartment they found the half-butchered body of his latest victim lying on an old camp-bed, along with the remains of three other women in various states of dismemberment and preparation. Beneath the bed was a pot of cleanly rendered human fat and a saucepan full of human fingers. In the refrigerator and closet were stores of sausages left for curing before being sold on the open market. Based on laboratory analysis the victims had all been killed within the past three weeks. After his arrest, the 58-year-old Grossman, like Denke, would hang himself in jail before he could be thoroughly questioned and examined by psychiatrists.

Had either of these men lived long enough to give their side of the story it might have provided us with a greater understanding of their motivations than the simple cataloguing of the horrific facts which turned up in the ensuing police investigations.

Georg Grossman's bloody story has been immortalised in a song by an Australian 'grunge' band by the name of Blood Duster, but otherwise he, like Denke, has been largely forgotten, which is probably for the best.

Nine

Candy from a Baby:
Albert Fish (1924–34)

On 19 May 1870 Albert Fish was born into a relatively prosperous, middle-class family who made their home in Washington DC. His mother was a homemaker and his father, Captain Randall Fish, piloted a riverboat along the Potomac. It seemed a reasonable start in life, but it all went sour when his father died of a heart attack in 1875. Left with no income, and unable to bring up her children alone, Albert's mother was forced to place him in St John's Orphanage. There the five-year-old's life took a dramatically wrong turn.

Always fragile and small for his age, Albert made an easy target for the bullying of older, bigger boys. When his fellow orphans were not beating him up, the matrons were. Along with the official beatings came liberal warnings – often punctuated with passages from the scriptures – of the punishment that awaited those who strayed from the straight and narrow path, practised the sins of the flesh or disobeyed scriptural admonitions. Albert did his best to do what was right. He even sang in the St John's choir between 1880 and 1884, but somehow the pain and the punishment, and what he believed God expected of him, got all muddled up in his head. Finally, at the age of fifteen, Albert Fish left the orphanage and found his way to New York where he was apprenticed as a house painter.

Ever the dutiful son, once he could afford his own apartment he brought his widowed mother up from Washington to live with him. In 1898 the 28-year-old Albert married a nineteen-year-old woman with whom, over the next sixteen years, he had six children. Although standing only 5 feet 5 inches and weighing not much over 8½ stone (120lb), Albert worked hard and did his best to be a good father. He never struck any of his children, or his wife, and insisted that grace be said before every meal. There were, however, strange, recurring episodes that may have been a prime factor in the upcoming destruction of his family.

Somewhere along the line, Albert Fish had developed a religious mania that would have been completely recognisable to the medieval flagellants. It would seem likely that he began his self-torture in secret, but soon he forced his children to watch as he administered ever more severe and bizarre punishments to himself. Sometimes he used a nail-studded paddle to whip himself to a bloody pulp; other times he shoved pins under his fingernails while his offspring watched in shocked silence. On at least one occasion the Fish children witnessed their father standing on a hill, arms raised, shouting 'I am Christ!' Eventually, it all became too much for his wife to bear. In 1917, three years after the birth of their sixth child, she packed up the kids and left.

Although it was undoubtedly the only sane choice for the stressed-out spouse and offspring, the separation did nothing to settle the troubled mind of Albert Fish. His self-torture slowly turned to self-mutilation. He soaked cotton balls in alcohol, inserted them between the cheeks of his rump and lighted them. He began sticking pins into the soft flesh between his scrotum and rectum, shoving some of them in so deep they became lost in his flesh. He also became convinced that the Almighty, as well as Christ and the angels, were speaking to him personally. In these hallucinatory fits, Fish became convinced that God ordered him to torture and mutilate children as some sort of sacrificial act. Sometimes Fish would ramble on, 'quoting' his own delusional scriptures. 'Happy is he that taketh thy little ones and dasheth their heads against stones.' Integral to the delusions was the belief that he needed to castrate little boys.

Alone and increasingly unstable, Fish continued painting houses for a living, but he began to wander from town to town and state to state, carrying his sickness with him wherever he went. He seldom stayed in any one place for very long. Sometimes people just got a weird feeling from him; other times, terrible things happened to children in neighbourhoods where the strange little painter was working. There was never any evidence to connect him with anything, but people just did not want him around. For no particular reason, in the summer of 1924 Albert Fish found himself working on Staten Island, a borough of New York City.

One warm July day of that summer, Anna McDonnell was sitting on her front porch nursing her infant daughter. Nearby, her eight-year-old son, Francis, was playing quietly by himself. Glancing up towards the road, Anna saw the strange figure of a small, rumpled man apparently staring at her. He had grey hair and a droopy moustache and wore a battered suit and bowler hat, both of which were covered with dust. He was obviously a workman of some kind, but why was he standing in the middle of the street staring? More disturbingly, he seemed to be talking to himself and he kept clenching and unclenching his hands. Not one to be intimidated, Anna returned his stare. Finally, the man tipped his dirty hat, nodded and wandered away.

Later that afternoon, a small man in a dusty, well-worn suit was seen watching a group of boys playing baseball. One of the boys was Francis McDonnell. When the elderly man called Francis over to the fence surrounding the ball field, the other boys paid no attention, focusing their young minds on their game. A few minutes later, both the old man and Francis were gone.

No one really noticed his disappearance until he failed to return home for dinner. Francis' father, a policeman, lost no time rounding up the neighbours and organising a search party. As they scoured the area around Charlton Woods, someone said they had seen a boy who seemed to match Francis' description go into the woods with an old man who looked like a bum. Deep in the woods, the searchers found what was left of Francis McDonnell.

The boy's clothes had been ripped from his little body before he was beaten to a bloody pulp. Finally, his own braces had been used to strangle the life out of him. The local police were immediately called in to examine the crime scene and their best detectives were certain that the 'bum' must have had an accomplice. A man as small and frail as the one Anna McDonnell, the boys from the ball game, and her neighbour had all described just couldn't have been strong enough to do so much damage to Francis.

In her statement to the police, Anna McDonnell described her encounter with the old man. The thing that seemed to stick out in her mind was that 'everything about him seemed faded and grey'. From this strange appraisal, the unknown assailant became known as the 'Grey Man'. But just like a puff of grey smoke, the Grey Man vanished completely – at least, it was nearly three years before his next recorded appearance.

Billy Gaffney was four years old. On 11 February 1927 he and his best friend, a three-year-old also named Bill, were playing in the hallway outside their parents' apartments. A neighbour's twelve-year-old son was trying to keep an eye on them, but his attention was divided between the boys and his little sister who was asleep inside. At some point, while the older boy was checking on his sister, the boys disappeared. With the help of Bill's father they found the three-year-old in the hallway on the top floor of the apartment building, but Billy Gaffney was nowhere to be found. When they questioned his little friend about Billy, all he could find to say was, 'The bogeyman took him.'

The bogeyman, a small, grey-haired man in a worn suit, had taken Billy to a nearby trolley stop. The trolley driver noticed that the boy obviously did not want to get on board with the old man. He kept crying for his mother and the man had to forcibly keep him in his seat during the ride and then drag him off at the stop in Brooklyn. What happened to Billy Gaffney from that point is best left to the words of Albert Fish as he recalled the incident years later.

I brought him to the Riker Avenue dump. There is a house that stands alone not far from there. I took the boy there. Stripped him naked and tied his hands and feet and gagged him with a piece of dirty rag I picked out of the dump. Then I burned his clothes. Threw his shoes on the dump. Then I walked back and took the trolley to 59th Street, at 2 am, and walked home from there.

Next day about 2 pm, I took tools, a good heavy set of cat-of-nine-tails. Home made. Short handle. Cut one of my belts in half, slit these halves in six strips about 8 inches long. I whipped his bare behind till the blood ran from his legs. (After describing in blood-chilling detail his torture, mutilation and murder of the child, Fish recounted his dismemberment of his small victim.)

I stuck the knife in his belly and held my mouth to his body and drank his blood. [Then] I picked up four old potato sacks and gathered a pile of stones. Then I cut him up. I had a [small suitcase] with me. I put his nose, ears and a few slices of his belly . . . in my [suitcase] with a lot of paper. I put [the remaining pieces of the body] in sacks weighted with stones, tied the ends and threw them into the pools of slimy water . . . along the road going to North Beach.

I came home with my meat . . . I made a stew out of his ears, nose, pieces of his face and belly. I put [in] onions, carrots, turnips, celery, salt and pepper. It was good.

Then I split the cheeks of his behind open . . . I put strips of bacon on each cheek . . . and put them in the oven. Then I picked four onions and when the meat had roasted for about ¼ hour, I poured about a pint of water over it for gravy and put in the onions. At frequent intervals I basted [him] with a wooden spoon. So the meat would be nice and juicy.

In about 2 hours, it was nice and brown, cooked through. I never ate any roast turkey that tasted half as good as his sweet, fat little behind. I ate every bit of the meat in four days.

While Albert Fish was torturing, murdering and devouring Billy Gaffney, Billy's father had called in fellow police officers from across the five boroughs of New York. They organised a massive search and interviewed everyone they could find who might have seen the boy. The one thing they did not do, however, was take much notice of three-year-old Bill when he kept trying to tell them that the bogeyman had taken his friend Billy. Even when he tried his best to explain that it was a skinny old man with a moustache, no one made the connection between Bill's bogeyman and the Grey Man who had abducted and murdered Francis McDonnell almost three years earlier. Once again, the Grey Man would simply vanish like vapour. Fifteen months later he reappeared.

When Delia Budd answered the door to her family's shabby New York City tenement on Monday 28 May 1928 she found herself face-to-face with a small, frail-looking man at the top end of middle age. He was wearing a rumpled, worn suit and a battered old bowler hat that he removed politely when Mrs Budd asked who he was. He said his name was Frank Howard and he had come in answer to an advertisement placed in the *New York World* by Edward Budd.

Mrs Budd asked Mr Howard to come in and told her youngest daughter, Beatrice, to go and find her brother Ed. While they waited, Delia sized up the stranger who had answered her son's request for employment on a farm. He seemed quiet, almost shy; his diffident air was only accentuated by his silver hair and drooping moustache. He was polite even if he did look a bit shabby, but that was just what you might expect from a farmer who was unaccustomed to coming into the big city. Besides, the Budds were so poor that almost anybody looked good by comparison.

When the strapping, eighteen-year-old Edward arrived, Frank Howard appraised him with a smile. He explained that he had a small farm in Farmingdale, Long Island, and that he ran it with the help of a few farmhands, a cook and his six youngsters. Unfortunately one of his hands was leaving and he needed a good, strong young man to take his place. There was no doubt that Ed Budd was strong, but was he willing to work hard? Edward assured Mr Howard that he was and in return the man offered him $15 a week along with room and board. Ed Budd was delighted. Replacing his hat, Albert Fish – in the guise of Frank Howard – promised he would return on Saturday to pick Ed up and take him to the farm where he could begin work immediately.

Leaving the 15th Street tenement, Fish stopped at a hardware store long enough to buy the tools he would need to murder and dismember Edward Budd. He bought a meat cleaver, a hacksaw and a butcher's knife, asking the clerk to wrap them up for him.

Saturday 2 June came and went without any sign of Mr Howard. A telegram from him did arrive, however. In it he explained that something had come up making Saturday impossible, but that he would be at the Budds' on Sunday morning. True to his word, an hour before noon the next day the Grey Man appeared at the Budds' door. This time he was bearing gifts. He handed a small pot of soft cheese and a box of strawberries to Delia Budd, explaining that they were produce from his farm. Delighted at such thoughtfulness, Mrs Budd insisted that he stay for Sunday dinner. Demurely, Fish accepted the invitation.

As the family and their guest were seating themselves round the table, a beautiful, dark-haired, pale-skinned, ten-year-old girl appeared in her best Sunday dress. Mrs Budd introduced her as their daughter Gracie, who had just come home from church. Albert Fish was enraptured. Asking the child to show him how well she could count, he handed her a wad of money that amazed the entire Budd family. Scooting herself on to the old man's lap, Gracie carefully counted out the $92 and 50 cents. When Fish beamed at her, she kissed him on the cheek as though he were her favourite uncle. Albert Fish made an immediate change of plans.

After dinner, Fish told the Budds he would be back later in the evening to pick up Ed, but that he had to go to his sister's house because it was his young niece's birthday and he had been invited to the party. Almost as an afterthought, he asked Mrs Budd if it would be all right if Gracie came along. Delia was uncertain, but her husband – a man whose face showed every beating life had doled out to him – shook his head. 'Let the poor kid go,' he said to his wife. 'She don't see many good times.' The matter was settled and Mr Howard promised faithfully to have little Gracie back by nine o'clock at the latest. It was the last time the Budd family ever saw Gracie.

Fish took Gracie by train from New York to rural Worthington in Westchester County. From the railway station they wandered down country lanes until they came to a deserted house that Fish had reconnoitred for the occasion. His disposition of Gracie's small life appears below in Fish's own words.

When we got there, I told her to remain outside. She picked wildflowers. I went upstairs and stripped all my clothes off. I knew if I did not I would get her blood on them.

When all was ready I went to the window and called her. Then I hid in the closet until she was in the room. When she saw me all naked she began to cry and tried to run down the stairs. I grabbed her and she said she would tell her mamma.

First I stripped her naked. How she did kick, bite and scratch me. I choked her to death.

It would appear, from a disjointed, later version of his statement, that Fish then drained Gracie's blood into an old paint bucket he had found lying in the house. We now return to Fish's own version of the story.

[I] then cut her in small pieces so I could take my meat to my rooms, cook and eat it. How sweet and tender [she] was, roasted in the oven. It took me nine days to eat her entire body.

When Gracie Budd failed to return home her family became frantic. In the morning Ed Budd went to the police station to report her disappearance and probable abduction. He gave them all the information he had on the mysterious Mr Howard, including the location of his farm in Farmington and the address he gave for his sister's apartment. It only took the police a few minutes to discover that both addresses were fictitious. Anxious to track down the man calling himself Frank Howard, the police asked the Budd family to go through the mugshots of all known kidnappers, child molesters and mental patients known to be at large. There was no sign of Albert Fish.

The New York Police Department put an extraordinary effort into the case. More than twenty detectives and officers were assigned to the Gracie Budd disappearance and 1,000 fliers were printed and posted off to police stations all over the East Coast.

Eventually solid evidence did turn up. They located a street vendor who had sold the strawberries and cheese to the little man with the grey moustache and found the Western Union office from which Fish had sent word that he would be delayed in picking up Edward Budd. Fortunately, Western Union still had Fish's original, handwritten copy of the telegram against which a possible ransom note could be compared. Because both the street vendor and the Western Union office were in East Harlem, this area was scoured for any sign of Gracie or a man matching Mr Howard's description. No suspects were found and no ransom demand ever arrived.

Four and a half years later any hope of finding Gracie Budd had long since been given up. Still, there are always officers who refuse to give up no matter how 'cold' a case has become. One of these was Detective William King of the New York Metropolitan Police. Like a dog worrying a bone, he continued toying with the Budd case. Occasionally he would leak some tiny bit of information to the press which, true or not, would hopefully make the unknown suspect reveal himself. On 2 November 1934 King placed one such item with gossip columnist and radio personality Walter Winchell. Winchell broadcast the story, stating that a break had come in the Gracie Budd case and an arrest was expected at any time.

Ten days after Winchell's radio broadcast, the Budds received a letter from Albert Fish. In it, he rambled on about cannibalism in general, gave a fictitious account of how he was introduced to eating human flesh and, finally, gave the graphic description of how he killed and ate their daughter, which was included above. A few lines from the letter will serve to illustrate its tone.

My Dear Mrs. Budd,
On Sunday June 3, 1928, I called on you at 406 W. 15 St. Brought you pot cheese, strawberries. We had lunch. Grace sat on my lap and kissed me. I made up my mind to eat her.

He ended the letter with what, for the monstrously deranged Fish, may have been intended as a note of reassurance: 'I did not fuck her tho I could have had I wished. She died a virgin.'

Fortunately for her, Delia Budd was illiterate. But when she handed the letter to her son Edward, now twenty-three, he ran straight to the police in a blind fury. Since the only person who was still up-to-date on the case was Detective King, Ed Budd and the letter were directed to him.

The letter was carefully examined and compared with the original, hand-written version of the telegram. The handwriting matched. King also noticed that the envelope was imprinted with the letters NYPCBA inside a hexagonal shield. This turned out to be the logo of the New York Private Chauffeurs' Benevolent Association. While police checked through the Association's membership cards trying to find a handwriting match, King requested any association member who had knowledge of any blank stationery which had left the club's offices to come forward. A janitor at the NYPCBA, Lee Siscoski, admitted he had taken a few sheets of stationery and some envelopes for his own use and carried them back to his rooming house on 52nd Street.

When Detective King interviewed Siscoski's landlady, she said that of course she knew a man who fitted that description. It was Albert Fish, and he had been a tenant in her house until very recently. When King explained the situation, the woman was shocked to say the least, but said she expected to hear from Mr Fish again. It seemed that his son often sent money to him and Fish had asked her to hold any letters that might arrive for him. It took almost exactly a month, but on 13 December the landlady called Detective King to inform him that Albert Fish was in her parlour. When King arrived, Fish was calmly balancing a teacup on his knee.

As King stepped into the room and asked if he was Albert Fish, the Grey Man stood up and nodded yes. But before King could even announce his arrest, Fish whipped a straight razor from his pocket and made a slash at the detective. King grabbed the old man's arm, twisted it aside and handcuffed him.

It seemed only fair that after having cracked the case it was Detective William King who took Fish's first statement. Amazingly, Fish seemed completely cooperative. He stated that young Edward Budd had been his intended victim right up until the minute he laid eyes on sweet little Gracie. He described where he took her and what he had done to her. Appalled, King asked him the most obvious question in the world. Why? Fish answered calmly, 'I never could account for that.' That cold, detached reply was to become typical of Albert Fish's attitude throughout the remainder of his examination and trial – it was the same attitude he had when describing dozens of other murders he had committed.

The next day he led King and other officers to the abandoned house in Westchester County where they recovered the scant remains of Gracie Budd; and he did so without the slightest sign of emotion.

During their routine investigation into Fish's background, police found that even though his most horrible crimes had gone undiscovered, Albert had been a very bad boy. His record began in 1903 with a conviction for grand theft. There had been six subsequent arrests including several for sending obscene letters, but each of them had been dismissed. Still, there had been several trips – some extended – to mental institutions. But each time he had been committed, Albert Fish, murderer and child eater, had been released as 'cured'.

The only thing left to do before formally charging Fish with the murder of Gracie Budd was to call in the Budd family for a formal identification of the suspect. Gracie's father and brother Edward agreed to undertake the nasty job themselves. When the Budds entered the room where Fish was being held, Ed launched himself towards the old man shouting, 'You old bastard. You dirty son of a bitch!' Only quick action by King and several officers kept him from tearing Fish limb from limb. Amazingly, Fish hardly blinked during the fracas. Gracie's father stared at the little man for a minute before he could ask, 'Don't you know me?' Fish answered politely, 'Oh, yes. You're Mr Budd.'

With Fish safely in custody, the police sent out requests for anyone who might be able to tie him to any unsolved crimes regarding children. In a matter of days witnesses started bringing in their evidence. From Staten Island came a man who recognised Fish as the person who had tried to lure his son into the woods in July of 1924, only three days and a few hundred yards from the spot where Francis McDonnell was found beaten and murdered. A retired trolleybus driver from Brooklyn identified the man he had seen in 1927, dragging four-year-old Billy Gaffney on and off his trolleybus. Others led police to connect Fish to crimes in which the Grey Man had never even been a suspect. One tied him to fifteen-year-old Mary O'Connor who had been found mutilated in woods near her home in Far Rockaway in 1932. At this point, Fish's approaching trial seemed to be no more than a formality. The only question was, was he sane enough to be held responsible for all the obscene things he had done?

The court ordered a mental examination which was carried out by the noted psychiatrist, or 'alienist' as they were then known, Dr Fredric Wertham. Wertham's initial reaction to Fish was identical to everyone else's: 'If you wanted someone to entrust your child to, he would be the one you would choose.' Fish was cooperative and chatty, never stinting on the details of his life and crimes, but almost as universal as his willingness to talk was his complete emotional detachment. He showed no more interest in what he was saying than someone reading the telephone directory. He told of his childhood and his feelings towards pain: 'I always had a desire to inflict pain on others and to have others inflict pain on me. I always seemed to enjoy everything that hurt.' Knowing full well that he would be put on trial for his life, he talked about that, too, 'I have no particular desire to live. I have no particular desire to be killed. It is a matter of indifference to me. I do not think that I am quite right.' Jumping on this last statement, Wertham asked Fish if he thought he was insane. 'Not exactly,' he answered, 'I could never understand myself.' At no point did Fish seem to think he had done anything wrong and attached this belief to his religious delusions. 'What I did must have been right or an angel would have stopped me, just as an angel stopped Abraham in the Bible [from offering his son as a sacrifice].'

When Fish began to recount his history of self-inflicted torture, Wertham simply could not believe what he was hearing. He ordered X-rays to be taken to verify Fish's claims that he had shoved needles so far into his groin they could not be removed. To the surprise of everyone but Fish, the X-rays showed 29 needles embedded deep in his pelvic region. Wertham's notes catalogued Fish's bizarre history of tortures. '[He described] experiences with excreta of every imaginable kind [both] active and passive. He took bits of cotton, saturated them with alcohol, inserted them in his rectum and set fire to them. He also did this with his child victims.' It would seem that Albert Fish, the mild little man with the droopy moustache, had more sexual fetishes than the psychiatry of the day had names to describe.

Fish's recounting of his innumerable murders led Wertham to conclude that while claiming to have killed – and sometimes eaten – more than 100 children in 23 states, he had, in fact, been guilty of at least fifteen murders and responsible for over a hundred mutilations from which the victims survived. Fish credited his long run to having satisfied himself primarily with black children. The police, he said, were never as interested in finding them as they were when it was white children who disappeared. Tragically, he was all too right.

Although the degree, and amount, of Fish's ghoulish fetishes were unique, Wertham unearthed records showing that Albert was the predictable product of a family with a history of problems. 'One paternal uncle suffered from a religious psychosis and died in a state hospital. A half-brother also died in a state hospital. A younger brother was feeble-minded and died of hydrocephalus [water on the brain]. A paternal aunt was considered "completely crazy". A brother suffered from chronic alcoholism. A sister had some sort of "mental affliction".'

Wertham's conclusion was that Albert Fish suffered from 'sado-masochism directed against children, particularly boys [and had a] sexually regressive development.' In an elaboration of that conclusion, Wertham wrote:

> I characterized his personality as introverted and extremely infantilistic . . . which I diagnosed as paranoid psychosis. Because Fish suffered from delusions and particularly was so mixed up about questions of punishment, sin, atonement, religion, torture [and] self-punishment, he had a perverted, a distorted – if you want, an insane – knowledge of right and wrong.

Charged with the first-degree murder of Gracie Budd, Albert Fish was brought to trial on Monday 11 March 1935 in White Plains, New York. Appearing for the defence was James Dempsey; the prosecution was presented by Assistant District Attorney Elbert Gallagher.

Dempsey's strategy was simple. He would not refute the charges against his client, but would try to prevent his execution by pleading insanity. To accomplish this he would rely on the findings of Dr Wertham and two additional defence psychiatrists and, in the process, discredit the testimony of the four psychiatrists the prosecution was planning to call to the stand.

Dr Fredric Wertham recounted his findings, closing with, 'However you define the medical and legal borders of sanity, this is certainly beyond that border.' The other defence psychiatrists, as expected, gave similar opinions.

The prosecution psychiatrists were harder for Dempsey to deal with, particularly Dr Charles Lambert from Belleview Hospital who had declared Fish 'both harmless and sane' after a stay there in 1930. With his reputation on the line, Lambert was not about to give Dempsey anything to work with. In a masterstroke of obfuscation Lambert declared Fish to be a 'psychopathic personality without a psychosis'.

In his cross-examination of Lambert, Dempsey asked, 'Assume that this man not only killed this girl but took her flesh to eat it. Will you not state that that man could, for nine days, eat that flesh and still not have a psychosis?' As though he had been asked to comment on the colour of Fish's necktie, Lambert flippantly answered, 'There is no accounting for taste, Mr Dempsey.'

Dempsey also put several of Fish's children on the stand to testify to his kindness towards them even while exhibiting perverse forms of personal torture and religious delusions. Although they all agreed he had been kind and gentle in his treatment of them, they refused to visit their father in prison.

Dempsey also introduced evidence to indicate that his client could be suffering from 'lead colic', a term then used for the nerve and brain cell destroying lead poisoning that sometimes afflicted painters in the days of lead-based paint. In his closing remarks, Dempsey reminded the jury that the question was not whether or not Albert Fish had murdered and defiled Gracie Budd, but whether a man could chop up and eat children and still be considered sane.

After ten days of testimony, cross-examination and exhibits that included the shattered skull of little Gracie Budd, the judge gave the jury their instructions and sent them to ponder their verdict. Less than one hour later they returned. In a clear voice, the foreman announced, 'We find the defendant guilty as charged.' The insanity plea had been rejected; Albert Fish, aged sixty-four, would be put to death in the electric chair at Sing Sing Penitentiary.

Amazingly, Fish thanked the judge profusely for the sentence. Later, he admitted to Dr Wertham, 'What a thrill it will be if I have to die in the electric chair. It will be the supreme thrill. The only one I haven't tried.' On 16 January 1936, Albert Fish experienced the supreme thrill. He was so excited that he even helped the guards fasten the straps to his legs. His children did not step forward to claim the body and Albert Fish was buried in the prison cemetery at Sing Sing.

As an odd footnote to this story, and a comment on the public's perception of the psychiatric system in general, several of the jurors later stated that they believed Fish to have been insane. Because he had been institutionalised and released on more than one occasion, however, they felt it their duty to do the only thing they could to guarantee that the monstrous Grey Man would never be let loose on society again.

Ten

The Shallow End of the Gene Pool: Ottis Toole and Henry Lee Lucas (1951–83)

When 29-year-old Ottis Toole and his future associate, Henry Lee Lucas, forty-two, first met in the soup kitchen of a Jacksonville, Florida, homeless shelter, it was a marriage made in hell. As alike as two peas in a very rotten pod, they took to each other like bluebottles to a dung-heap. Not only were they kindred spirits in a greater variety of depravity than can be imagined but they had already carved out individual careers as killers. As is so often the case in life, their combined talents would produce far more gruesome results than the sum of their individual parts. The politically correct might have described Ottis and Henry Lee as 'economically deprived practitioners of an alternative lifestyle'. Everyone else in America would have been more likely to describe them as 'white trash'.

What makes Ottis and Henry Lee unique among their ilk is the question: how many of the crimes they claim to have committed are real, and how many are either completely fictitious or a case of their taking credit for someone else's handiwork? It is a question which has never been satisfactorily answered. Consequently, at least some of what you will find in the following tale is open to question and controversy; it is, however, no less than what Henry Lee and Ottis claimed to be the truth, at least some of the time.

Henry Lee Lucas was born at the end of the Great Depression in the backwater village of Blacksburgh, Virginia. The year 1936 was not a good one anywhere, but in Blacksburgh no year was good. The Lucas clan lived in a dirt-floored shanty beyond the edge of town – beyond the point where electricity, telephone and running water stopped. Sharing the shack with the infant Henry Lee was his vicious prostitute mother Viola, his moonshine-making father Anderson, generally known as 'No Legs' ever since he stumbled, dead drunk, under a freight train, Viola's pimp Bernie and Henry's eight brothers and sisters, at least some of whom were Anderson's.

While Viola terrorised both her children and husband with an endless string of invective and savage beatings, she seemed to take a particular delight in abusing Henry Lee. While No Legs hid from Viola, drinking as much of his homemade whiskey as possible, Henry Lee was forced to watch his mother entertain an endless string of paying customers. If he turned away, she beat him. On at least one occasion she beat him so severely that he lay semi-conscious for three days before Bernie the pimp took him to the hospital. Thanks to the constant abuse Henry Lee began hearing 'voices' and noises in his head. His papa tried to shelter the child from Viola by making him the full-time guardian of the family still. Consequently, by the time he was ten years old Henry Lee was already an alcoholic. Once Henry was old enough to attend school his mother delighted in sending him off in a dress just to see what the reaction would be. Years later, a former teacher would recall him as being dirty, malnourished and seriously disturbed. Not surprisingly Henry dropped out of school after the fifth grade.

With nothing much to do, Henry Lee fell under the increasing influence of Bernie the pimp, who showed him how to torture animals and have sex with them – either before or after he killed them. Extending this fledgling interest in sex, by the time he reached his early teens Henry had begun raping his half-brother to while away the hours. Henry Lee's problems only got worse after No Legs crawled out of the cabin into a snowdrift and froze to death. Having no one and nothing to keep him at home, Henry Lee began terrorising the surrounding towns. According to his own account, he beat, strangled and raped a teenage girl in Lynchburg when he was fifteen, burying her body in a nearby wood. The disappearance of seventeen-year-old Laura Burnley would not be solved until Henry Lee's confession in 1983.

A string of crimes, arrests, time at juvenile detention facilities and the loss of one eye did little to improve Henry Lee's attitude or looks. By late 1959 the 23-year-old Henry Lee was living in Michigan with his sister when his loving mother turned up demanding that her boy come back to Virginia to take care of her. After a few hours of serious drinking and shouting, things got ugly. When Viola hit Henry with a broom handle he pulled a knife and stabbed her, taking time to rape her 74-year-old body before going on the run. Five days later he was arrested in Toledo, Ohio, and confessed to the whole thing.

After being sentenced to 20 to 40 years in prison for the murder of his mother, Henry Lee began telling his guards that he was hearing the 'voices in his head' again. This time it was his mother's voice telling him to kill himself in retribution for what he had done to her. After two unsuccessful attempts at suicide he was transferred to Iona State Mental Hospital where he was diagnosed as a 'suicidal psychopath', a 'sadist' and a 'sexual deviant'. The four-and-a-half years of drugs and electroshock treatment that followed only served to make him crazier than before. In April 1970 Henry Lee came up for parole and, as is usual in such cases, was sent to plead his case before the parole board. According to Henry's recollections, when a member of the parole board asked him, 'Now, Mr Lucas, I must ask you, if we grant you parole, will you kill again?' he answered, 'Yes, sir! If you release me now, I will kill again.' Three months later, Henry was out on the streets.

As a parting shot, Henry claims to have told the guards, 'I'll leave you a present on the doorstep.' He later insisted that he murdered two women that same day, leaving one of their bodies within sight of the prison walls, but no evidence of the crime has ever been discovered. True or not, once free Henry began robbing, raping, killing and doing the occasional stretch in the pen until late in 1975 when he wandered into Jacksonville, Florida, where he would eventually meet Ottis Toole.

Jacksonville was Ottis' hometown and a far cry from most tourists' conception of sunny Florida. When Ottis was born in 1949 Jacksonville, like much of Florida, was still rural and poor. The flood of tourists and money had not yet filtered much beyond the limits of Miami, St Petersburg and Fort Lauderdale. Like so many poor, southern backwater towns, Jacksonville was permeated by a hard-core, hyper-fundamentalist version of the Christian religion. This was the 'hell-fire and brimstone' Christianity that relies more on being 'God fearing' than on love and forgiveness. Like so many people attracted to this simplistic religion, Ottis Toole's family were dirt-poor, underfed and only semi-literate. Add to this mix the fact that, like Henry Lee's family, Ottis' parents were alcoholic, and the makings of disaster were close at hand.

The combination of poverty, malnutrition and an alcoholic mother ensured that Ottis Toole had little chance to make the most of whatever potential he might have possessed. Eventually, testing would show that he had an IQ between 54 and 75, which teeters on the edge of retardation. Later examinations would also show that Ottis suffered from 'frontal and limbic brain damage' resulting in periodic seizures and occasional blackouts. Ottis was sent to special education classes, but he gave up and dropped out in the eighth grade.

If anything more could have been added to this mix to guarantee Ottis would turn out bad, it would seem that at least some members of his family had a peculiarly bizarre take on their religion. In Toole's own words, 'If you believe in God, you believe in the devil. If you believe in the devil, you believe in God.' To some in Ottis' family it would seem that it mattered little to which of these powers they gave their allegiance. According to some sources, Toole's grandmother was a Satanist who liked to take little Ottis along while she dug up bodies to use in her cult's worship services. Along with desecrating the bodies of the deceased, the group allegedly partook in the eating of human flesh and sex orgies.

Perhaps as a result of his early indoctrination into this twisted cult, or possibly due to a chemical imbalance related to his brain damage, Ottis was always fascinated by fires – a bent which he nurtured until he became a fully-fledged pyromaniac: 'The bigger the fires, the more I get excited.' As though to make Ottis even more unacceptable to society at large, he was a homosexual and an occasional transvestite. Once, talking about his feelings towards women, he simply said, 'Tried 'em. Don't like 'em.' It was probably not an attitude that went down well in the fundamentalist atmosphere around Jacksonville.

Trapped with a mentality that went entirely against the grain of the world at large, Ottis tried to drown himself in a tidal wave of cheap booze and drugs. He started by stealing his mother's barbiturates and steadily worked his way up to anything he could find or steal. 'Oh, shoot, I would take it all. Whatever I could get my hands on, is what I would take. Something to get me real high, you know.'

By the time he was in his early teens, Ottis Toole spent his time in a self-imposed altered state of reality, setting fires and paying for his drug and booze habit by dressing in women's clothes and prostituting himself on the streets. At six feet in height, snaggle toothed and jug eared, how Ottis got any takers is a mystery, but he must have done so because in 1963, a travelling salesman picked up the fourteen-year-old Ottis. Bored, drugged out, or just plain crazy, Ottis changed his mind and proceeded to run the man over with his own car. Fleeing the scene, by the time he crawled back to Jacksonville some years later, he was a leading suspect in four other murder cases.

Late in 1976, Henry Lee Lucas and Ottis Toole were both living in Jacksonville, on the edge of existence. Without funds to support their drinking habits, without employment and evidently not in the mood to steal or kill anybody, they were reduced to taking their meals at homeless shelters. One day, they wound up in the same line at the same soup kitchen where, by pure chance, they struck up a conversation and were amazed at how much they had in common.

Because Henry Lee was living rough or at homeless shelters, Ottis invited him to come home with him to Springfield, a run-down suburb of Jacksonville where he lived with his mother, her husband of the moment, his nephew and niece, Frank and Becky Powell, and his own wife, Novella. It is unlikely that anyone seemed surprised when Ottis turned up with Henry Lee; he was always bringing home a man to have sex with – sometimes for pay, sometimes not. Everyone seemed to get on well. Novella was sent to live with neighbours, Henry Lee moved into Ottis' bed and spent his spare time making friends with the mildly retarded Becky Powell. But even the good life can get boring and before long Henry Lee and Ottis hit the road looking for adventure.

From state to state they stole cars, killed people and robbed anywhere that looked easy – mostly convenience stores, but occasionally they would 'knock off' a bank just for the thrill of it. Sometimes they killed to steal a car, sometimes for sex and sometimes just for the fun of killing. They both swore that when they were in too much of a hurry to stop and murder a hitchhiker they would simply run them down and keep driving. Anything for a laugh.

On one occasion, after terrorising the clerk at a convenience store, Henry Lee killed her and waited while Ottis raped the corpse. But Henry Lee said it was the woman's own fault for being killed; she just wouldn't be quiet and lie still like he told her to do. Ottis, on the other hand, never bothered with the niceties of a few threats before he shot someone. According to Henry Lee, 'Now, see, that's the difference between me and Ottis. He just kills 'em when he feels like it. At least I warn 'em first. He's the worstest killer in the world.'

No matter how much fun it was robbing shops, the homicidal pair's greatest joy was wreaking mayhem out on the open road. Sometimes they would pick up hitchhikers, other times they would pretend to be hitchhikers. Sometimes Ottis would be in drag, sometimes not. They did whatever it took to lure some poor, unsuspecting soul close enough for one of the lethal pair to kill them. Toole later explained, 'We picked up lots of hitchhikers, you know, and Lucas killed most of the women hisself, and some of them would be shot in the head and the chest, and some of them would be choked to death and some of them would be beat in the head with a tire tool.' Henry Lee was a little more blasé about it all: 'Just about everyone I pick up, I kill 'em.' The reason Henry Lee killed his victims – beyond preventing them from identifying him and Ottis – was that he liked a lot of sex and preferred to have it with dead people: '. . . to me a live woman ain't nothing. I enjoy dead sex more than I do live sex.'

But even Henry Lee was adaptable. On one occasion, while the pair was cruising along Texas interstate I-35, they approached a young couple thumbing a ride after having run out of gas. Stopping the car, Ottis jumped out, shot the man nine times in the head and chest, rolled his body into a ditch and dragged the terrified girl into the back seat of their car where Henry Lee proceeded to rape her. Not liking Henry Lee to have sex with living people other than himself, Ottis jammed on the brakes, hauled the girl out of the car and shot her six times. They left her body where it fell and continued on their way.

However their victims were killed, whatever sexual indignities were committed before, or after, death, it was nothing compared to Ottis' favourite means of disposing of the corpse. Although neither of the pair was ever formally charged with cannibalism, Ottis never made a secret of the pleasure he took in barbecued human flesh. Sometimes Henry Lee would join in at one of these obscene feasts, but normally he abstained. His problem lay not in the concept of eating people, but in his partner's cooking methods. In Henry Lee's own words, 'I don't like barbecue sauce.'

Shortly before his death in 1996, Ottis Toole granted an interview to freelance journalist Billy Bob Barton. During the conversation, the subject of Ottis' dietary preferences came up. When Barton said he understood that Ottis liked to eat young boys, Toole expounded: 'I've eaten my share. First I go out and catch me a little boy . . . grab him, tie him up, use a gag, put him in the trunk of my car and drive him out to my place.' After detailing the sexual depravities he would visit on the child, Ottis went on to explain his favourite method of preparing and cooking the victim: '. . . you strip them naked and hang them upside down by the ankles; then you slit their throat with a knife, slit the belly and take out the guts, the liver, the heart. Cut off the head. Let the blood drain. [I use] a pit. A barbecue pit. Charcoal so there ain't much smoke. Take down the body, put the metal spit through them. Put it into the asshole, through the body and out the neck . . . [and] put it on the spit-holder over the coals. Damn tasty.'

When asked to comment on the taste of a child's flesh, Toole waxed loquacious. '[It tastes] same as a roasted piglet. Boys and girls taste about the same when you roast them eight to ten years old. The flavour is a shade different when they're teenagers. The boys are gamier than the girls. Give me the roasted meat of a boy age fourteen and a girl age fourteen and I can tell the difference . . . Teenagers make a nice roast; I do favour a rump roast from a teen. Younger ones I think I prefer ribs. Juicy. Tasty. You ought to try some . . . People eat pigs, cows, horses. I like to eat people. It's good meat, too. You ain't tried it, don't you be saying it ain't tasty. You might like it.'

When Barton asked Ottis how many people he had killed and eaten, he replied, 'Just me killing them alone or the ones I killed and ate with Henry?' Unaware that Lucas had been in on this particular aspect of their partnership, Barton enquired what their combined number might have been. Toole's reply was, 'Oh, about one hundred and fifty or so.'

During a recorded conversation between Lucas and Toole, the subject of their cannibalism again came up when Ottis commented, 'And you know one time, you filleted some of them bodies, and I did too . . . tasted like real meat when it got barbecue sauce on it, don't it?' In response, Henry confirmed his dislike for barbecue sauce in general and Ottis' in particular.

If Henry Lee and Ottis' adventures in social and culinary abominations while roaming the highways of America were not strange enough, once the pair met a man by the name of Don Meteric they became even stranger. According to Toole and Lucas, Meteric was involved with a Satanic cult calling itself the Hand of Death. They claim that Meteric and Ottis had already known each other for some time when Henry became involved, bringing up the question as to Meteric's possible involvement with the devil worshippers from Toole's youth. According to Toole and Lucas, Meteric asked them if they might be interested in carrying out executions for the mysterious cult – the pay would be $10,000 per job. Since they already did similar work for the pure joy of it, they were more than happy to agree. As with all such societies, the Hand of Death required initiates to undergo a secret ritual.

In the best tradition of grade 'B' horror movies, Toole and Lucas were taken deep into the Florida Everglades where a group had gathered to celebrate a black mass. After they had been introduced, one of the celebrants was pointed out to Henry Lee and Ottis as the man whom they would be required to kill before they would be fully accepted into the cult. Luring their victim towards the beach with a bottle of whiskey, when the man tipped his head back to take a swig, Lucas slit his throat from ear to ear so cleanly that, according to Lucas, 'The liquor just spilled out the bottom of his throat.'

After the victim had been used in whatever ceremony the Hand of Death preferred, his carcass was cooked and eaten by the congregation. Later, Ottis described one of his favourite parts of the flesh-eating ritual as practised by the Hand of Death. 'Cut off the peter, cut off the balls [and] it's put in like a little stew pot. The guy who cooks it makes it like a soup or stew. It's a secret recipe from about a thousand years ago . . . The balls are damned good when fried. Use a little batter and a fryer and it's a real treat. Crispy. Like crispy chestnuts. Fresh fried balls is one of my favourites . . . I prefer to eat ribs, actually, but I go along with what's being served at the ceremonies.'

Evidently, there was no sexual discrimination among the Hand of Death and, as one might assume, virgin sacrifice played a central part in their rituals. Again, the best explanation of what took place comes from Ottis himself. 'We were working for that cult and we'd grab little kids for the human sacrifices . . . I liked working for the Hand of Death. They'd let me have the corpses when they were done . . . and I could take a prime cut.'

When asked where all this bizarre activity took place, Ottis insisted the cult had a ranch in Mexico which was used for the enactment of rituals and it was from here that he and Henry Lee would venture to Texas where they would kidnap girls and women at the behest of Meteric. Curiously, although no official proof of its existence has ever been disclosed, the Hand of Death has also been mentioned by those other noted maniacs, Charles Manson and David 'Son of Sam' Berkowitz in connection with their own reigns of terror.

The exact dates of Toole and Lucas' connection with the Hand of Death remain vague, but it would seem that they severed relations with Meteric and his group in 1981 when Ottis' mother and sister died. Particularly distressing to Toole was the fact that with no one left to take care of them, his nephew and niece, Frank and Becky Powell, had been placed in a juvenile home. Travelling back to Florida, Ottis and Henry Lee sprang the kids from the children's home and started hauling them along on their continuing travels. It was not long before Henry Lee and slow-witted Becky – who was then just twelve years old – developed a close relationship, which Lucas insisted was purely platonic. Whether this was because he actually respected the child or simply because he had no interest in sex with a living person is unclear. Whatever the case, Henry Lee and Becky's relationship put too much strain on Henry and Ottis' love life and the pair split up, Henry Lee and Becky heading west towards California.

Convinced that he had been betrayed by his best friend and his niece, Ottis went on a rampage of killing and burning. In 1983 he found himself under arrest and awaiting trial on charges of arson and murder in his native Florida. While behind bars, Ottis was finally given a thorough psychiatric examination. The report, released in 1985, described Ottis as:

a creature of impulse that seems incapable of pre-meditation. He has always acted instantly on impulse without the slightest sense of right or wrong at the time. Life itself, to him, is so unmeaning, and the distinction between living and dead people so blurred, that killing to him is no more than swatting an annoying fly is to normal people. He trivializes the distinction between living and dead, believing himself to be dead. Retarded and illiterate, he has been out of control since early childhood. A severely drug dependent individual, he is unsafe under any conditions outside of a secure prison, and perhaps unsafe there. He is neurologically damaged, definitely in the frontal area, and the psychological evaluation indicates other neurological defects. He is a classic case of severely diminished capacity to control his impulses.

Because of his diminished capacity, Ottis could not be given the death penalty. He was, however, sentenced to six consecutive life terms for arson and murder. Under close scrutiny, and placed on a regular diet that included the anti-psychotics Thorazine and Dilantin, Ottis regained enough equilibrium to remain under control without the use of physical restraints. Meanwhile, Henry Lee and Becky were exploring the great American West.

Eventually, although Becky never seemed to mind Henry Lee's habit of killing people, she began to develop an understanding of Christianity through the good graces of a religious community that had, unwittingly, taken them in. Immediately feeling threatened, Henry Lee took her to a field where he stabbed her to death. Before chopping the corpse into small pieces he finally had sex with her – something he insisted he had never done while she was alive. When Becky's disappearance was noticed by one of the elderly women who had given the pair shelter, Henry gave her the same medicine he had administered to Becky, incinerating the dismembered corpse in a wood-burning stove.

Amazingly, with an ever-lengthening trail of blood spewing out behind him, even when Henry Lee was captured and taken in for questioning in relation to two murders in October 1982, he was released for lack of evidence. Finally, in June 1983, he was arrested on a minor weapons charge but once behind bars he got the confession bug and started telling everything he knew, everything he thought he knew and everything he could imagine. His first confessions were in relation to the deaths of Becky Powell and Kate Rich, the woman who had sheltered the fugitive pair. After being convicted of Becky's murder, Henry even took a minute to congratulate the prosecuting attorney for presenting such a good case.

Now safely locked up in Monroe, Louisiana, Henry continued to confess to one unspeakable deed after another. 'I've killed by strangulation. I've killed by hit-and-run, by shootings, by robberies, by hangings. Every type of crime, I've done it.' For a while, nobody was quite sure if Henry Lee Lucas was the biggest mass murderer in history or just confession happy. Still, no police officer worth his salt can afford to leave any stone unturned so, from all over the USA they began to descend on Henry Lee's jail cell. By October 1983 investigators were convinced that Lucas – and by extension, Toole – was responsible for at least 69 murders. By the following January Henry had convinced them of his culpability in a dozen more. By spring 1985 Henry's confessions had apparently solved 90 murders. When his own foul deeds were added to those committed in the company of Ottis Toole, the number jumped to 198. Although formally charged with thirty murders in addition to those of Becky and Kate Rich, the one for which he was sentenced to death was the case of a woman known only as 'Orange Socks' – a pseudonym given to the unidentified victim based on the only articles of clothing found with the body.

During the years he was incarcerated while awaiting execution, Henry Lee whiled away his time leading police and FBI agents all over the country in search of the endless stream of corpses he happily admitted to creating. With the list now nearing 600 it was a full-time job. When a name came up in which Ottis was allegedly involved, half-way across the country in Florida, Toole would do his best to corroborate Henry's story with such details as he could remember.

But according to Henry Lee, the entire thing was a ruse. 'I'd go through files. I'd look through pictures, everything that concerned that murder. And when the detective come from that state, or that town, I'd tell them all about that murder.' But

Henry suddenly stopped confessing and began insisting his confessions were lies. Inevitably he was shifted back to death row. So why did he recant? According to Henry himself, he found religion. 'I'm not some kind of saint, but I do believe I'll go to heaven.'

Down in Florida, Ottis Toole had another explanation for Henry Lee's change of heart. 'Henry wants to deny everything now because he's trying to avoid being executed. I'm too crazy for execution so I can tell you how it really was. Henry killed a lot of people, I know, I was there. I helped him do the murders. I have everything I want in prison. Except I miss the freedom to drive down the highway robbing and killing from town to town. That's excitement at its best. And I miss being able to barbecue a boy when I get the urge. I do like to barbecue . . . anyone who wants to write me and get a recipe for my homemade sauce, I'll send it free. Just send a few stamps for the reply letter.'

On 15 September 1996, Ottis Toole died in prison from cirrhosis of the liver. He was forty-seven years of age.

Still imprisoned in Texas, Henry Lee Lucas was scheduled to be executed on 30 June 1998 for the murder of 'Orange Socks'. Curiously, on 27 June, Governor George W. Bush commuted the sentence. It was not a temporary stay of execution while the evidence was re-examined, but a permanent reprieve which, Bush insisted, was based on new evidence that Henry Lee had been hundreds of miles away at the time of the murder. Given the number of murders Henry Lee had committed, and the fact that (then) Governor Bush had pulled the switch on 152 other convicted killers during his tenancy in the governor's chair, it seems too odd not to ponder. Henry Lee Lucas died on 11 March 2001 at the age of sixty-four. We have no idea how many deaths he and Ottis Toole were actually responsible for, or how many children Ottis may have barbecued.

1. Cannibalism among the Tupi-Guarani in South America as viewed by Europeans. Note how the mothers feed select morsels to their children, possibly after pre-chewing them.

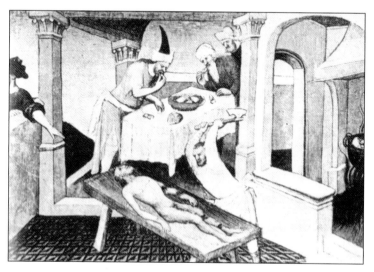

2. Cannibalism in the Andaman Islands as imagined by medieval travellers.

3. Woodcut of a mid-sixteenth-century 'barbecue' in Brazil.

4. Use of a 'barbecue' among the Tupi-Guarani in South America.

5. *Hunger, Madness and Crime* by Antoine Wiertz: note the cooking pot over the fire.

6. Babies in the cooking pot, a detail from a typical eighteenth-century view of the Witches' Sabbat.

7. A sixteenth-century impression of South American cannibals preparing a meal of human flesh, by Theodore de Bry.

8. In this sketch for a painting of the *Wreck of the Medusa* we have a classic example of cannibalism for survival.

9. Alf Packer in his prison uniform.

10. Albert Fish seated between his defence attorneys before sentencing.

11. Henry Lee Lucas opposite Sheriff William F. Conway, Montague County lock-up, Texas, on 15 June 1983.

12. Ed Gein.

13. André Chikatilo yawns loudly as the judge reads out his guilty verdict.

14. Issei Sagawa.

15. Jeffrey Dahmer.

16. Nicolas Claux.

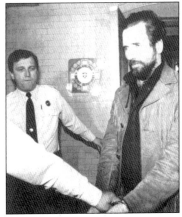

17. Gary Heidnik under arrest.

18. Armin Meiwes.

19. Bernd-Jurgen Brandes
– willing 'victim' of
Armin Meiwes.

20. Marc Sappington.

Eleven

Psycho Killer qu'est-ce que c'est? Ed Gein (1954–7)

Wisconsin in the 1950s was about as quintessentially small-town America as any place could be. People still farmed the land, went to church, watched *I Love Lucy* on television, voted, helped their neighbours when they could and sympathised with them when they could not. All that changed for one Wisconsin town and, by extension, for the nation in 1957, when the Ed Gein case broke into the national news. In a very real sense, America, and the way we look at it, has never been the same since.

Edward Gein was born in La Crosse, Wisconsin, in 1906, the second child of George and Augusta. A brother, Henry, had been born seven years earlier. Like most people at the time, the Geins were God-fearing people who largely kept themselves to themselves. But in the Geins' case, it was not just a matter of respectful privacy. Augusta, a harshly strait-laced woman, was unquestionably the head of the family and it was her firm belief that most of their neighbours, like most people everywhere, were irredeemable sinners and to be avoided at all costs.

In a more balanced family Augusta's husband might have been able to keep her religious excesses in check, but George Gein was a weak-spirited man who chose to hide in a bottle of whiskey rather than face the wrath of his hard-edged wife. Consequently, Augusta was left to bring up her sons as she saw fit. To keep the boys pure and safe, she alternated severe and nearly constant scolding with hefty doses of biblical scripture, concentrating on those passages which promised hell-fire and damnation for transgressors. She also saw to it that the boys had as little contact with the sinful, outside world as possible. But no matter what she did, she could not entirely blot out what she saw as the 'sinkhole of filth' that was La Crosse.

In 1914 Augusta sold the small, family-owned grocery store in La Crosse and moved the family to an isolated 160-acre farm seven miles outside the town of Plainfield. With the nearest neighbours more than a quarter of a mile away, Henry and Eddie should be safe. Unfortunately, even in Plainfield they had to go to school, so Augusta's brow-beatings and threats of damnation only increased. To keep the boys on the straight and narrow, she pounded into them the evils of loose women, the sins of the flesh and the dire consequences awaiting fornicators on the day they faced their final judgement.

Henry, who was the more outgoing of the two, seemed able to cope with his mother's tirades, but for small, awkward Eddie, life was nearly intolerable. The kids at school shunned him and teased him for being a 'Mama's boy' and a 'sissy'. Where other children with socialisation problems might have found solace at home, Eddie – desperate for love – only found Augusta's wrath and his father's alcohol-dulled indifference. The only one he could really talk to was brother Henry.

Neither of the boys ever really integrated into society, remaining distant, lonely bachelors all their lives. But shy little Eddie had the worst of it. Despite her terrible temper, Augusta had convinced him that only she could love him and take care of him, constantly drawing him close while simultaneously driving him away.

Henry did his best to provide some stability for Eddie, particularly after their father died in 1940 and managing the farm became almost too much to deal with. To earn extra money, Henry took the occasional odd job in Plainfield and when he went into town he took his little brother along, hoping that seeing how normal people lived and interacted might help balance out the worst aspects of life at home. He even got Eddie his own small jobs mowing lawns and babysitting. Eddie liked babysitting best. He could relate to children better than he could to adults, and children didn't frighten him the way adults did.

But at home, the situation was deteriorating. As Henry grew towards adulthood he became more open in his criticism of his mother. He told her to leave Eddie alone and let him grow up. The rows were awful and they confused Eddie more and more as time went on. How could brother Henry talk like that to their mother who loved them? But, of course, he loved Henry, too.

Ed's life took a wrenching turn on 16 May 1944, when Henry discovered a grass fire not far from the family barn. Calling Eddie to help him put it out before it spread to the outbuildings, the two soon became separated in the choking, swirling smoke. That evening, when Eddie returned to the house, Henry was nowhere to be found. Augusta contacted the police who arrived with a search party to scour the charred field. Curiously, although he insisted he did not know what happened to Henry, Eddie took them right to the spot where his brother's body lay. The grass beneath him had not been touched by the blaze and there were bruises on his head, but no one seemed to question the circumstances. The coroner ruled death by asphyxiation, and poor little Eddie was left alone to the tender mercies of his tyrannical mother – but not for long.

A few months later Augusta suffered a stroke which left her bedridden. Eddie did his best to take care of her, but going into town for his odd jobs was now out of the question. His mother quickly became his entire world. He prayed fervently that she would get well and not leave him alone in the sinful world, but on 29 December 1945 Augusta Gein died during a second stroke. At thirty-nine years of age, Ed Gein was on his own for the first time – emotionally dependent on a dead woman who had always provided him with direction.

Thanks to a government-sponsored soil conservation grant, Ed was able to give up farming and use his time however he wanted. But he didn't know what it was he wanted. Dazed and confused, he wandered around the ramshackle farmhouse, slowly closing off the rooms that had been his mother's private domain. The door to her bedroom was boarded up first, then the entire upper floor of the house. Next the parlour and the dining room were sealed off, leaving Ed with only the kitchen and one other room which he used as a bedroom.

With nothing to occupy his time he began reading voraciously. Reading was the one thing he had been good at in school and had always provided him with an escape from the noise and confusion of his oppressive world. His choice of reading material, however, was distinctly bizarre. He read about cannibals and head-hunters who had once inhabited the South Sea Islands. He read death-cult exposés, books about Nazi atrocities and the unspeakable experiments carried out by Dr Joseph Mengele at the Auschwitz death camp. He read books on taxidermy and the preservation and tanning of skin to make leather, and he read anatomy books and tales of grave robbers such as Burke and Hare.

Now almost completely lost in his own, increasingly strange world, Ed only rarely went into Plainfield unless he needed groceries or someone called and asked him to do some odd job or other. The only times he opened up a little bit were on those rare occasions when he stopped in at Mary Hogan's Tavern, a roadhouse next to the highway that ran between the Gein farm and Plainfield. Mary was a pleasantly plump woman at the top end of middle age who, like almost everyone who knew Ed, felt sorry for him. Being of a charitable nature, she referred to him as a 'poor soul' or called him 'Eddie', as though he were still a child who had somehow not quite grown up. More callous types just called him 'Weird old Ed'.

It was only the town's kids who really gave him a hard time. They taunted him mercilessly. Among younger kids the Gein home had the reputation of being haunted, and the boys would dare each other to run into the yard and throw stones at the house or get close and peer in at the windows. On more than one occasion a terrified child would run home with tales of 'dead people's heads' hanging on the walls inside the house. On the one occasion when a customer at Mary Hogan's brought his son's ramblings up to Ed, Eddie laughed and said that he did have heads on the wall at home. His cousin had been in the Pacific Islands during the war and had sent back some Maori shrunken heads that now hung in his bedroom. Ed probably got some strange looks for that comment – but everybody knew Ed was a little strange. When he had 'had a few' he would ramble on about head-hunters and Nazi experiments and the sex-change operation that Christine Jorgenson person had had, and odd things like that. But then, Ed had always been 'different', but he was harmless. He wouldn't even go hunting with the guys from town because he said he just couldn't shoot anything. Certainly, he didn't seem any more peculiar now than he had been before his mother died. Or so it appeared.

Thanks to his bizarre library, Ed developed a fascination with female anatomy for the first time. Never having allowed himself to have any sexual feeling for fear of being seduced by an evil woman and sent straight to hell, Ed had no idea how to deal with these new, disturbing thoughts. He wasn't even sure how they related to his mother who had been the best and purest woman he had ever known. What Ed did know was that women were stronger than men. He knew this because of the way his mother had dominated him and Henry and their dad. But now that she was gone, Ed didn't have anywhere to turn for that kind of strength. If he were a woman, it would all be different. With reality now slipping further and further away from him, Ed could no longer tell if he just wanted to look at women, or to touch them or, maybe, to be one of them. What would it be like to have breasts and a vagina? Would he feel different . . . stronger?

For a while he contented himself with dressing up in his mother's clothes and telling himself what to do. It must have seemed a relief to have his mother near him again, advising him and taking away the confusion. Later, he toyed with the idea of castrating himself, but gave up the idea; it still wouldn't make him a woman. He needed something else.

One day in 1947, while reading the newspaper, Ed's attention landed on the obituary column where he saw the funeral notice for a local woman. Finally, Ed knew what it was he wanted to do. He called one of his few friends, another old farmer named Gus, who was a few sandwiches short of a picnic, and told him he needed some help with a little project. When Gus came over, Ed explained that he was doing some medical experiments and needed a human body. Since grave digging was hard work, Ed wondered if Gus would mind giving him a hand? Gus had no objections, so together they robbed the grave the night after the funeral and took the body back to Ed's place. Over the next few years, Ed would enlist Gus's help any number of times. On one occasion they even robbed Augusta Gein's grave. Gus never knew what Ed was doing with all those cadavers and, so far as we know, he never asked. It was just part of Ed's experiments. Things went on this way until the day Gus was committed to an old people's home and Ed was left without anyone to help him rob graves. But grave digging was hard work and Ed was not quite up to doing it himself. He would have to find another way to get women's bodies.

On the afternoon of 8 December 1954, police got a call from a customer who had stopped off at Mary Hogan's Tavern and found the place standing wide open but with no sign of Mary. The police found bloodstains behind the bar leading all the way through the back door and into the parking lot. On the floor of the taproom was the spent cartridge from a .32 calibre pistol. But with no body and no other evidence, they had little to base an investigation on. It wasn't the first disappearance in that part of Wisconsin, either. In the past seven years two other girls had vanished. On 1 May 1947, eight-year-old Georgia Weckler had disappeared on her way home from school, in the town of Jefferson, and was never heard from again. Six years later, a fifteen-year-old La Crosse girl named Evelyn Hartley had vanished while babysitting. In the house, police found Evelyn's glasses and shoes and several miles away they discovered some of her clothes, but no trace of the girl was ever found. Mary's murder seemed to form part of a pattern, but there just weren't enough pieces to solve the puzzle.

Meanwhile, life around Plainfield stayed pretty much the same. New owners took over Mary's Tavern, Eddie Gein came into town now and again, only stopping in at the grocery store, the hardware store or the bar for a few 'quick ones' before driving back to the increasingly dilapidated farmhouse.

One of the occasions when Ed dropped into town was on 15 November 1957. On his regular rounds he stopped at Worden's hardware store where he chatted with Bernice Worden, who had run the place since her husband's death some years earlier. Sometimes her son, Frank, came in to help her out but he worked as a local deputy sheriff, so his time was limited. That day, Frank was in the store and both he and his mother took time to chat with poor old Eddie. They exchanged pleasantries and Ed asked Frank if he had been out deer hunting yet that year. Frank said not yet, but he was going out the next day. Ed mumbled something to Bernice about needing some anti-freeze for his Ford, but left without buying anything.

Late the next afternoon Frank called at the hardware store on his way back from hunting. He hadn't had any luck and was tired and cold, but decided to take a minute to see his mother before he went home. The door was open and the lights were on, but there was no sign of Bernice. Frank called for her and looked around for a minute before he realised the cash register was gone. On the floor behind the counter was a coagulating pool of blood. The only thing near the spot where the cash register should have been was a receipt for a half-gallon of anti-freeze – made out to Ed Gein.

Frank decided that Ed must have come in the afternoon before to find out when he would be away, and then returned to rob the place. Obviously he had got into a struggle with Bernice and something terrible had happened. Frank immediately called his boss, Sheriff Art Schley, and repeated his findings and suppositions. They agreed to meet at the Gein farm and Schley told deputies Chase and Spees to scour the area for any sign of Ed Gein and arrest him on suspicion if they located him. Almost before Sheriff Schley arrived at the Gein farm, Chase and Spees were driving past Hill's grocery store just as Ed was backing his battered pick-up truck out of the parking lot. When they pulled up behind the truck, Ed offered no resistance, but mumbled, 'Somebody framed me.' 'Framed you for what?' Chase demanded. Ed looked at the officer as though he were confused. 'Well, about Mrs Worden.' He answered. 'What about Mrs Worden?' 'Well, she's dead, ain't she?' Without another word, Chase and Spees hauled Ed to jail.

By the time Art Schley and Frank Worden got to Ed's house it was already dark, both inside and out. Ed was not there, but Frank and Art decided to try the doors. The main doors were locked, but the door to the old summer kitchen, which Ed used as a woodshed, was slightly ajar. Since there was no electricity at the house, the two had to use their electric torches. Fumbling around in the near dark, Schley felt something bump against his shoulder. Raising his light, he saw what, at first, appeared to be a field-dressed deer. The carcass was hanging from the ceiling, legs splayed, its torso slit from pelvis to throat, the innards, genitals and anus removed. It took a minute for the men to realise what they were looking at. It was the body of Bernice Worden. Nearby, in a box, were her intestines but her head was nowhere to be seen.

After a few seconds of frozen horror, the men stumbled outside to be violently sick. Once they gathered themselves enough to function, Art Schley called his office and demanded reinforcements. Within minutes more than a dozen officers had answered the frantic summons. While some of the men scoured the grounds and outbuildings, Art, Frank and the rest forced their way into the house. What they found would make Jack the Ripper look like a rank amateur.

Using their torches and kerosene lamps, the men stumbled through a maze of reeking filth and collected garbage. Boxes of junk, piles of newspaper, magazines and rotting food waste were everywhere, but it was what lay mixed in with the mess that told Ed's real story. In a pan on the stove lay a human heart and in the refrigerator were piles of human organs, some fresh, others quietly putrefying. The kitchen chairs had been reupholstered in human skin and the same material had been used to recover the lampshades and wastebasket. More skin had been used to turn an old 2lb coffee can into an Indian style tom-tom. The odd-looking bowl on the table was the top of a human skull. The finds in Ed's bedroom were even worse. A broken table had been propped up with a human shinbone and skulls grinned at them from the top of the bedposts. Beneath the bed they found a box of women's vaginas – the one painted silver turned out to be Augusta Gein's. On the walls were what appeared to be a collection of shrivelled Halloween masks. They were actually the facial skin of nine of Ed's victims. The main wall decoration was a preserved human head – the one the boys had been babbling about and could not get anyone to believe them.

Hour after hour the dazed deputies combed through the mess, uncovering one nightmare after another. In the wardrobe, the dressing table and scattered around the room were Ed's clothes.

There was a waistcoat of human flesh, the breasts still in place, a pair of hip-length stockings made of flesh and bracelets of plaited skin. Finally there was an entire bodysuit: it was anatomically correct, breasts, vagina and all. There was even a lovingly crafted mask to go with the bodysuit: the face, like the suit material, had once belonged to Augusta Gein. Finally, around 4.30am they found Frank Worden's mother's head inside a burlap bag. Nails had been driven into her ears and a length of twine tied to each of them, as though Ed were going to hang it on the wall next to his other trophies. In all, the remains of more than a dozen female bodies were scattered around the pigsty of a house.

The days that followed were a nightmare of confusion for everyone connected with the case. Local deputies and State Police combed every inch of the Gein property looking for whatever new horrors they might uncover, while forensic experts from the state capital in Madison came and went, carting away the finds in an effort to – quite literally – piece together the exact number of Ed's victims. The number they eventually came up with was fifteen, but they admitted it was only a 'best estimate'. How many more had been done away with entirely, no one could say.

While one group of officers grilled Ed in the Watoma County Jail, others tried to connect Ed – or some of his 'trophies' – to the long-missing girls, Georgia Weckler and Evelyn Hartley, and to the disappearance of saloon owner Mary Hogan.

At first, Ed simply refused to talk about anything but finally, after more than a day of intensive questioning, he admitted culpability in the death of Bernice Worden. He insisted that although he did remember going to the hardware store, he didn't remember killing her. He said he was confused and felt dazed before and during the murder. He did remember taking the cash register, but insisted he had not meant to rob the store – he just wanted to take the register apart to see how it worked and Frank was welcome to take back the $41 that had been in the cash drawer.

As to the rest of the body parts that littered the Gein home, Ed insisted they were all the pickings of his forays into the graveyard but, with the exception of his mother, he couldn't be sure who they all were. He was, however, happy to give the officers all the names he could remember. The whole story was reeled off in a completely matter-of-fact way. Sometimes Ed even seemed to enjoy telling it. He appeared to have no concept of the enormity of what he had done. In an attempt to verify, or dismiss, Ed's story Sheriff Schley asked the local judge for an exhumation order to dig up the graves Ed had so far admitted to desecrating. All of the coffins in question proved to have been tampered with, some of their contents missing entirely, while others were only missing some parts of the body.

Eventually, Ed admitted to killing Mary Hogan, explaining that both she and Mrs Worden had reminded him of his mother. It seemed that slightly overweight, middle-aged women were the only type he was interested in – and only because they looked like Augusta Gein. The question of how, exactly, his brother Henry had died cropped up again, but Ed staunchly denied any involvement. Finally, investigators gave up trying to connect Ed Gein with the disappearance of the two schoolgirls or his brother's death and turned him over to the Wisconsin mental health authorities who placed him in the Central State Hospital for the Criminally Insane, in Waupun, for further examination.

It did not take long before everyone in Plainfield, and the surrounding territory, knew what kind of awful things had been going on at the old Gein place, but it was not until the story broke a few days later in the local press, the *Shawano Evening Ledger*, that it became really big news. In a matter of days Plainfield was swamped with reporters, photographers and television and radio people. Nothing like this had ever happened anywhere, and the stunned people of Eisenhower-era America were both fascinated and repelled by the horrific tale. In December 1957, only weeks after the event, two of America's three biggest magazines, *Life* and *Time*, ran the story of Ed Gein's 'House of Horrors'.

While the people of Plainfield tried to be patient with the onslaught of the paparazzi, they also wished they would just go away and leave them alone. It was mostly the kids, with their 'I-told-you-so' attitude, who made the most of their tiny town's notoriety. They started telling tasteless 'Geiner' jokes that soon swept the country. The Geiners ran something like this.

Q. What did Ed Gein say to the sheriff who arrested him?
A. Have a heart!

Q. Why did they let Ed Gein out of jail on New Year's Eve?
A. So he could dig up a date.

There were even limericks, one of which ran as follows:

> There once was an old man named Ed
> Who wouldn't take a woman to bed
> When he wanted to fiddle
> He cut out her middle
> And hung up the rest in his shed.

It was all too sick, but to children who could not understand the very real implications of what was happening, it was just great fun. What was not so much fun for the people of Plainfield was the announced auction of the Gein farm and its contents, particularly when the auctioneers announced they would charge 50 cents for anyone to look around the place before the auction. The townspeople were outraged. The last thing they needed were throngs of morbid curiosity seekers ploughing through their town, gawping at the 'murder house'. Although Sheriff Schley refused the auction company permission to charge admission, there was nothing he could do to stop the sale.

Somehow, when the local volunteer fire brigade was called to the Gein farm in the early hours of 20 March 1958, people were far more relieved than surprised. A lot of head-nodding went on over the next few days, but not a great deal could be done to find the vandals who had started the fire. When Ed's doctors told him his house had burned down his only comment was 'Just as well'.

Not to be deterred by the loss of the house and its filthy contents, the auctioneers went ahead with the sale as planned. The land and outbuildings were sold to a local developer for use as a Christmas tree farm and most of the old farm equipment was sold for scrap. But Ed's 1949 Ford sedan was another matter altogether – this was the vehicle in which he had carried off the bodies of Mary Hogan and Bernice Worden. The first round of bidding involved no fewer than fourteen prospective buyers and by the time the bidding ended the car had brought $760. The buyer was a carnival sideshow operator named Bunny Gibbons from Rockford, Illinois.

Bunny first put the 'Ed Gein Ghoul Car' on display in July 1958 at the Outgamie County Fair in Seymour, Wisconsin. A huge placard outside the tent screamed 'See the Car that Hauled the Dead from Their Graves! Ed Gein's Crime Car!' The first weekend more than 2,000 people paid 25 cents each to look at the dilapidated old Ford. Local authorities shut the show down at one location after another and the car finally vanished from sight. Ed, however, was still being poked and prodded at Central State Hospital.

The eventual findings of the psychiatric evaluation board was that Ed Gein was both schizophrenic and a sexual psychopath, suffering from conflicting emotions about women that had been engendered by his love–hate relationship with his mother. Ed Gein was the most curious case of necrophilia, transvestism, cannibalism and fetishism that any of the doctors had ever heard of, let alone encountered. In short, Ed was not, at this time, mentally competent to stand trial.

It was not until January 1968, just over ten years after his arrest, that Ed Gein was declared legally sane enough to be tried for the murder of Bernice Worden. On the advice of his psychiatrists and lawyers he entered a plea of not guilty by reason of insanity.

The trial itself did not take place until November of that year and only seven witnesses took the stand to testify, most of them psychiatrists and members of the forensic team who had been charged with the grisly job of identifying the body parts found in Gein's house. Despite the small number of witnesses, their testimony was long, involved and almost entirely scientific in nature, and it took a week for them to deliver their findings. To no one's surprise, Ed Gein was found not guilty by reason of insanity and escorted back to the Central State Hospital for the Criminally Insane.

Ed seemed to have improved a lot over the years. The hospital administrator, Dr Schechter, always described him as a model patient who never required anti-psychotics or tranquillisers to remain calm. He always appeared at ease during his therapy sessions with the doctors and enjoyed working in the craft centre where he learned stone polishing, rug weaving and other forms of occupational therapy. It is unlikely that he was ever allowed to do leatherwork. By and large, he kept to himself, but when he mingled he got along well with the other patients and staff, except for the disconcerting way he would occasionally stare at the female patients and nurses – especially the ones who were plump and middle aged.

In 1978, at the age of seventy-two, Ed Gein was transferred to the Mendota Mental Health Institute where he died in the geriatric ward six years later.

Even though the world at large had long since forgotten about Ed Gein, there were a few who remained fascinated by America's most famously twisted killer. Only months after his arrest in 1957 internationally famous horror writer, Robert Bloch, began work on a novel based on the Gein case. Because the world was still not ready for all the gory details, the tale was toned down and made more psychological than graphic. When the book, entitled *Psycho*, came out in 1959, master film producer, Alfred Hitchcock, immediately picked up the movie rights. The following year Anthony Perkins' portrayal of the mother-fixated killer, Norman Bates, made audiences shiver all over the world.

In 1967 Ed became the model for the lead character in the film *It*, in which Roddy McDowall portrays a psychopathic museum curator who keeps his mother's decaying body at home in her bed. Gein again surfaced on celluloid in 1974 as Leatherface in Tobe Hooper's splatter classic *The Texas Chainsaw Massacre*. But Hollywood was still not done with poor Ed. In yet another, and probably not final, appearance, Ed was transformed into the transvestite killer 'Buffalo Bill' who, like Ed, wore a suit made from women's skin. The book *Silence of the Lambs* was written by Thomas Harris in 1988 and three years later the story brought to the screen by Jonathan Demme. We can probably assume that Ed Gein, like his victims, will be dug up again at some point in the future.

Twelve

From Russia with Hate: André Chikatilo (1978–90)

L ife has always been hard in the Russian states and it was especially true in 1936 when André Chikatilo was born in the Ukrainian village of Yablochnoye. The peasants who worked the land in the once fertile expanses of the Ukrainian steppes were suffering through their fifth year of famine. Unlike most famines this one was man-made; it was dictator Josef Stalin's personal revenge for the Ukrainian people's resistance to handing over their farms to the Soviet collective system. Year after year the Russian soldiers confiscated the livestock and the harvest, including the seed grain needed to replant the fields. Sometimes they cleaned out the peasants' cupboards and larders too for good measure. By 1936 an estimated ten million had starved to death. One of the side-effects of the famine was an epidemic of cannibalism as hunger-crazed people were forced to choose between eating their dead relatives or watching while their children wasted away. The Chikatilo family had already lost an elder son, Stephan, to a band of cut-throats who had probably kidnapped him to be sold as meat at a local market.

As if this were not enough to ensure that little André Chikatilo was off to a less than hopeful start, he was born with hydrocephalus – a condition once known as 'water on the brain' – which can cause damage to the frontal cortex along with a variety of physical impairments. One of the immediate effects of André's condition was an inability to control his bladder at night. In a peasant culture where the entire family slept on a single, raised platform the presence of a bed-wetter was immediately noticed by the entire family. While André's father and sister tried to make light of the problem, his foul-tempered mother, Anna, constantly humiliated him. Years later, André's sister, Tatyana, would remember her mother as 'very harsh and rude. She only yelled at us and bawled us out. She never had a kind word.'

By the time André reached the age of five, in 1940, the already intolerable situation in the Ukraine became even worse when the armies of Nazi Germany invaded the Soviet Union. One entire army was dedicated to subduing the Ukraine in an effort to seize its vast oilfields to fuel the German war machine. As with almost everywhere the Nazis invaded, the killing and terror was beyond belief. Along with everyone else, André was constantly exposed to the sight of dead, mutilated bodies littering the streets and mass executions carried out in reprisal for the smallest infractions of German rule. For unknown reasons, André's father was arrested by the Germans and sent to a forced labour camp, leaving an increasingly embittered Anna to bring the children up alone.

When the Germans were finally driven out of the Soviet Union, André's father returned home, but there were new problems. By the time he reached puberty André was no longer wetting the bed, but he had begun experiencing uncontrollable ejaculations. Unlike most boys, who occasionally experience night-time emissions, André's were almost constant and seldom accompanied by an erection.

Bullied at home, he received the same treatment at school because he was so shy and awkward. As a defence mechanism, André increasingly withdrew into a fantasy world filled with sadism and violence. To a boy who had seen so much suffering and cruelty, and felt such intense humiliation and inadequacy because of his physical problems, these nasty fantasies were the only thing which allowed him to feel he had any control over his world. On one occasion, when a friend of his sister came to the Chikatilo home, he tried to act out one of his fantasies. André was now sixteen and his younger sister's friend was ten or eleven. Grabbing the child, he tried to tear her clothes off as a prelude to rape, but found that although the sheer excitement of the violence caused him to ejaculate, he could not achieve an erection. The girl was terrified and he was completely humiliated.

Although André was a fairly bright student he failed the entrance exam that would have allowed him to enter the state university in Moscow, and escape his life in the Ukraine. Like most boys who did not qualify for higher education, André Chikatilo served his time in the Soviet armed forces. Again, every time he attempted to have sexual relations with a girl he met on leave he was incapable of the sex act, embarrassing himself with his impotence and nearly instantaneous ejaculation.

By 1960 Chikatilo was again a civilian and had taken a job with the Ukrainian telephone company. Desperate to live as normal a life as possible, he enlisted the help of his sympathetic sister in finding a girlfriend who would tolerate his shyness and sexual problems. Amazingly, she found one for him. The girl's name was Feodosia and in 1963 she became Mrs André Chikatilo. How they accomplished it can only be guessed at, but together they produced two children, a boy and a girl who, in the fullness of time, would make them grandparents. Determined to make the most of what he had, André took a correspondence course in Russian literature and by 1971 had not only graduated but obtained a position teaching in a boarding school at Novo Shatinsk near the city of Rostov-on-Don.

To his family, neighbours, friends and colleagues at school, André Chikatilo appeared perfectly normal, if a little withdrawn. Like most Russians he was an avid chess player, he seemed to get on well with his family and enjoyed the theatre. But inside

André's head something was terribly wrong. The first sign came when school administrators heard rumours that Chikatilo had attempted to molest some of the girls in his class. They may have dismissed the tales the first time, but in 1978 André was quietly asked to leave. As a member in good standing in the Communist Party, the school authorities must have provided him with a letter of recommendation because he soon found another teaching position in the mining village of Shakhty a few miles away.

While waiting for the government to provide him with suitable accommodation for his family, Chikatilo stayed in a run-down shack he had purchased in a Shakhty slum. When the new apartment came through and the Chikatilo family moved to Shakhty, André kept the shack but failed to tell anyone about it. It was to this place that, on 22 December 1978, he lured nine-year-old Yelena Zakotnova. Later, he would recall every minute of Yelena's ordeal. 'As soon as I turned on the lights and closed the door, I fell on her. The girl was frightened and cried out. I shut her mouth with my hands. I couldn't get an erection and I couldn't get my penis into her vagina. The desire to have an orgasm overwhelmed all else and I wanted to do it by any means. Her cries excited me further. Lying on her and moving in imitation of the sex act, I pulled out my knife and started to stab her. I climaxed as if it had happened during a natural sex act.' Chikatilo must have realised that this was as close as he had ever come to experiencing the tense excitement of intercourse; and all it had cost was the life of one small child.

Amazingly, he had been witnessed walking through the neighbourhood with little Yelena. When he was interrogated by the police in connection with her disappearance, his wife insisted he had been at home during the time in question and Chikatilo was released without charge. Later, a man named Aleksandr Kravchenko would be arrested, tried and executed for Yelena's murder.

For more than three years André Chikatilo kept the beast in his head under control, but it surfaced again in 1981 shortly after he got a new job with the Rostovnerund construction company in Rostov-on-Don. As Rostovnerund's supply administrator Chikatilo was required to travel a lot, sourcing the endless list of material and equipment his company needed in their work. When he got off the bus at Nvovshankhtinsk on 3 September he spotted seventeen-year-old Larisa Tkachenko standing in the bus shelter. He approached her and propositioned her; eventually she agreed to sex for a small price. By the time she realised just how high the price was going to be it was too late.

Together they walked to a nearby strip of woodland commonly used as an erosion break between fields all over the Ukraine. Once safely beyond prying eyes, Chikatilo strangled the girl, sinking his teeth into the tender flesh of her neck almost before she slipped into unconsciousness. He drank her blood as it gushed from the wound but quickly turned his attention to her breasts. He bit off her nipples, swallowing them whole before mutilating her genitals with a knife. The taste of flesh and blood was far more sexually exciting than just strangling a nine-year-old child. It would be more than nine months before André Chikatilo struck again, but in the second half of 1982 he would claim five victims. This time a little boy would be included in the list of casualties.

When the first body was discovered in early autumn 1982 it had lain so long in the tiny strip of woodland that only fragments of skin, hair and clothing remained intact. Police inquiries determined that her name was Lyubov Biryuk and she had been thirteen years old. She had been missing since 12 June – the day she met André Chikatilo. What police found most startling about the crime scene was how exposed it was. Although the body was found among the trees, the wooded area was only 50 yards wide and a main roadway ran only 20 yards beyond the tree-line. A well-worn footpath lay only feet from the body. If this seemed like a peculiarly exposed place to commit murder, the autopsy revealed just how horrifyingly odd the murder was. There were at least 22 knife wounds on the little body, the eyes had been savagely hacked out and although the corpse was badly decomposed there was clear evidence of knife wounds on the pelvic bone.

Local police knew all too well that the majority of murders are committed either during an argument among family or friends, the so-called 'crime of passion', or as a result of a robbery attempt gone wrong. Neither of these scenarios fitted the case in question and police assumed it had been a random act of violence, making it almost impossible to solve unless the assailant was clumsy enough to leave physical evidence at the scene. There was no such evidence anywhere near Lyubov's body. Considering the violence of the crime, police in the western world would immediately have considered the possibility of a serial killer, but in the Soviet Union there was, officially, no such thing. Serial killers, like unemployment, homosexuality and prostitution were sicknesses confined to the decadent, capitalistic West. The only thing left was to begin rousting all mental patients not under lock and key and any known sex offenders. The only obvious indicator was that the perpetrator was undoubtedly male. When the next body turned up it was found to be a boy. This completely confused the search parameters and, despite the fact that the wound patterns were the same as on the first body, the police could not believe that sexual assaults on a girl and a boy could have been committed by the same man. There must be two murderers at work and one of them was obviously a crazed homosexual. Former mental patients, convicted sex offenders and members of the tightly closeted gay community were rounded up, thrown in jail and grilled endlessly. One man who had served time for rape committed suicide, as did three members of Rostov's gay community.

While police were trying to make sense of the growing string of mutilated corpses and hordes of suspects, André Chikatilo was looking for ever more creative ways to satiate his unquenchable desires. Not only were young boys now on his list of victims, but how the grotesque, vicarious sexual encounters were acted out was becoming ever more bizarre. The mouths of most of the victims were now stuffed with dirt and grass; whether this was simply to keep them quiet or for some more subtle reason is not known. The earlier attacks had been swift and violent but now he was taking his time, making more and shallower cuts to prolong the victim's agony and his own sexual arousal. The genitals of most early victims, both male and female, had been cut out and Chikatilo would later admit that he carried them away with him to chew on as a way of reliving the attack. The police also began finding evidence of small fires near the bodies, but could not imagine how this might relate to the killings; the fact was Chikatilo had begun carrying a small pot along with him on his 'business trips' for the construction company, in order to cook the victim's genitals and eat them. If cannibalism had not been a part of his master plan, it had definitely evolved into an integral component. The tongues of many of his later prey were also found to be missing, having been added to the cannibalistic stew. The greater the indignity he could inflict, either before or after death, the more powerful Chikatilo felt.

Despite the best efforts of the police to keep the lid on a situation they were clearly unable to handle, rumours of what was happening to the missing children and young people were rapidly spreading beyond the Rostov area. Even if word of the fifteen children who had disappeared by May 1984 could have been kept secret, the continuing interrogations – which had now been carried out on more than 150,000 men – could not have gone unnoticed. But even on the rare occasions when the press mentioned one of the killings, or missing children, nothing was said to indicate there was any connection with past disappearances. There could be no serial killers in the Soviet Union.

Finally, in complete frustration, the head of the Rostov police detective bureau asked Moscow for help. It came in the form of Viktor Burakov from the Moscow Division of Serious Crime. At thirty-seven, Burakov was better at analysing physical evidence than any other detective in the Soviet Union and was noted for his absolute doggedness. There was no doubt the Rostov police needed all the help they could get; during the first eight months of 1984 the mutilated bodies of eight more children were discovered, along with those of two unidentified women. Unlike the earlier corpses, the eyes in these had been left intact, but the sexual mutilations were becoming worse with each attack: the autopsy on a fourteen-year-old boy showed more than 70 knife wounds. And not only were the attacks getting closer and closer together, they were starting to appear in places where earlier bodies had been found. The monster was revisiting his old haunts.

Because of the ferocity of the attacks, even Burakov was convinced that the assailant had to be someone with demonstrable mental problems. Twice, mildly retarded teenage boys were arrested and a confession was beaten out of them, but Burakov was astute enough to know that forced confessions were less than worthless. The only thing that seemed to link the two boys with the victims was the fact that they had both used public transport, and most of the victims had been found near bus or railway stations. But this was certainly not enough to convict anyone of anything. When yet another freshly murdered body turned up, Burakov was forced to turn his prime suspect loose – the boy had obviously been killed while the suspect was in jail.

It was only when forensic experts found semen smears around the rectum of one of the young, male victims that Burakov had his first, solid piece of evidence. The antigens in semen were known to match the antigens in blood, so the man now known as the 'Rostov Ripper' would have to have AB blood type, the same as the semen found on fourteen-year-old Sergi Markov. Unfortunately, none of the suspects in custody, and virtually no one on the possible suspect list, matched this type, but at least it was a lead that could be followed in future investigations.

At Burakov's request, the Minister of the Interior appointed a dozen more detectives to the case and a task force numbering more than 200 people in different capacities was now conducting the largest manhunt in the history of the Soviet Union.

Working on the theory that the Rostov Ripper was finding most of his victims at bus stops and railway stations, Burakov placed plain-clothes officers at nearly every public transport terminal in any town or village where bodies had been found. They were instructed to watch for anyone acting suspiciously, or approaching children or young women. A description of suspects was to be taken and if possible without arousing too much suspicion, their names acquired.

One of those who did, eventually, catch the eye of a detective assigned to the Rostov-on-Don central railway station was a slim, grey-haired man who appeared to be in his late forties, who consistently approached teenage girls and young women with whom he obviously had no connection. He had done nothing to warrant arrest so a few questions were quietly put to him. His name, he said, was André Chikatilo; he worked for Rostovnerund Construction and travelled a lot in and out of Rostov. Yes, he did talk to the youngsters. He used to be a teacher and still missed the company of young people. It all seemed perfectly logical and innocent, so the detective allowed Chikatilo to walk away. Still, there was something odd and furtive about the way the man kept looking around him even when he was not talking to the police. So the detective followed him.

When Chikatilo hired a prostitute to give him oral sex in a corner of the railway station he was arrested for indecent public behaviour. Under questioning Chikatilo admitted a weakness for prostitutes. It was a pretty unsavoury admission, but not a major crime, and Major Zanasovsky might have let him go if it had not been for the contents of his briefcase. Inside were a jar of petroleum jelly, a long kitchen knife, a piece of rope and a dirty towel, not the sort of things a businessman usually took with him on a buying trip for a construction company.

Handed over to Viktor Burakov for questioning, Chikatilo was given a blood test to see if his antigens matched those of the semen samples recovered from the victims. While the lab was carrying out its tests, Chikatilo was left to cool his heels in a cell in the hope that he might change his story. Burakov learned two things about Chikatilo: he was a member in good standing in the Communist Party and his blood was type A, not AB. One more in the parade of thousands of possible suspects was turned loose. A few months later, Burakov heard that André Chikatilo had been convicted of the theft of three rolls of linoleum and was sentenced to three months in prison. It would cost him his membership in the Party and probably his job, but petty theft certainly did not make the man the Rostov Ripper.

After August 1984 the killings seemed to stop altogether. A few more horribly mutilated bodies turned up, but they had obviously been murdered much earlier. Since his encounter with the police and arrest for theft, Chikatilo was keeping his head down and following the progress of the Rostov Ripper case in the now much-liberalised Russian press. He was clever enough, cautious enough and sufficiently in control to wait more than two-and-a-half years before he struck again.

Meanwhile, Viktor Burakov took a step unprecedented in Russian police history: he contacted a psychiatrist familiar with western methods of profiling serial killers. Dr Alexandr Bukhanovsky put together a six-page report that Burakov found interesting, but it did nothing to help him narrow down his search. By May 1987 Burakov was no closer to solving the case than he had been three years earlier, but his flagging interest was reinvigorated when Moscow police began reporting the murders of young boys – all stabbed repeatedly and sexually mutilated. Realising that there had to be a connection between these new deaths and the ones around Rostov, Burakov went back to Bukhanovsky, this time allowing the psychiatrist full access to every police report from every case tied to the Rostov Ripper. Bukhanovsky's new report ran to 65 pages and gave a detailed description of the unknown suspect. The man, Bukhanovsky said, was not psychotic because he could control what he did. He was heterosexual, he was a sadist and probably impotent – the knife serving as a substitute for entering the victim with his penis. Because the killings had almost all taken place during the middle of the week, the man probably had a job that allowed him to travel. His age was probably between forty-five and fifty years of age. Most unsettling was the conclusion that while the perpetrator was able to control his need to kill for extended periods, he would kill again and continue to do so until he was forcibly stopped. It was a good report, but how did Burakov go about finding one specific, impotent, travelling man in his late forties, among the hundreds of thousands of possible suspects?

In mid-1990 Chikatilo started killing again. After having abstained for so long, the frantic bloodlust that drove him had become stronger than ever and, once resumed, the murders and mutilations occurred at an ever-increasing pace. By July of that year the police in Rostov and Moscow estimated that the Rostov Ripper had accumulated a tally of 32 victims. Under increasing pressure to catch the man whom Dr Bukhanovsky had dubbed 'Suspect X', Burakov devised a new plan that he hoped would force the killer into the open. Every train and bus station in the greater Rostov area would remain under police surveillance, but now the officers at the majority of the stations would be in uniform to make their presence obvious. Those at the remaining stations would be in plain clothes, making it appear that only some stations were being watched. Burakov hoped that the suspect would avoid those stations where uniformed officers were stationed, limiting his activities to those which appeared unguarded. To cover every possible avenue, there would also be police stationed in any woodland near a rail or bus station; these men would be disguised as peasants and foresters so they would remain as anonymous as possible. It was a massive task requiring more than 350 officers.

One of the railway stations to be covered by plain-clothes officers was located in the village of Donleskhoz. While Burakov was still in the process of putting his plan into action the killer struck again. At Donleskhoz a sixteen-year-old retarded boy was abducted, stabbed 27 times and sexually mutilated. Almost immediately a nearly identical murder took place not far from the station in Shakhty. Frantically, Burakov got his men into the field but, once there, all they could do was wait and collect information on men who appeared 'suspicious'. One of the suspects on whom police did gather information was a man named André Chikatilo, aged fifty-four. He had been seen at the Donleskhoz station on 6 November – the day the retarded boy was abducted and murdered. Burakov instantly recognised the name and ordered his men to interview anyone who might have been in the area of the Donleskhoz station that day. The interviews produced information that told Burakov all he needed to know. On the day in question Chikatilo had been seen coming out of the wooded area near the station with grass and twigs on his coat and a red smear on one cheek. Later, he was observed washing his hands at a pump near the station. Immediately, Burakov had Chikatilo placed under surveillance.

While Chikatilo was being watched, Burakov dug deeper into the suspect's background and movements. The reasons for his dismissal from his teaching job were revealed, as was the fact that his travels for the Rostovnerund company coincided with the location of many of the murder victims' bodies.

On 20 November 1990, André Chikatilo was arrested on suspicion. The following day the police questioned him in the presence of his court-appointed lawyer. An inspector named Kostoyev, who had an enviable record of getting confessions out of even the most difficult suspects, handled the questioning.

Chikatilo insisted it was all a mistake, just as it had been in 1984. On the third day of questioning he admitted to certain 'sexual weaknesses' that drove him to hire prostitutes and that he did participate in 'perverse sexual activity', which he refused to specify. He did, however, admit that he was impotent; one of the motivational factors mentioned in Dr Bukhanovsky's profile of 'Suspect X'. Burakov was now so certain that he had the right man that he requested Dr Bukhanovsky to come to Rostov and question Chikatilo. While waiting for Bukhanovsky to arrive, Burakov ran into his first snag. Just as the blood test had shown in 1984, Chikatilo was type A, not the AB found on the murder victims. Improved methods of testing had come into existence over the past six years, however, and when Chikatilo's blood was retested in Moscow it proved to contain a recessive type B antigen, which could easily make it appear that his semen was type AB rather than type A. Such a result could be expected in less than one in a million men and it was only by this quirk of fate that Chikatilo had not been kept in custody six years earlier.

By the time Alexandr Bukhanovsky arrived in Rostov, little doubt remained in Burakov's mind that Chikatilo was the Rostov Ripper. The only thing left was to extract a full confession, and that was Bukhanovsky's job. Taking the slow, non-confrontational approach typical of those in the medical profession, Bukhanovsky began simply by reading his profile of 'Suspect X' to Chikatilo. Amazingly, after a dozen years of unspeakable murder, mutilation and cannibalism, that was all it took for Chikatilo to start talking.

He began at the beginning, with the December 1978 murder of Yelena Zakotnova, which must have caused some embarrassment since another man had already been executed for the crime. On and on he went, enumerating the crimes and describing what motivated him. 'The whole thing, the cries, the blood, the agony, gave me relaxation and a certain pleasure.' He described how he felt an 'animal satisfaction' in biting off women's nipples and eating vaginas, penises and testicles, both raw and cooked. He said that he especially enjoyed smearing his sperm on a newly excised vagina and then chewing on it.

He described how he varied the method of his hunt, sometimes stalking his victims for days or weeks and sometimes simply jumping out and attacking them at random. He admitted that the brutal stabbing was a substitute for intercourse and made a show of demonstrating how he knelt beside his prey in such a way that he could almost always avoid getting covered with blood. The one part of his rambling confession that everyone had most feared was the final body count. The police knew of 36 – Chikatilo's list included another 19 they had never found.

The unspeakable confessions and interrogations went on for more than eighteen months. Some of that time Chikatilo spent at the Serbsky Psychiatric Institute in Moscow, where he was examined by Dr Andrei Tkachenko. Included in Tkachenko's report was evidence that at least a part of Chikatilo's problem dated to his pre-natal hydrocephalic condition. 'We discovered in our research that Chikatilo had a whole range or neurological symptoms, which indicated that he had certain brain defects related to development before and during birth. In particular, using functional imaging, we found that he showed signs of dysfunction in the frontal sections of the right side of the brain.'

The trial of André Chikatilo, the Rostov Ripper, began on 14 April 1992 in front of a packed courtroom. Nearly all of the 250 seats were taken up by his victims' surviving family members. When Chikatilo was led into the room and locked inside a large iron cage, the public began to shout and scream at him, crying for justice and Chikatilo's death. Not at all cowed by this demonstration, Chikatilo shouted back at them. Throughout the trial his behaviour was disruptive, often degenerating into outright obscenity. He screamed, he sang the Communist anthem, the 'Internationale', he dropped his trousers and shook his penis at the judge and spectators, he insisted he was being 'radiated', he referred to his victims as 'enemy aircraft I had shot down' and, on one occasion, ripped open his shirt screaming, 'It's time for me to give birth.'

None of this grandstanding impressed the court. With 225 volumes of evidence and numerous psychiatrists testifying that although his crimes may have been monstrous, André Chikatilo was sane enough to control his urges when he wanted, or needed, to do so, the physical evidence presented at the trial was so horrific and so graphic that even one of the military guards stationed near Chikatilo's cage fainted.

The verdict was almost a foregone conclusion and on 14 October, six months after the trial began, Chikatilo was found guilty of 52 counts of murder. An appeal was immediately lodged, but turned down. On 15 February 1994, Chikatilo was taken from his cell, led to a soundproof room in the basement of the prison and shot once through the back of the head.

In 1995 a television film of the Chikatilo case, starring Donald Sutherland as Inspector Viktor Burakov, was released under the title *Citizen X*. In 1999 *Newsweek* magazine carried a story naming Rostov-on-Don as the serial murder capital of the world. According to the story, 'Twenty-nine multiple murderers and rapists have been caught in the area over the past ten years'.

Thirteen

Zombie Sex Slaves of Milwaukee: Jeffrey Dahmer (1978–91)

I f you had met Jeffrey Dahmer on the street the only thing you might have noticed about him was just how average he was. Born in the American heartland city of Milwaukee, Wisconsin, in May 1960, Dahmer was about as typically American as you can get.

With a population of about 700,000 Milwaukee is known for its hard-working, largely Germanic population, the fact that it produces about 20 per cent of all the beer in America and is the home of Harley Davidson motorcycles. Dahmer's family was just as typical as their city. His father, Lionel, was a chemist whose work, and PhD research, kept him away from his family more than he would have liked, but he tried to make up for it by spending as much 'quality time' with them as his schedule allowed. Joyce, Jeffrey's mother, was a slightly neurotic homemaker obsessed with her health. Like most kids, little Jeff had a dog and picked up injured birds hoping his dad could mend their broken wing. When he got a baby brother, David, in 1966, the family seemed complete. In Dahmer's own words, 'When I was a kid I was just like everybody else.' Well, not quite.

One summer day, when Jeff was four years old, his father was sweeping the debris from under the porch. Mixed among the leaves and twigs were a large number of bird carcasses. Jeff seemed almost morbidly fascinated by the tiny bones, playing with them and running his fingers through them. At the time,

Lionel laughed it off as a 'childish episode' but later remembered it as 'colouring almost every memory' of Jeff.

In the year Jeff's brother David was born, 1966, Lionel's new job as a research chemist forced a family move from Milwaukee to Akron, Ohio. In retrospect, Lionel believed that the trauma of a new brother, the move and his first year at school might have affected Jeff more than normal. In his book about his son, Lionel later wrote: 'A strange fear had begun to creep into his personality, a dread of others and a general lack of self confidence. The little boy who had once seemed so happy was now deeply shy, distant, nearly uncommunicative.' His parents were concerned but with a new baby, a new job, a new house and a new city to deal with their attention was divided. Besides, kids all go through phases. With Jeff, however, the phase did not seem to pass. In his book, his father remembered, 'His posture and the general way in which he carried himself changed radically between his tenth and fifteenth years. He grew increasingly shy during this time and when approached by other people, he would become very tense. More and more he remained at home, alone in his room or staring at television. His face was often blank and disengaged.'

In fact, Jeffrey was withdrawing into his own little world of nightmares brought on, at least in part, by his parents' dissolving relationship and the dawning awareness that he was gay, something his family's Christian fundamentalism would never understand. Unable to cope with the problems, Jeff simply withdrew. Still, he did his best to get along in high school. He worked on the school newspaper and joined the 4H Club (a youth organisation dedicated to agricultural and livestock raising, generally found in rural, faming communities), but his classmates always saw him as a loner and more than one of them noticed that Jeff was developing a drink problem, sometimes smuggling beer into school and more than once coming back from his lunch break a little drunk.

As Jeff's eighteenth birthday and his high school graduation approached, his parents' marriage collapsed in an acrimonious divorce. Almost simultaneously they left home, intending to sell the house later. Joyce took eleven-year-old David with her. Communication between her and Lionel had broken down to such an extent that each of them assumed the other was taking care of Jeff. As a result, one day Jeff came home from school to find himself deserted by his parents, without money, in a house with no food and a broken refrigerator. The confusion was eventually straightened out, but its effect on Jeffrey Dahmer was permanent. For the rest of his life he would be terrified of abandonment.

Only days after graduation in June 1978, Jeff picked up a casual acquaintance, eighteen-year-old Steve Hicks, who was hitchhiking to his girlfriend's house. Jeff offered to buy Steve a few beers at a local bar and, being in no particular hurry, Steve agreed. After a few beers they drove to Jeff's grandmother's house where, terrified of being alone once Steve left, Jeff beat his friend to death and stuffed the body into the void beneath the house. A week later, he returned late at night and dismembered the body, shoving the pieces into plastic bin bags and heaving the bags into the boot of his car. He then headed off to a nearby wood to bury the evidence. By this time, Jeff had had more than a few beers and his erratic driving was noticed by a passing policeman who pulled him over. When the officer asked the boy what the awful smell was, Jeff told him it was trash that he was taking to the local dump. The cop told him to watch his drinking and waved him on.

Later, Jeffrey Dahmer realised that the murder of Steve Hicks had irrevocably changed his life. During one psychiatric evaluation, he said: 'That night in Ohio, that one impulsive night. Nothing's been normal since. It taints your whole life. After it happened I thought I'd just try to live as normally as possible and bury it, but things like that don't stay buried.'

Worried that his son was becoming an aimless drifter, Lionel Dahmer, and his new wife Shari, tried to convince Jeff to cut down his drinking and get some direction into his life. Something. Anything. Finally, Jeff agreed to enrol in Ohio State University, but he spent most of his time in the local college bars and by the end of the first semester he had flunked out. Now completely frustrated, Lionel insisted that Jeff either get a responsible job or join the army. Jeff chose the army.

For a while after his induction in January 1979, Jeff's condition seemed to improve. He made it through basic training, became an army medic and was stationed at a US base in Germany. But his problems, especially the drinking, inevitably caught up with him. In early 1981 he was discharged on grounds of alcoholism. He moved back to Ohio, dug up Steve Hicks's bones, pounded them to dust with a hammer and scattered them across the woodland. Months later, in October, he was arrested on charges of drunk and disorderly conduct. No longer able to cope with his son, Lionel insisted that Jeff move to West Allis, Wisconsin – a suburb of Milwaukee – where his grandmother had a spare apartment he could rent. Maybe the move and the expense of living on his own would force him to become responsible.

The Jeffrey Dahmer who returned to the city of his birth looked like almost any other young man from the American Midwest. He stood just under 6 feet tall, weighed about 190 pounds, had dirty-blond hair and wore glasses. He had good manners, was well spoken and not at all bad looking. Although he found it almost impossible to make friends, people seemed to like Jeff Dahmer and he had no problem getting a job on the production line at the Ambrosia Chocolate Company. If he had a few drinks after work, who cared? Everybody in Milwaukee drank beer. Even when he dropped his trousers in a bar and was cautioned by the police, people just laughed it off. It was, however, a little different in September 1986 when he was caught masturbating in front of two young boys and was sentenced to a year's probation for indecent exposure. Still, as he had always done, Lionel stood by his drunken son, paid his lawyer's bill and, not for the first time, begged him to get help for his drinking. Jeffrey ignored the advice.

In September 1987, Jeff was drinking in a Milwaukee gay bar and fell into conversation with Steve Tuomi. After they rented a hotel room, Jeff proceeded to murder Tuomi and pass out: when he woke up there was blood on his mouth. Dahmer hurriedly bought a large suitcase, stuffed Tuomi's body into it, hauled his macabre luggage back to his grandmother's basement and had sex with the body before throwing it in the garbage. Jeff seemed to be amazed that he had killed for a second time. 'I just couldn't believe it happened again after all those years . . . I don't know what was going through my mind. I [have] tried to dredge it up, but I have no memory whatsoever.' Somehow, with the death of Steve Tuomi, a dam broke inside Jeffrey Dahmer's head. Whatever he had been trying to hold in check was about to drown out his entire existence.

The urge to kill and desecrate the body of another human being came again four months later. In January 1988 Dahmer picked up and murdered fourteen-year-old Jamie Doxtator who often loitered outside gay bars desperately trying to find someone to love him. Less than three months later, he did the same thing to Richard Guerrero. Events that had once seemed, to Dahmer at least, like terrible aberrations were now becoming a monstrous habit.

Although she was completely unaware of her grandson's unspeakable urges, Jeffrey's landlady-grandmother was exhausted by his loud, drunken lifestyle. In late summer 1988 she asked him to move and in late September he took an apartment in Milwaukee proper. As if released from the only remaining tether on his unbridled inhibitions, the next day Jeff found himself in serious trouble with the law.

On 26 September, Dahmer approached a thirteen-year-old Laotian boy and offered him $50 to pose for nude photographs. The boy was willing but Dahmer still felt it necessary to drug him so that he could have sex with him. Later, when the woozy boy staggered home, his parents realised something was terribly wrong. The hospital confirmed that he had been drugged, the police were called in and Dahmer was arrested while at work at Ambrosia Chocolate. Charged with exploitation of a minor and second-degree sexual assault, he was bound over for trial in January, but released on his own recognisance.

Anxious about the outcome of his trial, Dahmer decided to relieve the tension by picking up Anthony Sears. Amazingly, Dahmer even let one of Sears's friends drive them back to his house before he murdered the man.

Before Dahmer's case came up in May, he was ordered to undergo examination by three psychologists. Unanimously, they agreed that he was manipulative and evasive and should be hospitalised for intensive treatment. Dahmer's lawyer, Gerald Boyle, again hired by Jeff's father, argued that because it was Dahmer's first offence, he should not be imprisoned. Innocently, he told the court, 'We don't have a multiple offender here. I believe that he was caught before it got to that point.' In a statement to the court, Dahmer buttressed his attorney's argument. 'What I have done is very serious. I've never been in this position before. This is a nightmare . . . I do want help. I want to turn my life around.' The judge bought Dahmer's plea and put him on five years' probation with the first year to be spent under a 'work-release' programme whereby Dahmer could go to work every day but had to return to jail at the end of his shift. Ten months later, Jeff's behaviour seemed so exemplary that the judge offered him early release. At no time during his detention had he been ordered to seek professional counselling. Even a letter from Lionel Dahmer, urging the judge not to allow his son to go free until he was forced to get help, did no good. If no one else understood that Jeffrey Dahmer had real problems, his father did. He said he was afraid that his son 'would never be more than he seemed to be – a liar, an alcoholic, a thief, an exhibitionist, a molester of children. I could not imagine how he had become such a ruined soul. There was something missing in Jeff . . . We call it a conscience.'

Although he went back to stay with his grandmother temporarily, by May 1990 Dahmer had taken apartment number 213 at the Oxford Apartments located at 924 North 25th Street in Milwaukee. Knowing full well that he was living on the edge, in addition to the security system on the building's main doors, he installed a separate alarm system and security locks on his own apartment. They would be absolutely necessary for what he had in mind.

Now in a constant emotional frenzy, Dahmer increased both the frequency and ferocity of his attacks. In June he murdered Edward Smith; a month later it was Ricky Beeks. September was a bumper month that garnered him two playmates; the first was Ernest Miller and the second David Thomas. By now, Dahmer had honed his modus operandi to a fine edge. His targets were always young men with unsettled lives, and he often chose victims who, like himself, had drink problems or were frequently in trouble with the law. Many of them were members of racial minorities. He knew that the police never paid much attention when such people simply dropped out of sight.

The pattern of Dahmer's approach was as predictable as his victims' profile. He would pick a likely candidate at a gay bar or bookshop and fall into conversation with them. Being nice looking and articulate, he had no trouble getting them to agree to go back to his apartment; the ploy was either to watch 'porno' movies or pose for photographs. Once inside his lair, he would offer them a drink laced with prescription sleeping pills. When they were no longer capable of offering any resistance, he would strangle them with his belt or his bare hands, or simply slit their throat with a sharp knife. Then he would strip off their clothes, photograph them and have sex with the corpse. Now well into the swing of things, Dahmer would begin to mutilate the body, cutting it open, revelling in the heat emanating from the internal organs and photographing the entire process. Finally, he would dissect his prey, laying the best parts aside. Prime cuts, like biceps, hearts and thighs were wrapped in plastic and put in the fridge or frozen for later consumption. The sexual organs were cut off and preserved in jars of formaldehyde while the skulls were boiled clean and coated with granite-effect spray paint. Sometimes, he liked to pull out his growing collection of skulls and masturbate in front of them. The remainder of the carcass was dumped into a 55-gallon plastic container filled with acid that would reduce muscle and bone to a greasy sludge that could be flushed down the toilet. There were, of course, variations on the theme. Ernest Miller's entire skeleton was boiled clean and bleached, awaiting later reassembly. Later, one victim would be flayed, his skin tanned like a piece of leather.

One of the few cannibals ever to give an explanation for his predilection, Dahmer would later insist that he believed that by eating his victims he was able to make them a part of him and that, in a way, they would always be with him. In the most perverse way imaginable, Dahmer was ensuring that his one-off lovers would never abandon him and that he would always remain in control of the relationship. If possible, Dahmer's need for control and terror of rejection drove him to acts more bizarre than cannibalism. Even Dahmer found what he did so awful that he hesitated to talk about it. 'I didn't want to keep killing people and having nothing left except the skull . . . This is going to sound bad, but . . . should I say it? . . . I took the drill while he was asleep . . .' What Dahmer hesitated to describe was his attempt to make zombie love-slaves. He hoped that by drilling a $\frac{1}{16}$-inch hole in the head of his drugged victim and injecting muratic acid into their brain, he could, quite literally, turn them into zombies that would wait patiently while he was out and be ready to love him when he came home. It did not work. Most of the victims died almost instantly although a few hung on for several days as their brain was slowly eaten away. But still, Jeff kept trying.

In February 1991 he met and killed Curtis Straughter. The next month it was Errol Lindsey and the month after that Tony Hughes. Hughes' case was particularly tragic in that he was a deaf-mute and more than grateful to anyone who would spend a little time with him. Had he been alive, he would probably not have been so grateful when Dahmer left his body lying on the floor for three days before cleaning up the mess. Even Dahmer realised that his urge to kill was accelerating its pace. 'After the fear and terror of what I had done had left, which took about a month, I started it all over again. From then on it was just a craving, a hunger. I don't know how to describe it, a compulsion. And I just kept doing it, doing it, doing it.' And by the time he killed Tony Hughes he was 'doing it' almost once a week. At that rate, something was bound to go wrong.

On 27 May, the very evening he dissected Tony Hughes' body, laying aside the good bits and dropping the rest into the vat of acid, Dahmer went out hunting again. Later that evening he met a fourteen-year-old oriental boy named Konerak Sinthasomphone. Using the photo ploy Dahmer lured him back to his apartment, drugged him, raped him and drilled a hole in his head. Somehow, while Jeff was busying himself getting the muratic acid ready, Konerak stumbled out of the apartment, down the stairs and into the street. Minutes later, around 2.00am, he was spotted by two eighteen-year-old black girls as he wandered around naked, babbling incoherently, blood running all over his head and down his legs. One of the girls ran to help him while the other called 911 emergency. Even before the police cruiser arrived Dahmer was out in the street looking for Konerak. The girls managed to keep Dahmer and his victim apart until the police pulled up, and then tried frantically to explain to the cops what had happened. Dahmer interrupted, insisting that the boy was a lot older than he looked and was, in fact, his nineteen-year-old lover. The police never bothered to call in a request for background information on Dahmer – which would have revealed that he was on parole for molesting a child, who was, as it happened, Konerak Sinthasomphone's older brother. Neither did they seem to notice the blood covering the boy's head and legs. All they saw was an articulate, 31-year-old white male and two teenage black girls. Who were they going to believe? Joking that the whole thing was just a 'homosexual lovers' spat' they led Sinthasomphone back to Dahmer's door and handed him over. Minutes later Konerak was dead, his flesh was in the fridge, his skull waiting to join the rest of the collection.

When the story came out, the officers who had led Konerak to his death were summarily fired but took their case to court, won, were reinstated with full pay and later named Officers of the Year by the Milwaukee Police Union for their 'righteous' struggle to clear their good names.

Now in the last stages of his insanity, Dahmer finally decided what to do with all the skulls he had been collecting. Increasingly divorced from reality, he convinced himself that if he built a shrine to the devil he could conjure up the Evil One himself and convince him to fork over 'special powers and energies to help me socially and financially'. The shrine was to take the form of a long, black table with six skulls arrayed down each side and a complete skeleton at each end. He already had almost enough skulls and Ernest Miller's skeleton was just waiting to be wired together, so why not? Later, Dahmer would look back on this episode with mixed feelings about the devil. 'Am I just an extremely evil person or is it some kind of satanic influence, or what? . . . I have to question whether or not there is an evil force in the world and whether or not I have been influenced by it . . . I have no idea. Is it possible to be influenced by spirit beings? I know it sounds like an easy cop-out . . . but from all that the Bible says, there are forces that have a[n] influence on people's behaviour. The Bible calls him Satan. I suppose it's possible because it sure seems like some of the thoughts aren't my own, they just come blasting into my head . . . They do not leave.'

Whether or not the devil made him do it, Dahmer was doing it as fast as he possibly could. Only two weeks after nearly being caught trying to kill Konerak Sinthasomphone he was off to the Chicago Gay Pride Parade. There he met Matt Turner, and together they travelled back to Milwaukee by Greyhound coach. A few weeks later, on 5 July, Jeff was back in Chicago where he picked up Jeremiah Weinberger. Again, they went back to Milwaukee but there must have been something very special about this one – Jeff lived with him for four days before killing him. Maybe something Jerry found in the fridge made him want to get away and Jeff just couldn't bear to be deserted again.

A week later he picked up Oliver Lacey and only four days after Lacey it was Joseph Bradehoft's turn. Joe lay on Dahmer's bed for two days before the ghoul decided to dismember him. But even the best fun eventually comes to an end, and for Jeffrey Dahmer the end came on 22 July when he picked up Tracey Edwards. Tracey was thirty-two years old, as big as Dahmer, black and a far more formidable opponent than Jeff was accustomed to.

The two officers in the passing police car realised that something on North 25th Street was definitely wrong when they spotted the naked black man running down the street – a pair of handcuffs dangling from one wrist – frantically trying to wave them down. When they stopped he explained that he had just escaped from some 'weird dude' who had tried to drug him, handcuff him and threaten him with a knife. He had managed to punch the 'freak' and escape. Did they have a key to the 'cuffs? Finally, someone listened. The officers asked Edwards to show them where the suspect lived. Together the two uniformed officers and the naked black man went up to Dahmer's apartment.

A nice-looking white man opened the door and apologetically let them in, explaining he had been depressed over losing his job at Ambrosia Chocolate, had had a little too much to drink and got a little crazy. He was sorry and would get the key to the handcuffs. While one of the policeman stayed with Tracey Edwards, the other escorted Dahmer to his bedroom to get the key. When Dahmer opened a dresser drawer the cop noticed the pile of Polaroid photos of bodies – and parts of bodies. He also noticed that the refrigerator in the photos looked like the one in Dahmer's kitchen. Hadn't the naked black guy said something about seeing something 'nasty' in the fridge when he went to get a beer? Leaving Dahmer in the custody of his partner, the cop wandered into the kitchen and looked into the refrigerator. The thing on the shelf looked back at him. 'There's a goddamned head in here!' he shrieked. The head belonged to Oliver Lacey and next to it, in a plastic bag labelled 'to eat later', was his heart.

With that, Dahmer completely lost his wits. Fighting like a wildcat he was cuffed, hustled out to the cruiser and taken to the police station. Minutes later a throng of detectives and forensic experts were combing through Dahmer's apartment. It was like nothing any of them had ever seen, or would ever want to see again. In addition to Oliver Lacey's head and heart in the cooler compartment, there was a bag of human meat. The freezer contained the heads of Jerry Weinberger, Matt Turner and Joe Bradehoft. A chest freezer held the torsos of Matt Turner and Jerry Weinberger. In the kitchen closet was a soup kettle containing two hands and Anthony Sears' genitalia. A metal filing cabinet in Dahmer's bedroom contained the skulls of Konerak Sinthasomphone, Raymond Smith, Curtis Straughter and Anthony Sears, Errol Lindsey's skin, Ernest Miller's skeleton and 74 Polaroid photos of partially dismembered bodies. In all, portions of thirteen of Dahmer's seventeen victims were recovered from the slaughterhouse. There was also the 55-gallon drum filled with human sludge, the muratic acid, a hypodermic needle, an electric drill and a ⅟₁₆-inch drill bit to be used in the creation of sex-zombies and a circular saw for dismembering corpses.

While lab technicians and forensic experts ploughed through the gruesome souvenirs of Dahmer's life, the boy himself was spilling his guts to the police. His confession, which ran to just over 160 pages, contained some of the weirdest personal insights in history:

It's hard for me to believe that a human being could have done what I've done, but I know that I did it.

If I knew the true, real reasons why all this started, I wouldn't probably have done any of it.

If I'd been thinking rationally I would have stopped. I wasn't thinking rationally because it just increased and increased. I was very careful for years and years, you know. Very careful about making sure that nothing incriminating remained, but these last few months, they just went nuts.

If I hadn't been caught or lost my job, I'd still be doing it. I'm quite sure of that. I went on doing it and doing it and doing it . . . How arrogant and stupid of me to think that I could do something like this . . . as if nothing ever happened.

I should have gone to college and gone into real estate and got myself an aquarium, that's what I should have done.

Appearing for Dahmer's defence was Gerald Boyle who had defended him on the child molestation charges three years earlier. Against Boyle's advice, Dahmer changed his plea from innocent by reason of insanity to guilty but insane. Now Boyle had to convince the jury just how crazy his client really was, even if it was obvious that he had murdered seventeen men and boys.

The security around the Dahmer case was like nothing ever seen in America. Everyone who went into the courthouse was 'patted down' for weapons and scanned electronically. The courtroom was constantly swept for bombs, both electronically and by sniffer dogs, and an 8-foot high bullet-proof glass screen protected the defendant from the hordes of people who wanted him dead. Prospective jurors were warned, 'You are going to hear about things that you probably didn't know existed in the real world.' And the entire, grisly affair was to be broadcast on nationwide television.

It was the prosecution's intention to persuade the jury that although what he did was the act of a madman, Jeffrey Dahmer was completely sane. Ultimately, as is the case in most such trials, it would be the psychiatrists' job to convince the jury of the accused's state of mind at the time of his crimes. There were a wide variety of professional opinions on why Dahmer did what he did; Dr James Fox, Dean of the College of Criminal Justice at Northeastern University in Boston said, 'If he felt at all uncomfortable about his own sexual orientation, it is very easy to see it projected on to these victims and punishing them, indirectly, to punish himself.' It was all great theatre, but the jury did not buy any of it. After three weeks of testimony it only took the jury five hours to find Jeffrey Dahmer both sane and guilty on all counts.

Although nothing was going to ameliorate his sentence, after being found guilty Dahmer read a four-page apology to the families of his victims. 'I know how much harm I have caused . . . Thank God there will be no more harm that I can do . . . I ask for no consideration.' He got none. He was sentenced to fifteen consecutive life terms without hope of parole. Had he lived so long, Jeff would have been up for release in 957 years.

After his sentencing, Dahmer commented, 'I couldn't find any meaning in my life when I was out there. I'm sure as hell not going to find it in [prison]. This is the grand finale of a life poorly spent and the end result is just overwhelmingly depressing . . . it's just a sick, pathetic, wretched, miserable life story, that's all it is.' Later, he commented to his lawyer, '. . . if I was killed in prison, that would be a blessing right now'. It was one wish that Dahmer would have granted. On 28 November 1994, while on a toilet cleaning detail with two other inmates, Jeffrey Dahmer, aged thirty-four, along with fellow inmate Jesse Anderson, was murdered by the third man on their crew, a schizophrenic killer named Christopher Scarver, who believed himself to be a new messiah.

In 1996 the city of Milwaukee apportioned $400,000 to buy the entire contents of Dahmer's apartment and have them incinerated to prevent anyone from buying them to create a Jeffrey Dahmer museum. All things considered, it was probably a wise move.

Fourteen

Sushi Dreams: Issei Sagawa (1981)

W hen Issei Sagawa was born in 1949 his nation was undergoing a difficult rebirth. The Japan of honour, family values and dedication to the god-emperor had been virtually obliterated, along with Nagasaki and Hiroshima, when the USA dropped atomic bombs on those two cities in 1945. The new Japan – a nation with a morbid fascination for degrading game shows, corporate humiliation, prostitutes dressed like children and vending machines that dispense soiled women's underwear – had not yet come into existence. Along with his nation, Issei Sagawa would experience similarly difficult beginnings leading to an equally questionable outcome.

Although his mother had undergone a previous pregnancy without undue difficulty, Issei presented problems from the earliest stages of development. Born so premature that his father could literally hold him in the palm of one hand, Issei also suffered from anoxia: a severe, pre-natal oxygen deficiency that often causes brain damage. As a result of his delicate physical condition, Issei spent most of the first two years of his life – when most infants are bonding with their mothers – in the sterile surroundings of a hospital.

Once he was well enough to rejoin his family on a full-time basis, everyone did their best to include little Issei in family activities. At a new year's celebration during his third year, his father, Akira, and his uncle, Mituso, entertained Issei and his older brother with one game after another. In one of the games, Mituso pretended to be a child-eating giant while Akira took the part of a brave Samurai warrior who was sworn to protect the children. The men wrestled for possession of the boys while their small charges squealed with delight, simultaneously frightened and thrilled at the attention. At the end of the game, uncle Mituso defeated the Samurai and carried off the boys, running through the house growling and swinging them under his arms, insisting he was going to take them off to his cooking pot. It was a completely harmless bit of fun, but it affected Issei far more than it should have. Years later, Issei would recall that from that day onward he was tormented by dreams of cannibalism in which he and his brother were being cooked in a vast cauldron. The dreams began spilling into his consciousness, peppering his thoughts with images of cannibalism and human flesh, but now the roles were reversed. Rather than the helpless victim, Issei was the controlling cannibal who held sway over the fate of his prey. Flesh eating became the central focus of his inner mind and he read an endless stream of comic books and horror stories about cannibals. Eventually, as he neared puberty, the obsession took on decidedly sexual overtones. At one point, he attempted to explain his strange fixation to his brother. 'When I was sleeping with my brother I tried to tell him that when I saw a beautiful girl I wanted to eat her. But my brother didn't understand. He laughed, so I was very ashamed.'

If Issei's internal life was confused and disturbed, his external reality was not a lot better. Although he was extremely intelligent, he never fully developed physically and his health always remained precarious. 'I got ill very often . . . [and] I was not happy at school, especially when I was a high school student. Sometimes [the other students] said something that hurt me: "You are very small" or short, or thin, something like that. It hurt me very profoundly.' Indeed, Issei was noticeably physically different from the other boys. Even at maturity he stood just under 5 feet tall, had unusually tiny hands and feet and walked with a pronounced limp. To make matters worse, he had a high-pitched, effeminate voice. Not surprisingly, his self-image was something less than ideal and he knew he was never going to be the kind of man that women were likely to throw themselves at. Still, like Napoleon Bonaparte and Alexander the Great, Issei Sagawa was a very tiny young man with very big ambitions. While Napoleon and Alexander wanted to conquer large nations, Issei just wanted to conquer a large woman: a tall, blonde, Nordic-type woman to be specific. 'Because I'm so short and small, I admire tall and beautiful women. I prefer white girls.' While a lot of men want to pursue tall women, Issei Sagawa was one of the few who has ever believed that the ultimate consummation of the relationship would be to eat them. So long as he was surrounded by Japanese girls, there was no temptation to act on these morbid fantasies, but once he entered university, all that changed.

After high school, Issei entered Wako University in Tokyo where he majored in English Literature. As an elective course, he signed up for a class in German. The professor was a tall, blonde German woman with whom Issei instantly became obsessed. 'When I met this woman in the street, I wondered if I could eat her,' he once told a British reporter. It was obviously a question he needed to answer, if only for his own peace of mind.

One summer night, Issei crawled through his German professor's window fully intent on killing and eating her. Creeping through the apartment, he found the woman asleep in bed and began fumbling around, looking for something with which to bludgeon her senseless before taking the first bite out of her body. By the time he found an umbrella, and decided it was a suitable weapon, the racket had roused the woman who began screaming and shouting. Terrified, Issei stumbled back out of the window and fled the scene. Whether or not she recognised him, or how word of the incident got out, we have not discovered, but although no charges were brought against him, Issei was sent to a psychiatrist to discuss his little problem. It did not take long for the psychiatrist to label Issei Sagawa as 'extremely dangerous'. What other recommendations he may have made are unknown because Issei's father, Akira, was by now the head of Kurita Water Industries, extremely rich and extremely powerful. He engineered a cover-up and sent Issei out of Tokyo, to finish his bachelor's and master's degrees at the University of Osaka. By 1980 Issei was living in Paris and had signed up at the Sorbonne's Censier Institute to study for a PhD in English Literature.

All these years, Issei had been nursing his desire to eat a tall, beautiful blonde woman. He was certain he could do it, he just needed to plan it out better than he had the last time. Now over thirty years old, Issei knew that he would have to do it soon or the urge would drive him completely crazy. He already had one of his tools in place. On moving to Paris he had purchased a .22 rifle, insisting that he needed it for self-defence. Now, all he needed was a victim. The easiest source of meat he could think of were the local streetwalkers. 'During the day I was studying . . . but when it was dark, the obsession arrived and I went outside my apartment to look for prostitutes. Then, when I have them in my house, in my room, when they used the bidet, I tried to shoot them but I couldn't, really couldn't. It's not the sense of morality or something. I don't think so. I was scared.'

If Issei's quest left him unfulfilled, so did his social life at the Sorbonne. The tiny, frail oriental foreigner was almost completely ignored by his fellow students, so he was forced, once again, to retreat into a fantasy world to make friends. The newest object of his rapt attention was a 25-year-old fellow student named Renée Hartevelt. The extremely bright, Dutch beauty was everything Issei had ever dreamed about. 'I am amazed. She's the most beautiful woman I have ever seen. Tall,

blonde, with pure white skin, she astonishes me with her grace.'
Being outgoing and kind-hearted by nature, Renée took pity on
the lonely little man who sat near her in a class. Occasionally
she would take time out to talk to him, sometimes in English,
sometimes in French and, occasionally, he would try out his
limited German on her. They talked about everything from
Shakespeare to French Impressionist paintings. They even went
to art exhibitions, museums and concerts together and, on at
least one occasion, she invited him to her flat for tea. If Renée
felt a sad sort of affection for Issei, he was completely fixated on
her and devised a plan that would allow him to bring his morbid
fantasy to fruition.

Issei told Renée he wanted to hire her to tutor him in
German; since his father was rich he could easily afford to pay
her for her time. Like most students, Renée needed the extra
money and she rather liked Issei, so she accepted. To celebrate
their new arrangement, Issei invited her to his apartment for a
traditional Japanese dinner.

'After the meal I asked her to read my favourite German
Expressionist poem. As she reads I can't keep my eyes off her.
After she leaves I can still smell her body on the bed sheet where
she sat reading the poem. I lick the chopsticks and dishes she
used. I can taste her lips. My passion is so great. I want to eat
her. If I do, she will be mine forever.'

The next day, 11 June 1981, Issei asked Renée to come back
and reread the same piece of Schiller's poetry, explaining that he
wanted to tape it for one of his teachers back in Japan. She said
she had no particular plans for the evening and that she would
see him later.

When she arrived at Issei's rooms, he seated her on the floor,
Japanese style, and brought her a cup of tea liberally laced with
whisky in the hope that it would dull her senses. They chatted
amiably for a while until Issei was able to bring the conversation
around to his real feelings for her. He told Renée he loved her

and wanted to have sex with her. Embarrassed, Renée explained that while she really liked him, her feelings were purely platonic. She didn't want to lose him as a friend, but she really did not want to sleep with him. Resignedly, Issei shrugged his shoulders and said he understood. Then, changing the subject in an attempt to dispel the awkward silence, he suggested she read the poem again. Relieved, she was quick to agree. What happened next is best told in Sagawa's own words. He later recounted the entire incident in his semi-novelised autobiography *In the Fog* and has described the event innumerable times. Like everything else that has taken place in Sagawa's life since the incident, the book was an attempt to relive, and savour, the nightmarish events that followed.

> I turn on the recorder. She starts to read. She speaks in perfect German. I reach for the rifle hidden beside the chest of drawers. I stand slowly and aim the rifle at the back of her head. I cannot stop myself.
>
> I aim and I fire. There is a loud sound and her body falls from the chair on to the floor. It is like she is watching me. I see her cheeks, her eyes, her nose and mouth, the blood pouring from her head. Too much blood, her face all completely pale. I try to talk to her, but she no longer answers.

Later, Sagawa would comment that he was amazed at how quiet Renée became after he murdered her.

> I thought I would have to call the police or the ambulance, really, but suddenly I realized [that] for my fantasy I [had] killed her.
>
> There is blood all over the floor. I try to wipe it up, but I realize I cannot stop the flow of blood from her head. It is very quiet here. There is only the silence of death. I start to

take off her clothes. It is hard to take the clothes off a dead body. Finally it is done. Her beautiful white body is before me. I've waited so long for this day and now it is here. I touch her ass. It is so very smooth. I wonder where I should bite first. I decide to bite the top of her butt. My nose is covered with her cold white skin. I try to bite down hard, but I can't. I get a knife from the kitchen and stab it deeply into her skin.

Suddenly a lot of sallow fat oozes from the wound. It continues to ooze. Finally I find the red meat under the sallow fat. I scoop it out and put it in my mouth. I chew. It has no smell and no taste. It melts in my mouth like a perfect piece of raw tuna in a sushi restaurant. I look in her eyes and say: 'You are delicious.'

I cut her body and lift the meat to my mouth again and again. Then I take a photograph of her white corpse with its deep wounds. I have sex with her body. When I hug her she lets out a breath. I'm frightened, she seems alive. I kiss her and tell her I love her. Then I drag her body to the bathroom. By now I am exhausted, but I cut into her hip and put the meat in a roasting pan. After it is cooked I sit at the table using her underwear as a napkin. They still smell of her body.

Then I turn on the tape of her reading the German poem and eat. There is not enough taste. I use some salt and some mustard and it is delicious, very high quality meat. Then I go back to the bathroom and cut off her breast and bake it. It swells while it cooks. I serve the breast on the table and eat it with a fork and knife. It isn't very good. Too greasy. I try to cut into another part of her body. Her thighs were wonderful. Finally she is in my stomach. Finally she is mine. Finally, I was eating a beautiful white woman and thought nothing was so delicious. It is the best dinner I've ever had.

Afterwards I sleep with her.

Next morning she is still here. She doesn't smell bad. Today I must finish cutting up her body.

I touch the cold body again and I wonder where I should start. I start to cut off all the meat before amputating the limbs. While I cut her calf I suddenly want to taste it. I see the beautiful red meat beneath the fat. I grasp her knee and her ankle, and tear it with my teeth. It is tender. I slowly chew and savour it.

After eating most of the calf I look at myself in the mirror. There is grease all over my face. And then I start to eat at random. I bite her little toe. It still smells of her feet. I stab the knife into her arch and see the red meat deep inside. I thrust my fingers inside and dig out the meat and put it in my mouth. It tastes okay. Then I stab the knife into her armpit. Ever since I saw [her armpit] under her yellow sleeveless top I wondered how it would taste. I had no idea it would taste this good. The wonderful taste cheers me up and I devour her underarm up to the elbow.

Finally I cut off her private parts. When I touch the pubic hair it has a very bad smell. I bite her clit, but it won't come off, it just stretches. So I throw it in the frying pan and pop it in my mouth. I chew very carefully and swallow it. It is so sweet. After I swallow it, I feel her in my body and get hot. I turn the body over and open her buttocks, revealing her anus. I scoop it out with my knife and try to put it in my mouth. It smells too much. I put it in the frying pan and throw it in my mouth. It still smells. I spit it out.

It's been twenty-four hours now. Some huge flies hover and buzz in the bathroom. I try to chase them away, but they come back. They swarm on her face. They seem to tell me that I've lost her forever. It is no longer her. Where is she? She's gone far away. I try to use an electric knife to cut her body. It doesn't work. It just makes a loud sound. I use a hatchet. I strike several times. It's hard work. I strike her thigh. Her body jumps up. If she could feel, it would have hurt. Finally the thigh separates from her body. I bite it again, like I would bite a chicken leg. Then I cut off her arms. It is even harder than the thigh. I use the electric knife again. It makes a shrill sound, like the sound of her shrill voice. It works this time. Her hand still wears a ring and a bracelet. When I see her long fingers I am driven by another impulse. I use her hand to masturbate. Her long fingers excite me.

And then I see her face. It is still quiet. She has a small nose and a sweet lower lip. When she was alive I wanted to bite them. Now I can satisfy that desire. It's so easy to bite off her nose. As I chew the cartilage I can hear the noise. I use a knife to cut off more of the cartilage and put it in my mouth. It really doesn't taste very good. I scoop out her lower lip with my knife and put it in my mouth. It has hard skin. I decide to eat it later when I can fry it. So I put it in the refrigerator.

I want her tongue. I can't open her lower jaw, but I can reach in between her teeth. Finally it comes out. I cut it off and put it in my mouth. It's hard to chew. I see my face in the mirror. Her tongue entwined with my tongue. I try to close my mouth, but her tongue slips out. Finally I cut the skin off the tongue and taste the meat.

I try to eat her eyes. It's hard for me to stab into them, though it is the easiest part of her face. I can see tears coming from them. It frightens me. Her eyes are all that is left of her face. It is nearly a skull.

At last I have to cut off her head. It is the most difficult thing I have to do. I cut off the meat on her neck until I can see bone . . . I use the hatchet. It is surprisingly easy to cut through. With the head gone her body is now only flesh. When I grab the hair and hang up the head, I realize I am a cannibal. I put the head in a plastic bag.

[I] open the refrigerator. I recognize each piece of meat. This is part of her hip and this is part of her thigh. I fry them on the stove. I set the table. There is mustard, salt, pepper and sauce. I put her underwear beside the dish. I sniff it and look at a nude woman in a magazine. I try to remember which part of her is in my mouth, but it is difficult to connect the meat with a body. Each day the meat becomes more tender, each day the taste is more sweet and delicious.

At some point during this unspeakable chain of events, one of Sagawa's neighbours remembered hearing him howling and banging on the walls of his apartment.

By 15 June, four days after the murder, Sagawa realised that he would have to dispose of the rapidly putrefying carcass of Renée Hartevelt. Before stuffing the butchered remains into garbage bags, he went out and bought two immense, wheeled suitcases, lugged them home and proceeded to fill them with Renée's body parts. He then called a taxi, heaved the bags into the boot with the driver's help, and told the cabbie to take him to the lakes in the Bois de Boulogne park. The sight of this tiny, limping Oriental man lugging two huge suitcases over the vast expanse of lawn inevitably drew the curious stares and excited chatter of people in the park. Suddenly confused and terrified, Sagawa abandoned his burden and bolted for home, leaving the bags and their grotesque contents behind. Predictably the police were summoned and the suitcases opened. It only took two days for detectives to learn where the suitcases had come from and who had purchased them.

When the gendarmes arrived at Sagawa's flat, he made no attempt to flee. As they carried out a search that turned up various parts of Renée in the refrigerator, he went into great detail explaining exactly what he had done, why he had done it and the fact that he had once been to see a psychiatrist in Japan for his little problem. Shortly thereafter, the police hustled him off to the Henri Colin psychiatric ward in Villejuif where a team of three doctors tried to determine whether he was sane enough to stand trial for murder. They all agreed. Issei Sagawa was 'untreatably psychotic', legally incompetent and it was unlikely that he could ever be cured. By the time the trial came up in 1983, the presiding judge had no choice but to declare that Issei Sagawa was in a 'state of dementia' at the time of the crime and therefore unable to stand trial. Because it was unlikely that he could ever be cured, he would be committed to the Paul Guiraud Asylum in Paris where he would be detained for an indefinite period of time. It was the judges' intent that Sagawa be incarcerated for the remainder of his life, but somehow things did not quite work out that way.

After three years spent chatting with the doctors and corresponding with the seamier members of Japanese intelligentsia – who sent him a stream of books on cannibals and cannibalism – Sagawa came to a startling conclusion. 'I realized I was not so unusual.' Unusual or not, Akira Sagawa had no intention of allowing his little boy to rot in a French asylum, so he began making discreet enquiries as to how much it would cost to have him repatriated to Japan. The French authorities had no desire to feed and house Issei Sagawa for the next half-century or so, so they agreed to a deal. They would allow Issei to be flown back to Japan on condition that he be permanently institutionalised there. In May 1984, Issei was on his way back home where he was to be comfortably ensconced in the Matsuzawa Psychiatric Hospital in Tokyo.

Once at the hospital, two things seemed to happen simultaneously. First, he became the object of constant attention by a salacious Japanese press and, secondly, the doctors decided he was sane after all. Hospital superintendent Tsuguo Kanego went so far as to say, 'I think he is sane and guilty . . . he should be in prison.' Evidently, the Japanese police agreed and requested French authorities to hand over the evidence and legal transcripts that would allow them to build a case against Sagawa. The French adamantly refused to cooperate. If Sagawa was declared sane and allowed to stand trial, it would make the French psychiatric and legal system look incompetent – this they could not tolerate. Reluctantly but, it would seem, under intense pressure from Sagawa's father and his money, in September 1985, Issei Sagawa was released from the hospital.

After taking a small apartment near his parents' house, Issei set out to rebuild his life as a sort of renaissance man or, in his case, a renaissance cannibal. He wrote the fictionalised account of his French dining experience, previously mentioned and excerpted above, that sold over 200,000 copies. A Tokyo book reviewer wrote that *In the Fog* was 'Beautifully done . . . outstanding among recent Japanese literature.' With this first literary success under his belt, he began churning out a column for a porno magazine and appeared in a few cheap porno films, several of which featured re-enactments of his murder and consumption of Renée.

If the public's fascination with Japan's notorious woman-eater had died down since his days at the Matsuzawa Asylum, Issei did everything he could to revive it, mostly through his unrepentant attitude to having broken the great social taboo, which he was more than happy to expound on at every possible opportunity. His big break came in 1989 shortly after the capture of child murderer Tsutomu Miyazaki. A tabloid newspaper contacted Sagawa and asked him to comment on the Miyazaki case, and Issei made the most of the opportunity, parlaying his moment in the sun into a string of appearances on television chat shows where he revelled in his own crime, giving short shrift to that of Miyazaki.

The Japanese public were morbidly fascinated by Sagawa and quickly made him into a bizarre 'pop idol'. In 1994 he held a one-man seminar entitled 'Sagawa's World' in which he discussed his culinary preferences and aired a video predictably entitled *The Desire to be Eaten*. With some sort of sick fame now relatively assured, he took up more 'artsy', gentlemanly pastimes such as painting – mostly turning out rather pedestrian renditions of women's backsides. In a television drama he played a cult leader; he wrote a legitimate newspaper column and a string of seven books (to date) including a 1997 commentary on the fourteen-year-old Japanese serial killer from the city of Kobe, known as 'Youth A'. He turned his own crime into a 'Manga' style comic book entitled *Manga Sagawa-san*, published by Okura Shuppan. In the most obscene twist of all, he became a restaurant critic for the Japanese magazine of high culture, *Spa*; in one issue his smiling image even made it on to the magazine's cover. To ensure that the widest possible audience can share Sagawa's views on his dietary preferences he maintains his own on-line website.

More than a quarter century after his murder of Renée Hartevelt, Issei Sagawa seems to find as much pleasure in cashing in on his crime as he did in committing it. 'The public has made me the godfather of cannibalism, and I am happy about that. I will always look at the world through the eyes of a cannibal.' To this day he has never once expressed any regret at his heinous act, but does say that the only thing that can possibly save him is to be eaten by a young western woman. At least as disturbing as Sagawa's own sanguine attitude towards his crime is the continuing fascination of the Japanese public for their home-grown cannibal. One British foreign correspondent insists that their failure to condemn Sagawa 'is rooted in their perception of his victim as less than a person'. If this is true – and in light of the Japanese seeming willingness to kill and eat prisoners of war during the Second World War cited in chapter four, it well may be – then it is a sad and disturbing comment on the continuing Japanese attitude towards the West.

The best comment on the entire Sagawa affair may be found in the title of a Rolling Stones song which recounts Issei's crime: 'Too Much Blood'.

Fifteen

Even the Best of Families:
Hadden and Bradfield Clark (1984–92)

hen Hadden Clark proposed marriage to Flavia Scranton it seemed the perfect match. Both families were from the social stratum that Americans call 'good families'; in Britain they would be referred to as 'the right sort'. Flavia could trace her family's arrival in America back to the *Mayflower* and her ancestors had distinguished themselves in the American Revolutionary War. Her parents still maintained a small estate in Meriden, Connecticut. If Flavia's people were long established, Hadden's were newer, but no less successful. His father, Silas Clark, had been the Republican mayor of White Plains, New York, and Silas and his wife now lived in a mansion in Wellfleet on Cape Cod. Hadden himself had a Master's degree in business administration and a Doctoral degree in chemistry. Not only was he bright, he was also ambitious. Over the years he would be instrumental in developing plastic food wrap and the process by which carpeting could be made fire resistant. He was a young man who was going places.

As a family, the Clarks made all the right moves. They were liked by their neighbours and included in all the proper social circles. Between 1950 and 1959 they produced four children. Bradfield was the first, a year later came Hadden Jr, then Geoffrey in 1955 and Alison in 1959. But the good appearances were just that: appearances. Both Hadden Sr and Flavia drank heavily and loud arguments leading to fisticuffs were hardly a rarity. Anxious and restless, Hadden moved from one job to another faster than was good for him or for his family's stability. When the pressure got too great, Hadden would retreat to the garden shed to brood and contemplate his life. As a result of this unsettled atmosphere the children, particularly the boys, developed severe emotional problems.

From their earliest years both Brad and Hadden Jr proved unruly and hard to manage, each in his own way. Hadden developed into a touchy boy with a mean, vengeful streak a mile wide. The slightest criticism could make him lash out with every intention of hurting somebody. He was the kind of boy that other children went out of their way to avoid. On one occasion, he and younger brother Geoff were out riding their bikes when, for reasons unknown, Hadden grabbed the handlebars of Geoff's bike and pushed him over; Geoff toppled to the ground, cutting his head badly. Hadden left him to run home and tell their mother what had happened. His explanation was completely typical of his attitude: 'There's been an accident, but don't worry, the bike's okay.' Geoff's condition could not have concerned him less.

Flavia insisted that his odd behaviour was the result of having been delivered with surgical forceps and that he had developed cerebral palsy. Hadden Sr was more blunt, but no more accurate. When he had been drinking he simply referred to his son as 'the retard' – a slight specifically aimed at Hadden's speech problems and difficulties at school. At least part of the explanation for Hadden Jr's behaviour may have lain in the fact that Flavia had wanted her second child to be a girl. From his earliest years she dressed him in girls' clothes and, particularly when she was drinking heavily, called him Kristen. Thanks to his mother's insistence on feminising him, although Hadden was heterosexual, he became a transvestite and found it nearly impossible to develop normal relationships with women.

Although Flavia was at fault for Hadden's problem, she once criticised him for wearing women's clothes. He snapped back: 'I like my ladies' clothing. Don't try to change me.' It would seem that she already had.

Three of the Clark children went to university, as was expected of them. Only Hadden, who had never been the most accomplished of students, could not qualify. Determined that their son should have a respectable place in life, Hadden Sr and Flavia enrolled him in the prestigious Culinary Institute of America (CIA) in Hyde Park, New York. Amazingly, Hadden did extremely well there, excelling in his artistic ability as a sculptor of ice and tallow centrepieces. This is not to say that all of Hadden's problems disappeared at the CIA. He remained hypersensitive to criticism and would retaliate in nasty, insidious ways to even the smallest slight. On one occasion he urinated in a tub of mashed potatoes. He did, however, graduate in January 1974 and his entire family turned out for the occasion.

If Hadden's problems manifested themselves in violent behaviour, Bradfield became the rebel. Like many teenagers, Brad experimented with drugs and alcohol in high school. But where most kids give up the drugs and learn to control their drinking so they can get on with their lives, Brad did not. He was bright enough to earn two university degrees and became an early whiz in the emerging world of computer engineering despite his problems. But his deepening involvement in drugs, and the emotional baggage of his childhood, almost guaranteed that he would come to a bad end. By 1984 Brad was living in the San Francisco suburb of Los Gatos, California, where he worked as a computer software specialist in the booming computer industry. In June of that year he struck up a relationship with a co-worker named Patricia Mak, a charming, stunningly attractive woman of twenty-nine. On the 23rd of that month he invited her to his apartment for dinner and she accepted.

The evening seemed to be going well until Brad – fuelled by too much booze and drugs – moved a little too fast for Patricia's liking. He made a rude and clumsy pass at her, she slapped him and he attacked her. During the scuffle he slammed her head against a concrete block and proceeded to strangle her to death. Then, in a crazed and nearly incoherent fury, he dragged the body to his bathtub where he hacked her into eleven pieces with a large kitchen knife.

Still able to function, but clearly out of control, Brad cut off Patricia's breasts and took them out on to the patio where he lit his barbecue grill. After grilling and eating his girlfriend's mammaries he returned to the house where he stuffed the remaining body parts into several trash bags, stashed them in his car, and began planning where, and how, he would dispose of them. By now the drugs and drink must have begun to wear off and Brad started to realise what he had done. He wandered around for two days before finally attempting to kill himself. Later, in hospital, he confessed to the murder under a routine police questioning regarding the disappearance of Patricia Mak. When they asked where Patricia's body was, he replied: 'She's in the trunk [of my car].' Almost one year later to the day, Bradfield Clark was sentenced to eighteen years to life and shipped off to California's medium-security Deuel Vocational Institute.

No matter how much grief and anxiety Brad's actions may have caused his family, they could not possibly imagine that their nightmare had only just begun – and it was going to get a lot worse.

By the time Brad's life had gone down the tubes, his younger brother Hadden was a strapping 6 feet 2, thirty-year-old man with a wiry, athletic build who seemed well on the way to making a name for himself in the world of fine food. With his degree from the culinary institute he had his pick of secure, well-paid jobs all across the country. It might seem odd, then, that he could not hold on to any of them for very long. In addition to his uncontrollable temper he had developed habits that unsettled his co-workers and employers alike. Drinking cups of fresh beef blood from the carcasses delivered to the kitchen was only one of them but, at the end of the day, it may have been the most telling.

Hadden's earliest jobs were in the best restaurants and hotels in the resort town of Provincetown, located at the northernmost tip of Cape Cod. It was a renowned, up-scale market catering to singles, gay men and lesbians and the easy, free lifestyle in 'P-town' was every new chef's dream. But Hadden just could not seem to integrate into society. When he was not working, he spent his time alone, surf fishing along the sandy beaches of the Cape. He worked his way through all the town's better restaurants and finally had to leave to find a decent job elsewhere. Years later, he would claim that while in Provincetown he had killed several women and buried their bodies in the sand dunes. He claimed that on at least one occasion he had cut off the woman's fingers and used them to bait his fishing line. Like so much in Hadden's life, the truth of this story remains unclear. What *is* true, however, is that Hadden left Provincetown because he was no longer welcome.

He then went through a series of chef's jobs: working on a cruise ship, in banquet halls and even serving as a chef at the 1980 Winter Olympics at Lake Placid, New York, but he never stayed anywhere for very long. How Hadden felt about his transient life is unknown, but everyone he left behind seemed relieved to see him go. Finally, in desperation, he joined the Navy. It may have been a smart move for a down-and-out chef, but it was a very bad move for a transvestite. On the outside he wore regular issue US Navy fatigues, underneath was lady's underwear; obviously his shipmates found out and took exception. Hadden was regularly beaten. Once he was locked in the meat freezer for three hours. Transfers from one ship to another did not relieve the abuse, it only changed its venue.

The final beating came in March 1985 and the damage, caused by having his head slammed repeatedly against the steel decking of an aircraft carrier, put him in hospital. During his hospitalisation Hadden was interviewed by a military psychiatrist who appreciated the nature of his problems more than anyone else had. Hadden was diagnosed as paranoid schizophrenic, given a medical discharge and put on the antipsychotic Halidol, but as soon as he was released he stopped taking the medicine. Lost, frustrated, confused and angry he decided to go to his brother Geoff. In fact, he had little choice in where to turn.

During the years of his absence the Clark family had completely disintegrated. Older brother Brad was now permanently incarcerated, his parents had divorced, his mother had moved to Rhode Island and, a year later, Hadden Sr had committed suicide while living with daughter Alison in Rhode Island. After this terrible incident Alison had severed all ties with her unstable relatives and told people she had no family. Grandfather Silas Clark, to whom Hadden had been close, was also dead and his grandmother had moved from the estate at Wellfleet to a retirement home. That left only Geoff, who had problems of his own.

Geoff and his wife Marcia lived in Silver Spring, Maryland, where they moved when Geoff, a microbiologist, landed a job at the US Food and Drug Administration. Silver Spring was a nice, quiet community with shady tree-lined streets but was still within easy commuting distance of the FDA laboratories in Washington DC. Like his parents before him, Geoff's family life seemed fine. He and Marcia had three children and a good income, but there were problems simmering beneath the surface. There were arguments that turned into rows and the rows sometimes became violent. Eventually there would be a divorce, but for now things were stable enough for Geoff and Marcia to agree to rent the family room in their basement to Hadden.

When Hadden arrived at his brother's house on Sudley Road his entire life consisted of a few clothes, his prized collection of chef's knives and tools – which he kept securely locked in a metal toolbox – and the old Datsun pickup truck he was driving. Still, he settled in and tried to get on with Geoff, Marcia and their three kids. He even got a good job at an exclusive country club in nearby Chevy Chase, Maryland. But true to his established pattern, things did not remain calm for long.

This time, however, the problems were not at work, but at home. On one occasion Hadden was picked up for shoplifting ladies' underwear at a local department store and the incident did nothing to endear him to his brother and sister-in-law who had tried their best to ignore his transvestism. But because he was so 'different', his nieces and nephews would not leave their Uncle Hadden alone. They thought he was 'weird' and six-year-old Eliza called him 'retarded' just as his father had done all those years ago. Hadden developed a seething hatred for the children and all their obnoxious little friends. He got his revenge on the little wretches by masturbating in front of them. Obviously, they told their parents. It was the last straw. Geoff told Hadden he had to go. Furious, Hadden found a new place to live and began moving his things out of Geoff's house. He dragged out the process just to be infuriating, taking a few pieces at a time when he left for work, dropping them off at his new place in nearby Bethesda and then repeating the process the next day. By 31 May 1986 he only had one box still to be picked up.

It was not even an hour past noon but it was already hot – the kind of itchy, sultry hot that makes people short tempered – and when Hadden got to Geoff's house to find everyone out he was furious. The door was unlocked so he could get his belongings, but no one was there to say goodbye. As he stood in the driveway fuming, he saw a little girl in a pink bathing suit walking across the lawn towards him. He recognised her. Her name was Michele Dorr, the kid with the stutter. She lived two houses away with her divorced father, Carl, but only came to stay with him at weekends and then she and Hadden's niece Eliza hung out together almost constantly.

Michele had been playing outside in her plastic turtle-shaped swimming pool while her dad was inside watching television. Like all children, she got bored and decided to wander down to see if Eliza was at home. 'Is Eliza here?' she asked, staring up at Hadden.

In a flash Hadden knew how he would get even with his brother's snotty-nosed kids. He told Michele that Eliza was up in her room playing and it would be OK if she went up. As she skipped towards the door, Hadden walked to the back of his Datsun and raised the lid on the cap. Opening the toolbox, he stared at the collection of knives. There were boning knives, butcher's knives, fleshing knives, carving knives, filleting knives and meat cleavers – all sharpened to a razor edge. He selected a knife with a 12-inch blade, looked at it for a minute, and walked into the house and up the stairs towards his niece's bedroom.

Michele must have been surprised when he walked in on her, but he moved too quickly for her to react. He threw her on to the floor and slashed twice across her tiny chest, opening up a horrid V-shaped wound. When he thought she was going to scream, Hadden jammed one hand across her mouth. Imagine his surprise when she bit down on the fleshy part of his palm. How dare she? In blind fury he plunged the knife into her throat and blood began spurting everywhere. Hadden was suddenly confused. Which should he do first – rape the tiny, dying child, or clean up the mess? He decided on rape but, frustratingly, couldn't get an erection. Clean up the blood.

From his truck he gathered all the rags he could find and his old Navy duffle bag. On his way back through the house he stopped in the kitchen long enough to grab several large black garbage bags. He crammed Michele's limp body into a trash bag and then into the duffle bag, mopped the blood from the floor and jammed the rags, along with everything else that was blood-stained, into a second bag. When the room looked as normal as he could make it, he checked his watch. In twenty minutes he was due at work, and he had to hurry. This was not the day to be late. He stuffed the child-laden duffle into the back of the Datsun and roared off.

After work he drove to a nearby naval hospital to have a cut on his hand looked at and bandaged. Had it happened at work, or earlier at his brother's house? He couldn't remember. By the time he finished in casualty it was almost midnight, just time to take care of one last piece of business before going home. He drove in the direction of Baltimore until he came to a wooded area. There he stopped, pulled the duffle bag, a shovel and an electric torch from the back of the truck, walked a few feet into the undergrowth and started digging a hole. He was about to throw the body in and cover it up, when he paused. Killing the child had been a means to get revenge on Eliza – but didn't he owe himself some pleasure, too? He went back to the Datsun, selected one of his fleshing knives and sliced off a nice, choice, juicy cut of Michele Dorr. Then he buried the body, covering the freshly turned earth with a discarded mattress he found lying a few feet away. Finally, Hadden picked up the piece of meat he was going to cook for dinner, got into his truck and drove home to his new apartment.

While Hadden Clark was calmly cooking up meals at the country club, Carl Dorr had been looking for his daughter. At first he was not particularly worried when she was not in her little swimming pool; he assumed, correctly, that she had wandered over to Eliza's to play. But when she didn't come home for supper he decided he had better look for her. His first stop was Geoff Clark's house. The family were all together having a barbecue and none of them, including six-year-old Eliza, had seen her all day. Dorr scoured the neighbourhood before his rising anxiety sent him to the police station. He said he had last seen his daughter around 2.10 in the afternoon and that she had disappeared sometime between then and 5pm. The police would carry out a full investigation but were instantly convinced that Carl Dorr had done away with his own daughter. Tragically, the assumption was a lot more than police stupidity. In the vast majority of missing children cases a parent is ultimately found to be responsible. In consequence, while some of the officers grilled Carl Dorr, others spent the next day in a door-to-door search of the area around the Dorr home. One of the people they questioned was Hadden Clark.

Hadden was back at Geoff's house working on his truck when Officer Wayne Farrell called in. The police had already heard about Geoff Clark's weird brother and he seemed to be someone that should be questioned, so Farrell took him in to the station. Hadden was calm at first and said that he had been at Geoff's for a few minutes the previous day but had been at work about a quarter to three. Later, his time card at the country club confirmed that he had arrived at 2.46. The police thought it would have been nearly impossible for anyone to have done away with the child, ditched the body and driven from Sudley Road to the Chevy Chase Country Club between 2.10 and 2.46. But just to make certain Hadden was telling the truth they continued to question him. When they showed him a photo of Michele he broke down in tears, bolted out of the examination room, ran to the toilet and began throwing up violently. The cops were hot on his heels. While Hadden was still retching into the bowl they fired one question after another at him – shouting into the toilet cubicle. They pressed Michele's photo in front of his face. Had he seen her? What had he done with her? Hadden insisted he could not remember. Maybe he had done something to her. He just didn't know. After hammering away at Clark for hours they finally gave up. There was little doubt the guy was crazy as a loon, but even Superman could not have committed murder, hidden the body and made it to the country club in forty-one minutes. So they turned their attention back to Carl Dorr.

The police inquiry turned up a lot of circumstantial evidence that made Carl look guilty. He and his wife had had a turbulent marriage; on more than one occasion he had beaten her and threatened that if she left him he would kidnap Michele. Recently he had been in court with his ex-wife about overdue child support payments. Carl voluntarily took a polygraph test, was hypnotised and given sodium pentothal (truth serum) and passed every test, but it made no impression on the Silver Spring Police Department. Already shattered by his divorce and the disappearance of his daughter, under the pressure of the incessant, day-after-day questioning, Carl Dorr slowly became irrational.

Medieval torture-masters learned long ago that a person subjected to enough pain – either physical or emotional – would eventually say anything. This is exactly what happened to Carl Dorr. He never confessed to hurting Michele, but he did lose all grip on reality. He hallucinated; he thought the people on television were talking about him; he even believed that if he found his daughter – even if she were dead – he could bring her back to life. Finally, he was committed to a psychiatric ward for a seventy-two hour observation. The minute he was released the police picked him up and started the harassment all over again. In all truth, there was something Carl Dorr was not telling the police. The last time he had looked in on Michele had been noon, not 2.10 as he claimed. He was simply ashamed that he had neglected her for so long. That tiny lie had given Hadden Clark the extra time needed to appear innocent.

For Hadden, things were now going downhill fast. He lost his job at the country club and was thrown out of his apartment in

Bethesda, vandalising it before he left. Separating himself from human company entirely, he lived in the woods in the back of his Datsun. Sometimes he picked up odd jobs, mostly gardening, through a local homeless shelter; otherwise he kept to himself. More than once he checked himself into a mental hospital long enough to get a prescription for Halidol, and then scurried back to the woods. During one of his psychiatric evaluations, the examining doctor wrote: 'He is a potential danger to himself through poor judgement and self-defeating behaviour.' The danger was far greater to others than to Hadden, who even told one of his doctors 'I think I have a split personality.'

In 1989 he was arrested for having walked into a church during choir practice – dressed in women's clothes – and having stolen fifteen women's handbags and coats from the cloakroom. Most of the charges were dropped in exchange for a guilty plea. He should have received a three-months to two-year sentence but, instead, a sympathetic judge and public defender let him off with probation, despite the fact that he was already on probation in two states. The public defender, Donald Salzman, even wrote a letter for Hadden to give to any policeman who might arrest him in future. It was, in essence, a request that he should not be held responsible for his actions because he had serious mental problems. Of all the things that might have been done for, or to, Hadden Clark, this was the worst possible scenario for society at large, and it didn't take Hadden long to prove it.

The people at the homeless centre soon got him a job gardening for Penny Houghteling, a psychotherapist who lived in Bethesda. Penny believed she should 'practise what she preached' and as a professional who dealt with people with mental and emotional problems that meant giving them a little work when possible. Hadden worked hard at her lawn and garden and she was nice to him – in no time at all he fixated on her as a substitute mother. This did not mean he hesitated to steal from her, particularly small items of her clothing. When

Penny suspected Hadden of the thefts she confronted him. In response he lashed out at her verbally. His reaction should have set off alarm bells in her mind but, as on so many earlier occasions, Hadden got away with a shrug and a slap on the wrist. In spite of the occasional bump in their relationship, everything moved along relatively smoothly until the day Penny's daughter, Lisa, came home after graduating from Harvard.

Twenty-three-year-old Lisa Houghteling was not only exceptionally bright, she was a stunning 6-foot tall beauty who had everything in the world going for her. Hadden was immediately, insanely jealous. Why had this stranger come between him and Penny? As he had done six years earlier when he taught Eliza a lesson by killing Michele, he would teach Penny a lesson by getting rid of Lisa. On Sunday night, 18 October – while Penny was away at a conference – Hadden drove to the Houghteling house, took the spare key from its hiding place in the garden shed and let himself in. He was wearing women's clothes, most of them Penny's. Under his woman's raincoat he carried a .22 calibre rifle.

Creeping up to Lisa's room, he prodded her awake with the rifle and proceeded to terrorise her, insisting that he was really Lisa and she was an impostor. To show her what lying would get her, he was going to take her out to the woods where she could meet his friend Hadden. He covered her mouth with duct tape, but in his frenzy he covered her nose as well. When she passed out from lack of oxygen, he grabbed a pair of scissors and began hacking away at the tape, severing an artery in her neck. Within minutes Lisa Houghteling bled to death. Heaving the body into the back of his trusty Datsun, Hadden took Lisa to his hideaway in the woods where he buried her.

When Penny telephoned the police and told them her daughter was missing she mentioned the name of her gardener. The name was familiar: it was the same man who had been hauled in for questioning in connection with the Michele Dorr case eight years earlier. It took a month before the police had irrefutable evidence connecting Clark with Lisa's death but a faint fingerprint on a bloodstained pillowcase matched one of Hadden's. Although the body had not been found, in the spring of 1993 Hadden Clark was sentenced to thirty years in prison for the second-degree murder of Lisa Houghteling. Only after he was in prison did Hadden reveal the location of Lisa's grave. Had he told the court where she was buried any earlier he would have been convicted of murder in the first degree.

Once safely inside prison walls, Hadden seemed anxious to unburden himself of, or brag about, his crimes. His chosen confessor was another prisoner who bore a striking likeness to popular paintings of Jesus Christ. Believing his fellow inmate to be the Son of God, Hadden told him what he had done with Michele Dorr and the whereabouts of her body. Jesus, whose name has been withheld by prison authorities, repeated Hadden's confession to the warden. The information was accepted as validation of little Michele's death, but by that time police forensics experts were ahead of them. In 1999 mitochondrial DNA testing had matched a sample of blood found lingering in Clark's last apartment to a sample taken from Michele's mother. The proof was conclusive. Hadden Clark's cannibal dinner had finally caught up with him. That same year he was tried for Michele's death and given a life sentence for first-degree murder. In January 2000 he led police to the site where he had buried Michele's remains. After fourteen years, Carl Dorr was no longer the chief suspect in his daughter's disappearance.

But Hadden Clark made still more confessions to his pal Jesus. Over the years, he said, he had killed upwards of twenty women, sometimes eating them in the hope that if he consumed enough female flesh he would eventually become a woman himself. Outrageous as the claims sounded, he had led authorities to

Michele's grave, so maybe there really were more. Between January and April 2000 Hadden, prison guards and Jesus – who was allowed to go along because he was the only person who could control Clark when he was seized by one of his psychotic episodes – scoured sites in Massachusetts, Connecticut, New Jersey, Rhode Island and Pennsylvania looking for more bodies. To help keep Hadden calm and help him remember, he was provided with women's clothes for the outings. To date, no further bodies have been discovered.

Sixteen

Stocks and Bondage:
Gary Heidnik (1986–7)

Since the late eighteenth century, when Philadelphia, Pennsylvania, served briefly as the capital of the United States, it has been known as the 'City of Brotherly Love'. But, for at least one man who lived there in the late twentieth century, love had no place in his overall scheme of things.

A few people begin life with all possible advantages. Tragically, far more start out with no advantages at all, and such was the case with Gary Heidnik. Gary was born in November 1943 to severely alcoholic parents, Michael and Ellen Heidnik, of Eastlake, Ohio. A second son, Terry, was born eighteen months later and shortly thereafter Michael and Ellen divorced. The boys went with their mother, but by the time Gary was four Ellen's condition had deteriorated too far for her to care for her sons and they moved in with their father and his new wife, both of whom were violent and abusive to each other and to the children.

Although Gary was a bright child his fractured home life left him too emotionally damaged to do well at school. Withdrawing from society, he obsessed on two goals: making money and a career in the military. Undoubtedly he saw both of these aims as means of obtaining the stability so lacking in his life. If he did nothing else for his son, Michael Heidnik managed to get Gary into the Staunton Military Academy in Virginia, a good first step in becoming a career army officer. Although Gary got good grades at Staunton, he decided to drop out after two years and returned to live with his father. Gary tried two different high schools but finally dropped out altogether in 1961, at the age of eighteen, and joined the army.

His army aptitude tests showed that he had an above-average IQ of 130, and Gary was allowed to apply for specialist training as a medic. After completing medical training he was stationed at a field hospital in West Germany where he finally seemed to be getting his life on track. But during the summer of 1962, Heidnik began acting strangely, complaining of headaches, dizziness and disorientation. In August he was admitted to sickbay where a neurologist suggested that he be shipped back to the USA for further tests. There, a psychiatrist diagnosed him as having a borderline psychotic condition that 'often precedes breakdown to full schizophrenia'. Gary was discharged from the army with a full military disability pension and social security benefits, and committed to a Pennsylvania mental hospital for three months' observation. From there he was released with a diagnosis of 'personality disorder' and placed on tranquillisers.

By the beginning of 1964 Heidnik felt well enough to enrol for training as a practical nurse. A year later he had graduated and taken an internship at Philadelphia General Hospital. In his spare time, Gary enrolled as a part-time student at the University of Pennsylvania and eventually took a nursing job at the university hospital. As had happened so often before, things started out well, but his job performance declined and he was fired. He then enrolled at the local Veterans' Administration Hospital for training as a psychiatric nurse but was expelled because of attitude problems. Finally, Gary took a job at the Elwyn Institute, a training facility for mentally and physically handicapped people.

For a while, Gary seemed to do well at Elwyn. He got along well with staff and students, though some might have said he got on a little too well with the African-American and Hispanic women who attended classes there. But he worked hard, saved his money and by combining his pay with his government and Social Security pensions bought a large house in a ghetto neighbourhood where he rented out two apartments and lived in the third.

Still, Gary was forced to take occasional leaves of absence from work for trips to psychiatric hospitals. When he got word in 1970 that his mother had committed suicide, he had another breakdown and was institutionalised yet again. While under care he attempted suicide and retreated into a near catatonic state, only communicating with the staff by writing notes or through a series of signals he devised, including rolling up one trouser leg when he did not want to be disturbed. His personal habits also began to deteriorate and he had to be forcibly bathed by the staff. On his release, Gary decided that what he needed was a complete change, so he went to California.

California is the kind of place where strange things can happen to even the most normal people, and for Gary Heidnik its impact was profound. At some point in 1971, he decided to establish his own church, calling it the 'United Churches of the Ministries of God'. On his return to Philadelphia he duly registered the church, installed himself as 'Bishop' and gathered a flock of five followers including his brother Terry – who had also developed a pattern of mental and emotional problems – and at least one of the students from Elwyn, a black girl with whom he had developed a relationship. Eventually, the church picked up three additional members, again, entirely from Elwyn. Many bogus preachers use their position to milk cash out of their trusting followers, but Gary's congregation had no money. For him it was not cash, but power over his flock that was the attraction. Money, however, was one of the few things that had always interested Gary, and under US tax law churches pay no income tax. The opportunity was too good to pass up. Gary may have been crazy, but he was neither stupid nor lacking in cunning.

In 1975 he opened an account with investment brokers Merrill Lynch in the name of his church. Over the next dozen years his initial investment would grow from $1,500 to well over half a million. With his new-found riches Gary indulged himself by purchasing a fleet of luxury cars. There was a Rolls-Royce, a peacock blue van, a Lincoln Continental and a silver-white Cadillac Coupe DeVille with gold trim, custom wheels and a GMH monogram on the front doors. The 'Caddy' was Gary's pride and joy, the symbol of his success.

Despite the apparent stability in Heidnik's life, there were more disturbing undercurrents. His relationships with the female members of his little congregation, and other mentally handicapped students at Elwyn, should have sounded alarm bells somewhere. His liaisons all followed the same pattern: the women were all African-American, they were all underprivileged and they were all mentally handicapped to some extent. In short, they were easy victims for the manipulative Heidnik.

One of these was a young woman named Dorothy who was more seriously retarded than most of the others, and Heidnik took merciless advantage of her. Neighbours often complained to the police when his usual bad treatment of Dorothy turned into outright beatings. The complainants said they had reason to believe he often kept the girl locked up. The police cautioned Heidnik, but there was little more they could do unless Dorothy herself brought formal charges. A year and a half after the affair with Dorothy began, Heidnik persuaded her they should sign her sister, 34-year-old Anjeanette, also severely retarded, out of the institutional home in nearby Harrisburg, where she lived. Together, they got her out on a twelve-hour pass and drove back to Philadelphia. With no intention of returning her to the home, Heidnik proceeded to lock Anjeanette in an empty basement room where he systematically abused her both sexually and physically. When the hospital notified police of what had happened, they went to Heidnik's house and removed her by force. The medical examination showed that Anjeanette had been raped, sodomised, beaten and infected with gonorrhoea vaginally, anally and orally. On 6 June 1978, Gary Heidnik was arrested and charged with kidnap, rape, unlawful restraint, false imprisonment, involuntary deviant sexual intercourse and interfering with the custody of a committed person.

When Heidnik's case came to trial in November, a court-appointed psychiatrist stated that he found the accused 'manipulative and psycho-sexually immature'. Found guilty, Heidnik was sentenced to three to seven years in prison, but on appeal the sentence was overturned and he was transferred to a series of mental institutions where he spent the next three years trying to kill himself. The closest he came was the occasion when he ate a light bulb. Within four years of his arrest Gary Heidnik was back on the streets on condition that he remain under psychiatric care. Obviously, he didn't.

During his incarceration, Dorothy had disappeared without trace, and although police tried to link Heidnik with her disappearance, there was no evidence with which to work, so Gary blithely went back to his old habits. Not surprisingly, relations with his neighbours rapidly deteriorated; in late 1983 Heidnik sold his house, and in April of the next year bought a new one at 3520 North Marshall Street in the ghettoised Philadelphia suburb of Franklinville. To decorate the interior of the dilapidated house, Heidnik chose to display his wealth in an even more obvious way than with expensive cars. On the kitchen walls he glued coins and the upstairs hallway was papered with $1, $5 and $10 bills. But still life was incomplete; Gary was without a woman that he could control.

For his next foray into the world of human relations Heidnik went through a matchmaking service specialising in introducing oriental women to western men. After a two-year corre-spondence – throughout which he claimed to be a minister – Heidnik invited 22-year-old Philippine beauty Betty Disto to come to Philadelphia. Over the strenuous objections of her parents she agreed. On 3 October 1985 – four days after Betty's arrival in the USA – the two drove across the Pennsylvania border to Maryland where they were married. No more than two weeks later Betty returned home from a shopping trip to find Gary in bed with three black women. Understandably, Betty demanded Gary send her home, but he refused, saying it was his house, he was boss and having multiple sex partners was part of his life. If Betty would not join them, she could just watch while they had sex. When she complained he beat her. On one occasion he kicked her senseless and raped her anally while the other girls watched. Finally, after more than a year of abuse and frustration, Betty left, charging her husband with spousal rape, indecent assault and involuntary deviant sexual intercourse.

Two weeks later Gary Heidnik was arrested for wife abuse and only by a stroke of sheer luck the parole from his last imprisonment for abusing a woman had run out the day before. He only escaped being returned to prison because Betty failed to show up for his arraignment.

It was late at night on the eve of Thanksgiving, 1986, when Gary took his Cadillac on to the streets of 'Philly' to see what he could pick up. Pulling up to the kerb next to a group of girls who were obviously pulling in 'johns', he called out to a pretty girl of mixed black and Hispanic parentage. When she approached the big, white Cadillac, she could see the driver was a powerfully built man with a neatly trimmed beard, intense blue eyes and lots of expensive jewellery. She could also tell that he hadn't bathed in days. He smelled and his clothes were a filthy mess. Josefina Rivera always prided herself on being choosy, but the man's car and rings indicated she could get a good fee out of this one, so she agreed to go with him.

The neighbourhood in Franklinville, and the house he drove up to, were as dirty and rundown as Gary, but the fleet of expensive cars in the fenced-in rear yard immediately caught

Josefina's attention. Maybe this wouldn't be so bad after all. She was wrong.

After taking her upstairs for sex, Gary pinioned her arms and dragged her through the house to the basement where he manacled her to a length of chain fastened to a pipe running across the ceiling. Weirdly, after tearing off all her clothes, he laid his head in her lap and went to sleep. When he woke up, he went to a corner of the dingy cellar, picked up a shovel and pick and walked to a large piece of plywood lying on the floor. Pushing the wood aside, he revealed a pit hacked through in the concrete. Jumping into the hole, he started shovelling out dirt, digging deeper and deeper. While he worked, Gary explained that all he had ever wanted was a big family and that he had decided the best way to achieve it was to gather a harem of ten women, keep them in the basement and get them all pregnant. When the babies arrived, they would all live together down here in the dark. To demonstrate his sincerity, he took a break from his work and raped Josefina.

Obviously terrified, his prisoner tried to keep the madman talking while she surveyed her surroundings. With the exception of an old washing machine, a pool table and a chest freezer, the room was empty. The only light seeped in through a boarded-up window. There was nothing here to help her escape and her captor was too big to fight off, especially while she was chained up.

As he worked away at his hole, Heidnik explained that he was digging a 'punishment pit' and that any time Josefina was bad, she would have to spend time in it. Finally satisfied with the pit, Heidnik left his captive alone in the dark. After nearly a week of being raped repeatedly and fed sporadically, Josefina managed to work one of the ankle chains loose enough for her to reach the window. Pulling the boards loose, she worked her slim body far enough through the opening to get her head and shoulders outside. Then she began screaming for help. Unfortunately, the only person who heard her, or at least the only one who responded, was Heidnik. He pulled her violently from the window, beat her with a board, shoved her into the pit and threw the thick plywood on top of her, weighting it down with bags of dirt. To muffle her screams, he brought down a radio and turned it up full blast. Then he left to collect his next harem slave.

Twenty-five-year-old Sandra Lindsay was only mildly retarded but her speech impairment and a pronounced limp made life especially hard for her. Still, she was determined that with the help of her training classes at the Elwyn Institute she would find a job that paid enough for her not to be a burden on her mother and siblings. That November evening she was on her way to the drugstore near her home when one of the staff from Elwyn pulled up and asked her if she wanted a lift. Happy to see a friendly face, she got into Gary's car and disappeared.

When they returned to the house on Marshall Street, he dragged her to the basement, stripped her of everything except a blouse and chained her to the pipe on the ceiling. He then went over to the pit, removed the board and let Josefina out, chained her up next to Sandy, introduced them, and left. It took Josefina a few minutes to realise why her fellow prisoner seemed so 'out of it'. Then she understood: the girl was retarded. Slowly, Sandy explained that Gary was a friend from the Elwyn Institute and that they had often had sex in the past. Once, she said, he had got her pregnant but she had had an abortion and Gary was furious. Since then he had been demanding that she have his baby. She guessed that was why he had brought her here. Although she remained composed while she told her story, when she finished she broke down and wept. She just wanted to go home.

Over the next few days, Heidnik raped both women repeatedly and, not having planned far enough in advance for so many mouths to feed, began doling out bowls of the canned dog food he normally fed to his two dogs, which often wandered into the basement to visit his prisoners. While the girls had disappeared, they had not been forgotten. Sandy's mother had alerted the police who, in turn, had instituted a search of her neighbourhood. When news of the missing retarded girl began appearing on local television and in the newspapers, Heidnik forced Sandy to write a note to her mother, telling her that she had gone away for a while but would ring her soon.

Heidnik may have thought it was a clever move, but, desperate to find her daughter, Sandy's mother told police that her daughter had often mentioned a man from the Elwyn Institute named Gary Heidnik who lived somewhere on Marshall Street. The police followed up the lead and repeatedly visited Heidnik's house, but no one ever answered the door. Finally, lacking any firm grounds to order a search warrant, they abandoned that particular line of inquiry. Maybe Sandy would turn up somewhere else.

On 22 December yet another young black girl disappeared. Nineteen-year-old Lisa Thomas was a high-school dropout living on social security, but she enjoyed living, and dressing well. Attracted by her flashy clothes, the man in the white Cadillac pulled up to the kerb and asked if she was 'hooking'. She became indignant and started to storm away, but the big car crept along after her, the driver apologising and offering her a ride to make up for his rude behaviour. Attracted by the car and the expensive watch and rings on the man's hands, she finally agreed. Amazingly, Heidnik took his time with Lisa. They went out for dinner and during conversation, he offered to take her to Atlantic City the next weekend. Lisa was thrilled but said she didn't have any clothes to wear, so Heidnik offered to take her shopping. Again she agreed. After a spree at the local Sears Roebuck store, she also agreed to go back to Heidnik's house. That was a big mistake.

At first everything seemed fine. Heidnik even opened a bottle of wine, but it was 'spiked' and Lisa quickly passed out. When she awoke, Gary was taking her clothes off, but she wasn't too disturbed and was more than willing to have sex with him. It was only when he dragged her to the basement and chained her up with Josefina and Sandra that Lisa realised just how awful her situation really was.

Now faced with three 'wives', Heidnik had to make a few adaptations. Cleanliness was not a problem – they could just stay as dirty as he was, but thoughtfully, he bought a portable camper toilet for the girls to use. He also added another feature to their lives. In addition to the continual rapes, beatings and occasional trip to the pit, he added electric shocks. When the girls refused to behave, he would clamp the exposed end of an old extension lead to their chains and plug it in to an outlet. Any tiny deviation from Gary's rules could warrant such treatment. If they resisted his advances . . . zap. If he wanted to watch while they had sex with each other and they refused . . . zap. If one of them was 'bad' and the others failed to inform on her, they both got a good jolt. If they cried too loudly during their torture . . . they were zapped again. When he got tired of the shock treatment and the beatings, he suspended his victim of the moment from a ceiling beam by one arm, and left her dangling for hours, nearly pulling her arm from its socket. All the girls could do was huddle together and pray that somehow one of them would escape and rescue the others.

Ten days after he added Lisa to his growing collection, Heidnik introduced yet another victim. Deborah Dudley was captured on New Year's Day. At twenty-three Debbie was a pretty girl who had a mind of her own and a fiery temper. This one was going to be a challenge, but Heidnik liked that. As she struggled frantically against being hauled into the strange house and locked in chains, Heidnik beat her almost senseless.

While news of yet another lost girl sent shivers down the backs of Philadelphia residents, Gary Heidnik was busy devising new and better ways to control his slaves. He encouraged them to inform on each other for even the slightest infraction of 'the rules'. As a reward, the informer was ordered to administer a beating to the guilty party. If the punishment was not severe enough, they would both suffer. Soon, Josefina began to play up to Heidnik, informing on the others and telling Gary she was 'on his side'.

On 18 January, still another victim appeared at 3520 North Marshall Street. Eighteen-year-old Jacquelyn Askins was a tiny, fragile, retarded girl whom he had picked up while she was 'hooking' on one of Philly's main streets. When he got her to his basement, he stripped her, raped her, beat her savagely and told her it was just to show her who was boss. 'You'll do as you're told, or you'll get more of the same.'

If Jacquelyn thought she was alone in her nightmare, it only took minutes for her to realise there were four other women chained up beside her. Now, finally, there might be enough of them to overpower their jailer. Sadly, Josefina informed Heidnik of the plan. Furious, he meted out the usual round of punishments. He also decided that if they couldn't hear him coming and going, they would never know when it was safe to try to escape. To solve the problem, he jammed a screwdriver in each of the girls' ears in an attempt to shatter their eardrums. Only Josefina, who had revealed the plot, escaped the horrible punishment.

A few days after the escape plan failed, Sandy Lindsay committed some small infraction that displeased Heidnik. He placed her in the punishment pit, but she struggled to push aside the board and the heavy weights holding it in place. Infuriated, Heidnik hung her from a beam with a single handcuff. Her feet did not quite reach the floor and the weight of her body pulling against one wrist and shoulder socket quickly became excruciating. Heidnik simply walked away.

Day after day Sandy hung there, growing weaker and weaker, finally developing a fever. She refused to eat and when Heidnik tried to force-feed her, she vomited. Eventually, she lost consciousness. When Heidnik's vicious slaps failed to waken her, he unlocked the handcuff, allowing her to crash to the floor. He then kicked her into the pit and brought a treat of ice cream to the rest of the terrified women. Finally, he knelt over the pit and checked Sandy's pulse. She was dead. Calmly, without emotion, Heidnik pulled her body on to the floor, hoisted it to his shoulders and carried her out of the basement prison. Later, the girls trembled when they heard the high-pitched whine of a power saw filtering down from upstairs. Not long after, one of Heidnik's dogs wandered into the basement carrying a large, meat-covered bone. Settling down in a corner, he began gnawing away contentedly. The surviving prisoners became violently sick.

Upstairs, Heidnik was calmly butchering the remains of Sandra Lindsay. Roasts and chops were laid aside, while the odds and ends were puréed in his commercial food processor and mixed in with the dog food that was the main diet of captives and canines alike. The unprocessed pieces of meat were loaded into a bag and chucked into the refrigerator after being marked 'dog food'. Of course, there was still the problem of the head and ribcage. He had to render them down enough to dispose of them without rousing too much suspicion. The stench of overcooked human flesh, however, caused all the suspicion necessary for neighbours to call the cops.

In a ghetto neighbourhood screams and shouts don't get too much attention, but this stench was too much to bear. When the police came knocking on his door, Gary apologised, explaining that he had burned a roast and it was nothing to worry about. Once again the police left without demanding entrance.

A day or two later, Debbie Dudley, always hot-tempered, began fighting frantically every time Sandy's murderer approached. Calmly, Gary unchained her and led her upstairs. When she returned, Debbie was ashen faced and trembling. It took a while for her to calm down enough to explain what had happened. In a large stew pot on the stove, she had seen Sandy's head being boiled down to the bare skull. Inside the oven her ribcage was being roasted. He also showed her what was in the bags in the refrigerator and told her if she didn't stop causing problems, she was going to be next.

On 18 March Heidnik was going through his usual routine of rape and torture when some of the girls did something to displease him. Obviously the usual corrections were not working and some new twist had to be added to get their attention. Ordering Josefina to fill the punishment pit with water, one after another he threw Debbie, Lisa and Jacquelyn into the rising pool of sludge. When the water had risen to chin level he ordered Josefina to stop. Then he threw the plywood across the hole and piled the weighted bags on top. It was new, it was novel, but it still wasn't enough. Taking the electric cord he used to administer shocks through the girls' chains, he lowered the bare end into the water and told Josefina to plug it into the socket. In a split second the water was alive with electricity and the girls were shrieking and screaming, jerking uncontrollably as the current surged through their bodies. Gary told Josefina to cut the power, but decided one more good jolt was needed to drive his point home. This time the end of the wire came in direct contact with the chain around Debbie Dudley's neck. She jerked violently and fell forward into the water, dead. Jacquelyn and Lisa shrieked even louder than before and, this time, Heidnik pulled the wooden cover from the pit. Dragging Debbie's lifeless body from the hole, he smiled at the other girls and asked, 'Aren't you glad it wasn't one of you?'

Leaving Debbie's body where it lay, he forced Josefina to write a statement saying she had been the one to electrocute Debbie. He then told her that if she ever had any ideas about going to the police he would use the statement to prove she was guilty of murder. The following day, with Josefina's acquiescent help, he wrapped the body in plastic, heaved it into the chest freezer in the corner of the basement and left the house.

In the days that followed Debbie's murder, Josefina remained close to Heidnik's side, trying desperately to convince him that he needed her help if he was going to complete his collection of 'wives'. Slowly winning his confidence, she was allowed to accompany him on his occasional trips into the real world. She became his confidante, and on 22 March 1987 she helped him carry Debbie's frozen body to his van and drove with him to the desolate Pine Barrens section of New Jersey where they dumped the carcass in the undergrowth by the side of the road. Having thus proved her loyalty, when Heidnik started talking about abducting more women, Josefina suggested that she could help him. The following day they picked up another prostitute, Agnes Adams, and brought her back to the Marshall Street torture chamber.

Only a day later, 24 March, Josefina convinced Gary that if he took her home to see her family she could find him still more women to serve his needs. Excited at the prospect, he agreed on condition that if he dropped her off near her house, she would meet him at midnight at a nearby petrol station. Obviously, she agreed.

Once free of Heidnik, Josefina ran to the house of her former boyfriend Vincent Nelson where, nearing hysteria, she blurted out her incredible story. Vincent wanted to go to Heidnik's house and confront him, but Josefina insisted they call the police. When Officers John Cannon and David Savidge arrived at Nelson's she repeated her story to the sceptical men, telling them when and where Heidnik would be waiting for her. Finally convinced, they called in their report, demanding an immediate search warrant and back-up to help them search the house once they had Heidnik safely in custody.

At the appointed time the cruiser was parked discreetly across the street from the service station with Cannon and Savidge in the front and Josefina Rivera in the back. Minutes after midnight, Heidnik's Cadillac pulled into sight. Guns drawn,

Cannon and Savidge approached the car, calling for Heidnik to step out with his hands up. Casually obeying, he asked if it was something to do with overdue child support payments. They assured him it was more serious.

It was nearly 5am when a squad of heavily armed police kicked open the front door of 3520 North Marshall Street. Pushing her way to the front, Josefina directed them to the basement steps, shouting for them to hurry. In the dark, dank cellar, the shocked policemen were greeted by a sight that could have come straight out of a cheap horror movie. On the floor two women lay huddled together on a filthy mattress, the chains from their legs running up to a large pipe fastened to the ceiling. When the hysterical girls stopped screaming, Officer Savidge asked them if there was anybody else there. Mutely, they pointed to the covered punishment pit. Inside the police found Agnes Adams, curled in a foetal position in the mud. After ambulances had taken the starved and beaten women to hospital, the officers began searching the rest of the house.

Beyond the confines of the kitchen there was little to be found except filthy furniture and dirt, but that one room was mute testimony to the extent of Gary Heidnik's brutal insanity. The scorched and filthy cooking pot held a human skull and the yellow, gelatinous remains of human fat. This, along with a heap of charred ribs and selected roasts and chops, some cooked, some not, belonged to Sandra Lindsay. The industrial food processor on the counter had obviously been used to grind meat; there was already little doubt of what meat, but when one of the police opened the refrigerator, any lingering uncertainty was removed. On one shelf was a human forearm and elsewhere, neatly wrapped in plastic bags and labelled 'dog food' were 24lb of Sandra Lindsay's flesh. To one side was a pile of arm and leg-bones with varying amounts of flesh still clinging to them.

Over the following days, as police and forensic investigators scoured the house and garden, the newspapers, including the prestigious *Philadelphia Inquirer*, had a field day describing the 'House of Horrors', the 'Torture Dungeon' and the 'Mad Man's Sex Orgy'. It was shock journalism at its very worst. But for Gary Heidnik bad press was the least of his concerns. What he needed was a good lawyer. At least with the small fortune he had made playing the market he could afford one.

Chuck Peruto was one of Philadelphia's best, and flashiest, legal eagles and he charged accordingly. His standard fee for capital offences was $10,000 plus expenses. He believed that everyone, no matter how hopeless their case looked, was entitled to the best defence money could buy, but in Heidnik's case he was willing to make an exception. It was the kind of publicity he really did not need, so he told Heidnik that his fee was $100,000 plus expenses. He must have been surprised when Heidnik unhesitatingly agreed.

On 23 April 1987, Gary Michael Heidnik, aged forty-four, appeared in court for his preliminary hearing. Opposing Peruto was Assistant District Attorney Charles Gallagher who was determined to make every one of the eighteen charges – including murder, rape, kidnapping, aggravated assault, involuntary deviant sexual intercourse, indecent exposure, false imprisonment, unlawful restraint, simple assault, indecent assault and all the rest – stick like glue to the Marshall Street maniac. At the preliminary hearing it was a foregone conclusion that Heidnik would be bound over for trial, but Peruto insisted that his client could not obtain an impartial trial in Philadelphia because of the sensational publicity he was receiving in the press. The judge agreed and the venue was changed to Pittsburgh, 300 miles to the west.

When the trial opened on 20 June 1988 in the courtroom of Judge Lynn Abraham, Peruto already had his defence settled. He would, not surprisingly, plead insanity. District Attorney Gallagher countered by insisting that Heidnik had been too methodical in both his execution of the crimes, and the methods he employed in hiding his grisly work, for him not to have been completely aware of what he was doing. Peruto asked the judge to consider the possibility that Josefina Rivera was equally culpable. Judge Abraham agreed, but stipulated that if Heidnik was sane enough to enlist Rivera's help, he was certainly not insane. Peruto withdrew the suggestion.

The most damning evidence came from the captives' description of their time in Heidnik's homemade prison, but there was other, equally horrific testimony. Dr Paul Hoyer, of the county medical examiner's office, detailed the gruesome finds in Heidnik's kitchen, stating that the body parts had, apparently, been cut from the corpse with a power saw just as the girls had suspected at the time. Gallagher's final witness turned out not to be connected with the case at all. Robert Kirkpatrick, Heidnik's broker at Merrill Lynch, testified that Gary Heidnik was 'an astute investor who knew exactly what he was doing'. Peruto's defence was already badly damaged before he ever called his first witness.

Peruto limited his defence to establishing Heidnik's mental condition at the time of the kidnappings and torture. First to testify was Dr Clancy McKenzie who, for reasons unknown, refused to directly answer Peruto's questions concerning Heidnik as an individual, but rambled on about schizophrenia as a general condition. It was all Peruto could do to get him to admit that Heidnik probably did not know the difference between right and wrong. The following day Jack Apsche, a noted Philadelphia psychologist was slated to testify, but Judge Abraham ruled that the majority of Apsche's testimony was inadmissible. It was a severe blow to Peruto, but he had one final witness, Dr Kenneth Kool, a psychiatrist. Kool delivered his evidence but later, in a closed session with the judge, it came out that Kool had only spent twenty minutes with Heidnik who simply refused to say anything. When Judge Abraham asked him on what he had based his testimony, Kool admitted he gleaned his information from Heidnik's past clinical records. Like Apsche before him, most of Kool's statements were struck from the record. On 30 June, after ten days of testimony and arguments, the jury retired to consider their decision. Sixteen hours later they found Gary Heidnik guilty on all eighteen counts. Three days later Judge Abraham imposed the death penalty.

For eleven years, while one appeal after another wound its way through the court system, Gary Heidnik was incarcerated on death row at Graterford Prison at Rockview, Pennsylvania. On 6 July 1999 at 10.29pm, he died by lethal injection. No one came forward to claim the body.

Agnes Adams, Josefina Rivera, Lisa Thomas and Jacquelyn Askins have filed suits to claim shares of Heidnik's money in compensation for their ordeal.

Just as Ed Gein, whom we met in an earlier chapter, served as a model for the crazed killer in Thomas Harris's 1988 book *Silence of the Lambs*, so did Gary Heidnik. His penchant for keeping his captives in a pit in his basement became an integral part of the twisted character of Buffalo Bill.

Seventeen

Bringing Home the Bacon: Nicolas Claux (1990–4)

I n the late 1970s and early '80s a new, youth-orientated subculture arose out of the then-current music scene. Just as the hippies had arisen out of '60s hard rock, the new movement – known as 'Goth' – shaped itself out of the 'punk' and 'new romantic' musical scene. The name was derived from the nineteenth-century neo-Gothic movement in literature and architecture that provided the Goths with their look and lifestyle. Dressed in heavily romanticised versions of Victorian clothes, their hair dyed raven black, the Goths flock to their chosen musical venues where they listen to bands with names like Marilyn Manson, Sisters of Mercy and The Damned. There are enough Goths for them to hold parties and conventions all over the world. For most, it is no more than a weekend escape from the drabness and drudgery of modern urban life. For others it becomes a full-time lifestyle. Among the more serious and edgy members of the Goth community there is a predilection to adopt vampire-like personas taken straight from the pages of Bram Stoker's *Dracula* and Anne Rice's *Interview with the Vampire* novels. For 99.9 per cent of the Goths it is all just good clean fun but for a tiny minority it becomes something much more dark and disturbing. Nicolas Claux was one of the few who took it all just a little too far.

Nicolas Claux's father worked in the international finance section of a French banking firm and, as a result, travelled widely.

When Nicolas was born in 1972 his family was stationed in Cameroon, Africa, and moved to London when he was five years old. Two years later they returned to their native Paris. According to Claux, his parents never denied him any material necessity but were cold, unemotional people who seemed incapable of showing affection to their son. Nicolas seemed predisposed to return the favour, failing to display the normal emotions of a child. He was so withdrawn his mother was concerned that he might even be autistic. He was not, but insists that the only feeling he harboured for his parents was utter indifference.

One day, when little Nico was ten years old, he became embroiled in a heated argument with his grandfather. During the exchange the old man suffered a cerebral haemorrhage and dropped dead. Such a traumatic event would undoubtedly cause deep disturbance for even the most normal child, and for Nico it became one of the defining moments of his life. From that point on he was obsessed with every aspect of death. Funeral rites, wakes, cemeteries, mortuaries, all began to exert a morbid attraction on him. He began reading everything he could lay his hands on that discussed death and the possibilities of an afterlife. Of particular fascination were fantasy novels and comic books concerned with vampires, werewolves, black magic and the occult.

As his morbid streak grew and festered, more family moves – first to Portugal when he was twelve and then back to Paris at sixteen – only served to alienate him further from his family and people his own age. Seeking refuge from his loneliness, Claux began to wander through the famously elaborate graves and crypts of Parisian cemeteries. Between 1990 and 1993 he came to know the layout of these necropolises as well as most teenagers know their own neighbourhoods. Soon, the interests became more specific. 'I would examine rusty locks and evaluate the weight of cement [crypt] lids. My favourite things were mausoleums. The most impressive ones can be found at Père

Lachaise, Montmartre or Passy cemeteries. I would peep through their windows to see the inside. Some were decorated with furniture, paintings or statues.' But somehow, looking was not quite enough. He needed to be inside; to share the experience of the dead.

With a combination of lock-picks and crowbars Nicolas Claux began breaking into the tombs that fascinated him most. Sometimes, if rusty door hinges refused to budge, he would simply break in through a window. Once inside, he revelled in the dank, dark surroundings, feeling, in his own words, 'like an emperor reigning in Hell'. To prolong the eerily satisfying experience, he would break in during the day, remain there and creep out to wander alone among the graves and crypts during the dark of night. But just as peering through the windows and rusty grilles had not been enough to satisfy his ghoulish curiosity, neither was simply staring at the coffins resting on their lonely biers.

I woke up one day feeling this sinister urge to dig up a corpse and mutilate it. I gathered a small crowbar, a pair of pliers, a screwdriver, black candles and a pair of surgical gloves in a backpack. Then I took the metro [to] the Trocadero station. It was nearly noon. The gates of the Passy Cemetery were wide open, but nobody was inside. The undertakers were out for lunch.

Passy is a small Gothic graveyard with plenty of huge mausoleums, which were built during the nineteenth century. It is located right between two large avenues, so it is impossible to climb inside at night. But anyway, nobody could ever imagine that there was someone robbing graves at noon.

I had this special grave in mind. It was a small mausoleum, the burial site of a family of Russian immigrants from the 1917 revolution. I had already prised open the iron door a few days before, and I had closed it afterwards so it would seem that nobody had ever touched it. All I had to do was kick it open . . . At this point, my mind was in total chaos. I had flashes of death in my head. I took a deep breath, and I climbed down the steps leading to the crypt.

It was a rather small one, with damp walls, buried deep inside the cemetery ground. There was no other source of light than the candles I had brought. To begin, for more than an hour, I removed one of the heavy coffins from its stone casing. It was especially hard not to let the coffin fall all of a sudden to the ground, but somehow I managed to slowly lay it down without making too much noise.

I examined the casket for a while. It was solid oak and sealed with big screws. It looked brand new, so I expected to find a recently deceased corpse. First, I unscrewed the coffin, which took me less than 10 minutes. Then I prised it open with the crowbar. Once opened, a horrible stench of putrefaction came out of the box. It smelled like [embalming fluid] . . .

Then I saw the body inside. It was a half-rotten old woman, shrouded in a white sheet, covered with brown stains. Her face seemed to be smeared with oil, but it was simply the death fluids oozing from her skin. The stench was so intense that I nearly fainted. I tried to lift one side of the sheet, but it was . . . [stuck] to her skin like flypaper. The teeth were protruding from the mouth, but her eyes were gone. I stared into the empty eye sockets, and all of a sudden something broke into my mind.

That's when I picked up a screwdriver. The corpse inside the coffin started to move slightly, like it had guessed what would happen next. So I began to stab the belly, the rib area and the shoulders. I stabbed her at least 50 times. I really can't remember. All I can remember is that when I woke up my forearms were covered with corpse slime. I tried to sever her head, but I did not have the right tools. I took Polaroid snapshots [of the corpse].

After violating his first grave, Nico said he spent much of his free time searching the cemetery for new graves to desecrate, but even this did not satisfy his increasingly morbid urges. He needed to be even closer to the dead, so he began to collect souvenirs from the desecrated tombs and carry them back to his apartment. 'Throughout my apartment bone fragments and human teeth were scattered around like loose change; vertebrae and leg bones hung from the ceiling like morbid mobiles.'

More evidence of his fascination with death, pain and mutilation took their place along with the remnants of deceased bodies. There were 'hundreds of videocassettes, mostly slasher and hardcore [sadomasochist] flicks . . . Several bondage magazines were piled in a far corner.' On top of his television set were jars filled with human ashes.

In 1992, at twenty years of age, Claux spent a year in the French military working as a gunsmith, but decided that there was no fulfilment in working with instruments of death; it was death itself that he craved. In 1993 he applied to a Parisian mortician school but, for whatever reason, his application was declined. Taking the next, logical step, he got a job working as a morgue attendant at St Vincent-de-Paul's children's hospital. 'I found that it was the best way to be in contact with corpses . . . my first contact with a corpse there was when I assisted [in] the autopsy of a ten-year-old girl. The other attendant showed me how to stitch up her belly, and that was the first time I ever got to touch a fresh corpse. I was amazed by how red and clean her organs were.'

In December 1993 Claux left St Vincent-de-Paul's to take a similar job at St Joseph's Hospital. In addition to working in the morgue, Claux was required to deliver blood from the hospital blood bank to the operating theatres. Within a few weeks he was secretly removing any unused blood bags left over after the surgery, changing the labels to make it look as though the seal had been broken. Hiding them in his locker and taking them home with him, after re-cooling the blood in his refrigerator he would mix it with powdered protein or human ash and drink it in the best vampire fashion.

Still, it was the hospital morgue and working with the cadavers that were his real love. Later, in his confession, Claux stated: 'Most of the autopsies were done by us, the morgue attendants. We would do the Y-shaped incision, cut the ribs at the joints and open the skull with an electric saw. The pathologist only dissected the organs . . . I would be left alone with the body after the autopsy to do the stitches, which were my speciality.' During his tenure at St Joseph's, Claux moved from simply helping prepare the deceased for their final rest to the realm of desecrating the bodies that had been entrusted to his care. In addition to insisting that he had sex with some of the corpses, he claims to have begun eating the bodies.

'This is when I began eating strips of muscles from the bodies. I always checked their medical files first. I talked with a butcher once who told me that meat is better three or four days after death. This was something I had always dreamed of doing and this was the opportunity to do it on a regular basis. On some occasions, I would bring pieces of flesh back to my place where I would cook and eat those pieces as well . . . but my preference was to eat them raw. It tasted like steak tartare or carpaccio. Human meat tastes pretty good. It depends on what part you eat. The big muscles of the thighs and back were good, but there was no good meat in the breasts, only fats. People often ask me what went through my mind the first time I indulged my cannibalistic fantasy. Well, to be honest, I said to myself: "Wow! Now I'm a cannibal. Cool!"' From his tone, it is hard to tell if Claux was confessing or simply bragging to the police.

When in a more introspective, reflective mood, Claux had another opinion on the more spiritual aspects of cannibalism. 'It feels like touching the face of God. It makes you feel like you don't belong to the human race any more.' Most people would probably agree with at least the second part of that statement. But Claux tries hard not to become too reflective about his grotesque taste for human flesh, preferring to keep a light, chatty, yet informative flavour to his narrative. He has even written down his recommendations as to the best way to choose, and prepare, the human body for the dinner table. The following is taken from his on-line tome, 'Cooking with Nico'.

I personally recommend taking meat from someone who died less than 48 hours ago. Rigor mortis disappears more or less five hours after death, so it would be better to cut the meat the day following the cattle's demise.

I'm not the kind of guy who likes to eat disgusting stuff like offal, brains, etc. I only appreciate red meat. Therefore I recommend the following chunks of meat: Quadriceps – the two big muscles on the front of the legs. They provide big juicy steaks. [And the] calves, my favourite meat. Two muscles on each leg, easy to cut. [The] buttocks are the biggest muscles on the human body. But there's a good amount of fat tissue in them (especially in women), and I only eat girl meat so it's not my favourite meal. But when the girl is sporty, then it becomes my favourite meal. The other pieces of meat are too tiny (arms, neck) or covered with fat tissue (breasts) so I won't mention them. Once you have cut all the food, you can store it up to 3 days in a fridge. But first remove the skin, the fat tissues and the nerves.

I know it is more hygienic to cook meat before eating it. But sometimes you don't have the patience and you just bite into raw meat and feel the juicy proteins pouring down your throat. Other cannibals worldwide have described how they like to cook human meat and season it with spices. I am not that sophisticated. I won't tell you that beans are a good side dish, and that meat is best when flavoured with BBQ sauce. I personally think that any kind of spiced sauce will spoil the naturally sweet taste of human meat and blood. Human meat is a gift from the gods, and it is a shame to ruin its delightful taste. Bon Appétit – Nicolas Claux – Dec '98

For ten months Claux satisfied himself with doing his grocery shopping among the helpless cadavers of the deceased but, as had happened so often in the past, with the need for taking his cravings to ever greater heights, or depths, the pleasures of the morgue soon became no more than routine. If the already dead were good, how much better it would be to make his own corpses. Even being in a sadomasochistic relationship with a young woman who enjoyed being beaten did nothing to assuage his taste for violence. Only an actual killing could do that.

On 4 October 1994, Nicolas Claux awoke with the realisation that this would be a good day to kill someone. He wandered around the streets of Paris all morning looking for a likely victim and although none of the available prey seemed to his liking, an idea did come to him. That summer and autumn there had been an ongoing string of murders of gay men that had left the police completely baffled. One more murder buried among so many others should go almost unnoticed. Claux was also aware that many in Paris' homosexual community arranged their meetings on Minitel, an early version of the Internet. It would be a completely anonymous way to find and stalk his prey. So far as Claux could see, the plan had only one downside. 'Queers were an easy prey . . . but the bad side was that I couldn't mutilate them and eat some of their meat, because I don't like to touch men, and they have diseases.'

Late that morning, Claux logged on to Minitel and made contact with Thierry Bissonnier, a 34-year-old restaurateur and part-time classical musician who was already involved in a steady relationship. Thierry, however, seemed to enjoy the occasional meeting with a stranger for a bout of anonymous sex, particularly if it involved bondage and sadomasochism. Only a few e-mails passed between them before Bissonnier foolishly gave Claux his home address. Claux's own description of their meeting follows:

So I agreed to meet Thierry around noon. With me I carried a single shot 22-calibre handgun, which I hid under my jacket. When I arrived at his place, a one-room apartment under the roof of an old building, I knocked on the door and gave him the fake first name that I had given him on Minitel. He opened the door, I stepped inside, quickly turned around while he was closing the door and pulled out the gun.

I looked at his face just as he turned his head towards me and saw the gun pointed at his eye. After a few awkward moments passed, I pulled the trigger. He instantly fell face down without a word. It was really eerie. It all happened like in slow motion. Then I watched him bleed on the carpet. Soon I decided to see what the apartment was like and wandered around a bit.

When I returned to where he was lying I observed that he was still moving and making horrible breathing noises on the floor, like he was breathing through a straw. I reloaded the gun and shot again, this time striking him in the back of the head. I reloaded and fired a few more times, but he was still alive and making a noise. I was surprised that he was still holding on; I had expected the first shot to kill him.

After a few minutes, I went into his kitchen and found some cookies to eat and then sat in a corner of the room and watched him as I ate. When I was finished, I decided to get out of there quickly, so I shot him one last time in the back. I also lifted a huge plant container and smashed it on his head, partly crushing it. I then wiped down my fingerprints; picked up his cheque-book; a credit card and a wallet (with ID papers); his driving licence; an alarm clock, and an answering machine, and finally left the scene.

If Claux's description of the murder of Thierry Bissonnier sounds impossibly cold and detached, a statement he made in a later interview reveals much about his feelings towards his victim and, possibly, about his opinion of the human race in general. 'I didn't kill anybody. I just killed some insects. Not people. Insects.' We have no explanation for Claux's use of the plural in the above quote except that it raises the question of other killings with which Claux was never officially connected.

Bissonnier's body was not discovered for three days. When he failed to return repeated telephone calls from his parents, they went to his apartment only to discover the grisly remains of Claux's handiwork lying inside their son's door. Immediately, they rang the police.

To Chief Inspector Gilbert Thiel, Bissonnier's murder at first appeared to be just another addition to the growing list of gay men who had been brutally killed by a person, or persons, unknown. Homosexual hate-killings already accounted for one in three murders in Paris and the general assumption among the police and press was that a gang of neo-Nazis was taking its mindless revenge on a nearly invisible segment of the population. Obviously, this is exactly what Claux had hoped the official reaction would be to Thierry's death. Despite the similarities with the other gay murders, Inspector Thiel quickly realised that there were subtle differences in the Bissonnier case. There was no sexual mutilation or violation of the body as there had been in most of the other cases, and the items stolen from the apartment were certainly at the low end of a thief's wish list. It was almost as though robbery was not the motive at all. If it wasn't a hate-crime and robbery was not the real motive, what was? Why had Thierry Bissonnier been murdered?

Nicolas Claux might actually have got away with the murder if he had not tried to forge one of Bissonnier's cheques to buy a new VCR machine. As a form of identification, he gave the shop assistant Bissonnier's driving licence on to which he had made a sloppy attempt to insert his own photograph. Suspicious of the licence and the none-too-subtle forgery of Bissonnier's signature, the clerk rang the police. In panic, Claux fled the scene, leaving the forged driving licence – with his picture on it – behind. Inspector Thiel and the criminal squad now had a photograph linking a man with long, black hair and a small beard to the death of Thierry Bissonnier.

On 15 November 1994, six weeks after the killing, police had already obtained a search warrant for the home of the as yet unidentified man in the photo. The minute they found him they would be able to sort through his possessions so there would be no opportunity to destroy any evidence of the Bissonnier murder still remaining intact. When Claux got into a heated argument with a woman in front of the famous Moulin Rouge nightclub on the evening of the 15th, a passing policeman moved in to break up the fracas. Immediately, he recognised the face in the forged driving licence photo that had been circulated throughout the Paris Metropolitan Police and arrested him. Almost before Claux arrived at the police station a squad of detectives were ploughing through the morbid museum of human bones, teeth and violent videotapes that cluttered his apartment and life. One of the items they discovered was the .22 calibre pistol lying under his bed.

At first, Claux denied any knowledge of Bissonnier's death, but when ballistic tests on the gun came back as a match with the bullets found in Bissonnier's head he confessed. Initially, Claux insisted it was a simple robbery that had gone horribly wrong, but he quickly revised his position in the belief that it could work to his benefit if he said it was an act of revenge taken out on a random homosexual in retaliation for an argument he had had with another gay man. It was Claux's hope that by giving this cock and bull story he might get a lesser sentence on the grounds of diminished responsibility: what most people think of as temporary insanity. He also played on the bags of blood the detectives found in his refrigerator, insisting that he was a vampire. He went on to confess his predilection for grave mutilation and eating human flesh. If he hoped the police would think he was crazy, he was probably right, but faced with the mountain of evidence found in his apartment, they were equally convinced he was guilty.

If the wheels of justice grind slow, the French judiciary system seems to grind slower than most. For two years after his arrest Claux was remanded to the Fleury-Merogis jail where he underwent extensive psychological testing while the police were putting together an airtight case against him. The psychologists and psychiatrists who examined Claux came to the conclusion that he was psychotic with a penchant for necrophilia and sexual sadism. His response to Rorschach, or 'ink blot' tests, showed that he suffered from an 'inner void' which is accepted as a typical symptom of the schizophrenic personality. By December 1996 Inspector Thiel was content that he had sufficient evidence to press a solid case of premeditated murder against Claux and the case was handed over to the Office of Prosecution. Claux himself insists that he was also charged with desecration of graves and theft of blood from the hospital, but court records make no mention of any such charges.

The trial of Nicolas Claux opened on 9 May 1997. Presiding judge Waechter imposed a news blackout on the case, so many of the details of the proceedings are unavailable for review and confirmation. What is known is that Claux's defence counsel, Irène Terrel, entered a plea of 'not guilty' on Claux's behalf. Fully aware of this move, the prosecution opened its case by displaying photos of the crime scene, Bissonnier's body and shots of Claux's macabre apartment. The prosecutor insisted that Claux's style of living clearly showed his morbid and violent turn of mind and dubbed him a 'death addict' and a 'real-life vampire'. It all seemed to be going just as the prosecution had planned until they tried to connect Claux with the many other unsolved homosexual murders that had taken place in Paris prior to his arrest. Under cross-examination, Inspector Carcin, one of the detectives assigned to the case, admitted that there was no physical evidence to connect Claux to any murder other than the one with which he had been formally charged. The only defence he could offer for his assumption was that Claux matched the profile of a serial killer and there were witnesses who believed they had seen Claux in gay bars that other murder victims were known to have frequented. Again, the accusations of grave robbing, necrophilia and blood theft were never made in connection with Claux; charges the prosecution would undoubtedly have made if there had been any evidence to support them. After three hours of deliberation the nine-member jury found Nicolas Claux guilty of premeditated murder, armed robbery, fraudulent use of a bank cheque, falsification of a driving licence and an attempt to defraud a retail merchant of a videotape machine. For all of these crimes he was sentenced to only 12 years in prison.

It was another two years before Claux was transferred from Fleury-Merogis jail to the Maison Centrale Poissy maximum-security prison. To make good use of his time, Claux studied computer programming and took up painting, for which he seemed to discover a latent talent. He joined the prison's video staff and helped record concerts, football games and boxing matches and learned to edit the tapes they had made. Claux was released back into an unsuspecting world on 12 March 2002, after serving only seven years and four months of his sentence.

Deciding that he deserved a holiday after his imprisonment, he visited Sweden and England before settling back down in Paris. Always a great self-promoter, Claux immediately went to work establishing himself as the self-proclaimed 'Vampire of Paris', advertising his past life on several websites that he continues to maintain. One site is dedicated to the sale of his paintings which, not surprisingly, deal with scenes of autopsies and portraits of famous serial killers and cannibals of the past. Claux's artwork now adorns the official website of the Church of Satan and the covers and interior pages of several murder and cannibal-related books. On one of his websites he blithely provides instructions for would-be grave robbers and ghouls, expanding on his theme with the butchering and cooking instructions presented earlier in this chapter. Being every bit as promotion-minded as either Henry Lee Lucas or Issei Sagawa – both of whom we met in earlier chapters – Claux has turned his tawdry fame into a career by getting himself booked on to television chat shows and radio programmes where he happily expounds on his life as a 'reformed' vampire and cannibal. While he insists on one of his websites that 'I do not profit from my past', this is exactly what he is doing.

To keep his little ball rolling, and keep the money coming in, Claux attends Goth and vampire conventions where he lectures on his past lifestyle and sells paintings to his morbidly fascinated fans. If nothing else, Claux seems, through his newfound cult celebrity status, to have finally learned how to make friends with the living. They may not be the kind of friends that most people would want to have around, but if they keep him grounded enough not to kill, or eat anyone in the future, then they are doing their bit for civilisation.

He also seems to have calmed down a lot. He has a steady girlfriend and says he spends his spare time 'painting, watching horror flicks, working out and writing to other killers and watching documentaries on freaks or amputees'. He also insists that he has a fetish for murderesses: 'I like girls who kill. There should be more of them.' He does not, however, indicate whether or not his current girlfriend is a killer. While he claims to worship the devil, he simultaneously insists that he no longer eats human flesh and says, 'I do not encourage other people into doing the things that I have done. The spiritual and social prices to pay are far too high.' Odd sentiments for a Satanist.

Finally, if you, dear reader, wonder if Nicolas Claux, the Vampire of Paris, has any advice for you, the answer is yes. 'I have a message for people who smoke, do drugs, eat junk food and drink alcohol . . . You have no respect for your own body . . . Do some sport, stop smoking, go on a protein diet, take care of your arteries. You will feel a lot sexier.'

Eighteen

Spider on the Web: Armin Meiwes (2001)

Tragically, but possibly predictably, Armin Meiwes' childhood shared much in common with many of the dangerously deranged characters we have met previously in this book. By all accounts his father was – and as of this writing, still is – a kindly if rather weak-spirited man who was absolutely no match for his shrewish wife, Waltraud. Waltraud, commonly known as Ulla, was a sharp-tongued harridan who took delight in venting her spleen on her two sons and husband. She seemed to find a particular satisfaction in bullying Armin, the younger of her two boys, derisively calling him 'Minchen', a deprecating term once used by Germans to refer to their servants. Some of the Meiwes' neighbours insisted that Ulla was a witch, who was so evil that she must have been in league with the devil himself.

Torn between an unresponsive father and a cruel mother, Armin withdrew into a fantasy world shaped largely by old horror movies and the often disturbing characters from the traditional fairy tales collected by the Grimm brothers. Because his mother discouraged him from having any friends of his own, Armin invented friends. His favourite was a make-believe boy named Franky who shared his burgeoning interest in everything dark and macabre.

As if it were not bleak enough already, eight-year-old Armin's world took a decided turn for the worse when, in 1969, his father decided he had taken all he could of Waltraud. Packing up Armin's older brother and his belongings, he left, filing for divorce. He may have wanted to take Armin with him but, as is usual in such cases, the courts believed that young children should remain with their mother. In this case, the results of such an arrangement were to be disastrous. Now cut off from anyone who had even the slightest sympathy for him, Armin's retreat into fantasy increased at an alarming rate. Deprived of any model on which to build normal reactions to life and family, he invented his own rules based on the experiences of his sad life. With his real brother gone Armin fantasised about what it would be like to have another brother, one who would not abandon him as his own had done.

He decided that the only sure way to bind this fantasy brother to him permanently would be to eat him. In this mixed-up world, images from the Brothers Grimm came flooding back; the tale of *Hansel and Gretel* – the siblings abandoned in the forest by their parents – who found themselves captured by a wicked witch, only to be fattened up until they were tender enough to eat, seemed to make some kind of sense. Even those few boys at school that Armin would have liked to have had for friends could only be seen in terms of how satisfying, how reassuring, it would be to serve them up on a plate. But none of his fantasies would ever come true – at least not as long as his loving mother stood in the way of Armin making any real friends.

She followed him everywhere, never letting him out of her sight, never letting him gain even the slightest inkling of independence. When Armin was old enough to start dating, Ulla insisted on chaperoning them. When he joined the armed forces she even trailed along when his company went on manoeuvres. How and why the officers allowed this has not come to light, but it certainly did nothing to endear Armin to his peers. When the other young men in his company went on leave, Armin was instructed to come home with mother. And home with Ulla was not the place any rational person would want to be.

When Armin was sixteen Ulla had bought a house on the outskirts of Rotenburg, not far from the city of Kassel. A rambling, ancient, tumbledown, half-timbered farmhouse, it already had the reputation of being haunted long before Mrs Meiwes and her browbeaten son moved in. With more than thirty dusty rooms punctuated by sloping floors and bulging walls, it did, indeed, look like something out of a Gothic horror novel or the stereotypical 'haunted house' from a children's ghost story. If the place itself were not grim enough, the half-empty rooms with their hard linoleum-covered floors did nothing to impart the slightest hint of cheer, but it certainly fitted the mood of its inhabitants. When Armin was twenty years old his mother slapped a sign on the door of his room: 'Kinderzimmer' it read – 'Children's Room' in German. So cowed was Armin by his tyrannical mother that even after she died in 1999 he left the humiliating sign in place.

Once out of the military, Armin Meiwes continued to live in the ramshackle house and earned his living as a computer engineer. To acquaintances and neighbours he seemed a perfectly normal, if slightly shy, man. He was always polite, offering to mow the lawn for elderly neighbours, helping people work on their cars and even occasionally inviting someone from the neighbourhood in for dinner. One neighbour later described him as being almost 'childlike' in manner. What no one knew was that the dark fantasies of his childhood had completely taken over his private existence.

No matter how awful his mother had been, she was the only anchor in Armin's life and he simply had no idea of how to live without her. So, in his own way, he kept her alive. In an unbelievable reflection of the Norman Bates character from *Psycho*, Armin began wearing his dead mother's clothes, wandering around the decaying mansion talking to himself in her voice. He even put a mannequin's head on the pillow of her bed. If this was a newly created aspect of his fantastic inner world, there were still plenty of other, more familiar fantasies to occupy his time.

The twisted dream of having a brother or friend who he could keep with him for ever by devouring their body had begun to take on new and ever more bizarre aspects. From a variety of underground internet sites, Meiwes began downloading pictures of torture and cannibalism. Before long, despite thousands of images stored on his computer and printed out, Meiwes needed more. He needed to find real people with whom he could share his fantasies. That is when he discovered literally hundreds of cannibalism-related websites floating around the darker corners of the net. Trawling sites with names like 'Flesh and Bone' and 'Cannibal Café', Armin found that not only was he not alone in his desire to eat someone, but that there were hundreds of unstable people in the world who were more than happy to entertain the thought of becoming someone else's dinner.

Beginning late in the year 2000, Meiwes became a constant visitor to these sites, logging on to their bulletin boards and chat-rooms under the pseudonym of Franky, the name of his imaginary boyhood friend. In his personal ads, Meiwes solicited possible victims, specifying the type of person that he thought would look best in his oven. At first he asked for a man between the ages of eighteen and twenty-five, who was in good physical condition and would consent to be eaten. Although he would later raise the age limit to thirty, he always stated 'slim and blond' as a requisite. Between May and August 2001, Meiwes corresponded with over four hundred would-be cannibals and victims from all over Europe and the USA. Some of them answered his ad just to chat, but according to his computer files a total of two hundred and four men actually offered themselves up to sate his culinary peculiarities.

Literally thousands of these always grotesque, but frequently hysterical, exchanges survive. 'Hi!' one of them began, 'Being roasted alive, that is absolutely a beautiful concept.' To another applicant he wrote, 'I hope you can come quick to me, I am a hungry cannibal. Please tell me your height and weight and I will butcher and eat your fine flesh.' Even the details of portion control found their way into these odd correspondences: 'But keep in mind that with your weight there is about 35kg of your flesh available for eating.' Even the festive season was an integral part of this cannibalistic correspondence. In January 2002, Jorg, one of Meiwes' chat-room friends, enquired, 'Did you kill any young men over the holidays?' Armin responded, 'It was the only thing I didn't do over the holidays. Do you think that I have slipped out, [because] I want to kill a young man and eat him?' Jorg's blasé reply was, 'No, there is nothing sexier than to be killed like a pig.'

Just how 'sexy' being killed like a pig might be is probably best left unimagined, but it is beyond question that such an end requires specialised equipment. So, just to be ready for any eventuality, Meiwes constructed a slaughterhouse on the third floor of his house. The windowless, attic room was painted in horror movie shades of blood red and stygian black. There were meat hooks hanging from the beams, a slaughtering table and a wood and wire cage in the corner. No cheap flick from the Vipco Vaults of Horror could have looked any sleazier.

While there is no way of knowing how much of the ghoulish conversation carried on over the websites that had become Meiwes' secret world was nothing more than bored people letting their unwell imagination run wild, it is certain that some of the people who stumbled across Armin Meiwes were just as serious, and at least as sick, as he was. An Italian respondent, who identified himself as Matteo, asked if Meiwes would enjoy burning off his testicles with a blow-torch before crucifying him and then whipping him to death. Armin replied that he was not particularly into torture; he just wanted a friend who was willing to be eaten. At least one other applicant was also rejected by the discriminating Meiwes. When Alex from Essen, Germany, asked 'Franky' to behead him, Armin refused, saying that Alex was just too fat. In one instance, however, Armin came awfully close to getting what he wanted.

Later, Meiwes recalled that a man named Andres from Regensburg, Germany, 'wanted me to pick him up in a cattle truck and slaughter him like a pig. I told him to take the train.' Amazingly, Andres did exactly that. Meiwes remembered their encounter. 'I picked him up at the station and we went back to the butchery at my house. He wanted me to wear rubber boots, which I did. I wrapped him in cling film ready for slaughtering, but he backed out. So we just fooled around, drank beer and ate pizza.'

From as early as March 2001 Meiwes had been in almost constant communication with a man named Bernd-Jurgen Brandes who lived in Berlin. Like Meiwes, Brandes was a computer engineer and, since he also wanted to be eaten, the two had much on which to base their developing relationship. Whether Brandes originally got in touch with Meiwes, or it happened the other way round, seems in doubt, but certainly Brandes had his own posting on the Cannibal Café website. It read, 'I offer myself to you and will let you dine from my live body. Whoever REALLY wants to do it will need a REAL VICTIM.' However the two found each other, their relationship quickly evolved from chatty exchanges like the note Brandes sent to Meiwes in which he quipped, 'You don't have to buy meat again, there will be plenty left,' to far more serious affairs.

When Meiwes told Brandes how many of those who responded to his ad were not really serious, the 43-year-old Brandes responded with a line that may have been intended as an erotic tease. 'I hope you are serious because I really want it. My nipples look forward to your stomach.'

As the two came closer and closer to meeting, their conversations got correspondingly stranger.

Brandes:	Are you a smoker?
Meiwes:	Yes, but my teeth are still pretty white.
Brandes:	That's good, I smoke too. I hope you like smoked meat.
Meiwes:	Just bring yourself for breakfast.

Soon, the records of their conversations show that things had moved from the realm of sick fantasy to bloody, matter-of-fact reality:

Brandes:	What will you do with my brain?
Meiwes:	I'll leave it, I don't want to split your skull.
Brandes:	Better bury it, preferably in a cemetery; nobody notices skulls there. Or maybe pulverise it?
Meiwes:	We have a nice, small cemetery here.
Brandes:	You could use it as an ashtray.

In retrospect, it would seem clear that Brandes meant every word of what he said to Meiwes because before leaving Berlin for Rotenburg he took the time to have his will drawn up. Obviously, he had no plans to return home.

On the evening of 9 March 2001, Meiwes picked Brandes up at Rotenburg railway station and drove him back to his creaking old house. Once there, Brandes got the grand tour of the place, including the slaughterhouse room on the top floor. After a loving romp in Meiwes' bed, the men wandered downstairs to the kitchen where Brandes swallowed 20 sleeping pills, a bottle of night-time cold medicine and a bottle of schnapps. So as not to lose one minute of the action that was to follow, Meiwes dragged out his camcorder and trained it on the table where they sat discussing the forthcoming human feast. At some point, they started deciding just how to proceed with the business of doing away with Brandes. Finally, they determined it would be a fine thing if they could share some of Brandes' flesh before his final dispatch; it seemed like a last, friendly gesture to bind their deadly relationship.

While Brandes waited patiently, Meiwes got a butcher's knife and cut off his new friend's penis, bound the gushing wound, and sautéed the fresh meat in butter, adding a little garlic for flavour. When the meal was ready, they ate it together. Later, Meiwes remembered it as being 'tough and unpalatable', but such little inconveniences can be laughed off among friends. By the time they finished dinner, Brandes was becoming increasingly weak from blood loss and the drugs were beginning to take effect. There seemed little doubt that he would not last much longer, so Meiwes switched off the video recorder long enough to drag Brandes up the stairs to the bathroom where he placed him in a tub of warm water where he could, in Meiwes' words, 'bleed out'. While his friend lay slowly bleeding to death, Meiwes settled down with a *Star Trek* novel. How often Meiwes checked on Brandes' progress is unknown, but ten hours later the man was still not dead so Meiwes decided to help him along.

Retrieving a kitchen knife, Meiwes knelt beside the bathtub, cradled Brandes' head in one arm, kissed him gently on the lips, and plunged the knife into his throat. Hauling the carcass out of the tub, Meiwes proceeded to dismember and butcher the body of the man he had been having sex and dinner with only a few hours earlier. The result was 65lb of prime cuts, most of which were portioned out into freezer bags, neatly sealed and stashed in the chest freezer next to pizzas and other, more traditional foodstuffs. A small portion was kept aside for more immediate consumption. The scabrous leftovers – bones, skull, viscera and so forth – were taken to the garden where they were buried next to a barbecue grill that would later be used to prepare a few 'Brandes steaks' for the table.

To celebrate his first meal of fresh flesh, Meiwes set the table with his best linen, china, crystal and silver. The candles added a nice, intimate touch. In true Hannibal Lecter style, Meiwes chose a bottle of South African red wine as a proper accompaniment to the delicate flavour of the meat.

Although he would later admit that Brandes had been something of a disappointment as a person, having lied about his age and not wanting to spend more time together before submitting to the slaughter, in retrospect he wasn't such a bad guy. Meiwes insisted that Brandes had spoken much better English than he had, but once he began ingesting his friend his own English improved markedly. And there was a more romantic side to the coin as well. 'With every bite, my memory of him grew stronger', Meiwes would recall wistfully. And over the next ten months there were quite a few bites to enhance the memories.

The vast majority of Brandes would eventually be cooked and eaten, but well before the meat supply ran out Meiwes was back on-line looking for a new source of groceries. Meiwes complained to an on-line friend at one of the cannibal chat-rooms, 'I hope I will soon find another victim, the flesh is almost gone.' Now, as before, there seemed to be no shortage of people willing to sacrifice themselves to an on-line cannibal. In the coming months Meiwes would meet up with four of them, but in every case things seemed to go wrong at the last minute. Stefan from Kassel travelled to Rotenburg and got as far as the slaughter room, where Meiwes hung him on meat hooks, wrapped him in cling film and labelled the various parts to be dissected 'steaks', 'chops', 'ham' and so forth but, according to Meiwes, 'We called it off because it was so damn cold in there.' Whatever Armin Meiwes was, he was neither an out-of-control killer nor an inconsiderate host.

In the end it was one of Meiwes' own correspondents who tripped him up. An Austrian student who had entered into conversation with Meiwes thinking the whole thing was a joke, soon realised he was in contact with a real-life cannibal who had his eye firmly planted on some Wiener schnitzel. In July 2001, the student contacted the German police and told them everything he had learned about Armin Meiwes. For seventeen months the police tracked Meiwes' progress on the net before finally closing in in December 2002, arresting Meiwes, and confiscating the remaining 15lb of Brandes' body from the freezer. It was only a matter of days before a salacious international press was publishing photos of the German 'Internet Cannibal', his ramshackle house and the gory slaughter room on the third floor.

While Meiwes was sent off for examination by psychiatrists the local prosecutor's office, under the direction of Marcus Kohler, set about putting together their case. The preliminary psychiatric report was a prosecuting attorney's dream. Dr George Stolpmann described the 42-year-old Meiwes as having 'no evidence of a psychological disorder', but admitted that Meiwes did have a 'schizoid personality'. Explaining this apparent contradiction, Stolpmann said, 'What we have here is an inability to have warm and tender feelings towards others.' With such a clear-cut case dropped into their laps, prosecutors must have been deeply chagrined to find that Germany had no laws against cannibalism. Considering previous cases such as Karl Denke and Georg Grossman, who were covered in an earlier chapter, this would seem to be an egregious legal oversight. Even at this early stage, prosecutor Kohler knew that because of Meiwes' videotape of the killing, it would be virtually impossible to get a conviction for first-degree murder. Consequently, he decided to go for a charge of 'murder for sexual pleasure', with second-degree murder held in reserve as a back-up. The former charge would guarantee a sentence of fifteen years in prison, the second only eight-and-a-half. For good measure, they would also charge him with 'disturbing the peace of the dead'. Whatever they could get him on, Kohler would do everything in his power to keep Armin Meiwes behind bars for as long as possible. In

Kohler's words, Meiwes 'slaughtered his victim like a piece of livestock and treated him as an object of fancy'.

Meiwes' defence team knew there was no way their client was going to walk away when two hours of videotape showed his crimes in grisly, living colour, and the psychiatric report had already disallowed an insanity defence. They finally agreed on pleading guilty to 'killing on demand', a term usually used in cases of assisted suicide and euthanasia. This lesser charge would carry a maximum sentence of only five years in prison.

The trial began on 3 December 2003 with a slate of 38 witnesses to be questioned over 14 days. A major part of the prosecution's case would be an airing of the two-hour video of Brandes' death and dismemberment, but the three-judge panel requested that only the 'relevant parts' – those concerning 'what the victim is saying and doing before and during the killing' – be shown.

As he walked into court with his attorneys, Meiwes seemed amazingly relaxed, talking casually and joking. For his time on the stand, however, he was much more serious. Addressing the court, Meiwes explained that what he had done was a benefit to both himself and Brandes; saying that he had only wanted 'someone to be part of me' and that Brandes 'enjoyed dying, death. Bernd came to me of his own free will to end his life . . . For him, it was a nice death.' If he had any regrets it was in how long Brandes took to bleed out. 'I only waited horrified for the end after doing the deed. It took so terribly long.'

As much as anything, it was Brandes' state of mind that occupied the court's attention. While psychiatrists had declared Meiwes to be sane, had Brandes been emotionally capable and mentally stable when he invited his own murder? Could anyone in their right mind consent to be slaughtered and devoured? The testimony, like much in the case, was contradictory.

Brandes' father insisted that his son had never shown any signs of depression, and his most recent lover, 27-year-old René

Jasnik, agreed. He said Brandes and he were happy together, that Brandes had never entertained morbid or suicidal thoughts, and that they were in the midst of planning a summer holiday when Brandes took off for Rotenburg. Jasnik did admit that he had received a letter from Meiwes apologising for having eaten his boyfriend.

The flip side of this picture of Brandes as a stable, seemingly happy man came from a former, occasional sex partner who insisted that Brandes had once offered him 2,000 Euros to bite off his penis. At the end of the day, the only thing prosecutors and defence could agree on was the version of Brandes who appeared on video. 'The victim appeared to be fully aware of the situation. Videotape material definitely shows both him and the suspect engaged in eating his own flesh prior to his death.'

Although not directly related to the Brandes case, Detective Inspector Wolfgang Buch told the court that Meiwes was under investigation for the presumed disappearances of at least two other men – one from Frankfurt and one from Austria – with whom he had been corresponding through the Cannibal Café. Buch concluded, 'It is at this point impossible to say whether others among the 204 persons [with whom Meiwes had been corresponding] might also have been homicide victims.'

In his final statement before the court, Meiwes said, '[I] regret all that I have done', insisting that he would not kill and eat anyone else in the future. Expounding on this theme he added, 'I always had the fantasy and in the end I fulfilled it. I had my big kick and I don't need to do it again. I regret it all very much, but I can't undo it.'

On Friday, 30 January 2004 the court concluded that Armin Meiwes had no 'base motives' in his killing of Bernd-Jurgen Brandes, but that he was undoubtedly guilty of his death. He was convicted of second-degree murder and sentenced to eight-and-a-half years in prison. While Meiwes' defence attorneys seemed satisfied, the prosecution immediately lodged an appeal.

In April 2005 the German courts ordered a retrial and it seems likely that the case will make its way through the system all the way to the German Supreme Court.

While he waited to find out what would happen, Armin Meiwes whiled away his time in prison writing his memoirs. Since there is no law in Germany prohibiting criminals from making money by selling their story to the press, publishers and movie companies, Meiwes looks forward to being a very rich man whenever he is finally released. Already a German film company has been awarded a government grant equivalent to $25,000 to begin work on a cinematic version of Meiwes' story – tentatively titled *Your Heart in My Head* – and even Hollywood has its eye on the marketing possibilities of the Rotenburg Cannibal. Says Randy Sanchez, marketing director of a Los Angeles firm that analyses markets for the American film industry, 'It's all very Hannibal Lecter.' Meiwes hopes for a $1 million advance for the film rights to his story. The German heavy metal band Rammstein has already climbed on the bandwagon with a Meiwes-inspired song 'Mein Teil', or 'My Piece'. In German, 'piece' is a slang term for penis.

Thanks to the dogged persistence of Prosecuter Marcus Kohler when Meiwes' case was retried in May 2006, the internet cannibal's sentence was increased to life imprisonment.

Nineteen

Something Completely Different: Marc Sappington (2001)

Big cities worldwide harbour both the best and worst examples of the human condition. In this respect, the American midwestern metropolis of Kansas City, Kansas, is no different from any other city. The city centre and wealthy neighbourhoods in the suburbs stand in stark contrast to the crime-ridden, largely black ghettos of the north side. While drugs, guns and violent gangs rule the streets, good, honest, hard-working people struggle to survive in the face of poverty and despair.

When Clarice Sappington's son, Marc, was born in 1980, she vowed that no matter what it took her boy would be brought up properly. She knew from the start it would be an uphill struggle all the way. Marc's father had disappeared before he was born and Clarice, although a good church-going, hard-working woman, was plagued by recurrent bouts of mental problems. As often as possible she took, or sent, the boy to church, provided for his needs in every way she could and on those occasions when she had to attend the mental hospital, she sent him to stay with her parents who loved him as much as she did.

To all appearances Marc Sappington looked like one of those rare few who might actually escape the worst effects of the ghetto. He was never a brilliant student, but he did well enough at school and was liked by everyone who knew him. He was charming, articulate, funny and always greeted everyone with a smile. A former classmate remembers him as the class 'goofball' who joked a lot but was always ready to defuse a tense situation by quietly quoting a passage from the Bible. A neighbour once described him, saying 'nobody was afraid of him', which, in the violent youth culture of Kansas City's north side, was a compliment indeed. But his mother's schizophrenia, and the death of both of his maternal grandparents while he was still an adolescent, took a huge emotional toll on Marc. Still, he loved his mother and had the support of a few good friends. Chief among his buddies were Terry Green, who was four years his senior, Michael Weaver, who was in Marc's class at school and Alton 'Freddie' Brown, a skinny neighbourhood boy who was five years younger than Marc and looked up to him with the worshipful eyes of a kid brother.

By the time Marc graduated from high school in 1998, he had matured into a muscular, 5 foot 11 inch, 12-stone (170lb) man with the smiling face of an ebony cherub. But ultimately, the poverty of the ghetto began to take its toll on Marc. Unable to find work and bored out of his mind, he slowly drifted into drug use. He began smoking 'danks', cigarettes soaked in embalming fluid, and worked his way up to the deadly PCP, known as 'angel dust', which can have long-term, if not permanent, mental and emotional side-effects. His reliance on drugs reached a point where even those who had always supported and defended him were forced to admit he was a 'heavy smoker'. What no one could possibly know was that Marc was developing other problems, too. He had inherited his mother's schizophrenia and it was slowly eating away at his mind.

While wandering the streets one day early in 2001, Marc, now twenty-one, ran into sixteen-year-old Armando Gaitan, a casual acquaintance who was everything his mother had warned him against. Gaitan was one of those violent, foul-tempered tough guys who was well on his way to becoming what black youths refer to as a 'gangsta'. Wandering along the streets, getting deeper and deeper into conversation, Gaitan tried to enlist Marc's help with a little problem. It came out that Gaitan had bought a car from another kid named David Mashak but that only days later the car had been impounded by the police and Gaitan had been unable to get satisfaction from Mashak. With Marc's help, he was sure he could force Mashak to give him his money back. A year or two earlier, Marc would have turned him down flat, but now, for some reason, all he did was ask for more details. What would he have to do? Warming to his subject, Gaitan took Marc to where he had stashed an AK-47 assault rifle, showed it to him, and told him that together they would confront Mashak. All Marc had to do was stand there holding the gun while he, Gaitan, did all the talking. He assured Marc that once Mashak saw the gun there wouldn't be any trouble. Foolishly, Sappington agreed.

On the afternoon of 16 March 2001 Marc and Armando Gaitan confronted David Mashak while he was eating lunch in his garage. Gaitan threatened Mashak. Mashak threatened Gaitan and then, for no apparent reason, Marc Sappington opened fire with the AK-47. As the torrent of bullets sprayed across the walls of the garage, one of them ricocheted, striking Mashak in the back. As if the hail of gunfire was not terrifying enough, the look of pure glee on Marc's face sent Gaitan fleeing from the scene. He did not stop running until he reached Texas. Two hours after the assault, David Mashak was pronounced dead.

The long-running argument over the car soon led police to connect Armando Gaitan with Mashak's murder and only a few weeks later he was arrested and shipped back to Kansas City. Under police questioning, and later at the juvenile detention centre, he admitted his own, secondary role in the killing, but refused to give the name of the other man who had been seen entering Mashak's garage with him. The police assumed it was some 'honour among thieves' thing that kept him from talking.

It wasn't. Remembering the maniacal look on Marc Sappington's face as he wielded the AK-47, Gaitan was simply too scared to give them Marc's name. It would be a lot safer in prison than to risk coming face-to-face with that crazy man again.

If the Mashak killing was a disaster for Mashak and Gaitan, its effects on Marc Sappington were more subtle, but no less profound. In those few seconds, something inside him had snapped. Whether it was the incipient schizophrenia, the effects of the danks and the PCP, or a combination of the two, may never be known, but only days after the killing, something began talking to Marc. Something inside his head. And it was saying very frightening things.

Curiously, according to psychologists and psychiatrists, most people whose mental state is such that they imagine voices will ascribe the source of the voices either to God, the devil, or some kind of demon. If their background is religious, as Marc's was, they tend to believe that they are either being directed by the Almighty, or threatened by Satan. Marc was never able to determine who the voices belonged to, nor did he seem to care: all that mattered was that they were threatening him. If he did not do what they told him to do, they were going to kill him. It was as simple as that. Terrified, Marc agreed to do the voices' bidding. That's when they told him to kill people. They also told him there would be other things to do later, but for now, all he had to do was find someone to kill. In compliance with his orders, Marc began stashing weapons in a corner of his mother's basement, the one area of the house that was his and his alone. He gathered a shotgun, knives, an axe, all kinds of weapons. When he seemed to have enough to cover any possible eventuality, the voices told him it was time to go hunting. They did not, however, offer him any specific guidance. He would have to select the victim himself.

For days he wandered the grimy streets of the north side, staring at every passer-by, appraising their suitability and asking the opinion of the voices in his head. Him? How about her? What about him? But after three weeks of looking the voices remained steadfastly silent. Marc did not know what to do. If he didn't find a sacrifice soon the voices might make good their threat to kill him. Finally, pure chance made the decision for him.

On the afternoon of 7 April, his old friend Terry Green, now twenty-five, dropped by at the Sappington home to spend some time hanging out with Marc. Marc had barely opened the door when the voices told him this was the one. Nervously, Marc invited Terry inside and led him to his own, personal space in the basement. Minutes later, Terry Green lay dead on the floor, bleeding profusely from multiple knife wounds. His friend, Marc Sappington, was leaning over the body, furiously lapping up the spreading pool of blood as it oozed from Green's body. As the gore smeared across his face and hands, Marc looked up. He was sure he had heard a noise. Had his mother come home from work early? He was confused, but the voices told him to be calm and get rid of the body as quickly as he could.

Wrapping Terry's carcass in an old tarpaulin, he lugged it out of the house, heaved it into the boot of his mother's car, and drove through the city, across the Missouri river into Kansas City, Missouri, and then to a nightclub he and Green liked to frequent. Even at this early hour there were a few cars scattered around the edges of the car park. Marc tried one after another until he found one that was unlocked. Pulling up alongside the car, he lugged Terry's body out of the boot and into the back seat of the other car. He tossed the tarpaulin over the body and drove away.

When the body was found a short time later, Kansas City, Missouri Police assumed it was a Missouri murder, but alerted the police across the river in Kansas City, Kansas. The Kansas police were more than happy to leave the matter on the Missouri side of the river; they had plenty of murders of their own to deal with. It would be three days before Terry Green would be identified as a resident of Kansas and his connection with Marc Sappington would come to the investigating officers' attention. In those three days, Marc Sappington, and the voices living in his head, would be very, very busy.

On 10 April, a mere three days after Green's murder, Marc was wandering up and down the streets looking for the next person to sacrifice to the voices, but the voices had not been any more help today than on any other day. No one seemed to please them. Finally, wandering around the neighbourhood, he spotted his old classmate and friend Michael Weaver sitting on the front steps of his parents' house, so he stopped to chat for a while. They talked and laughed and agreed that they were both bored silly. Finally, Marc suggested they go for a ride in Michael's car. At least it was better than standing there on the street. Weaver agreed. They were still negotiating the narrow alleyways near Michael's house when Sappington pulled out a hunting knife, killed his friend and began drinking his blood. He had to. The voices told him to do it and he had no choice. But only moments after the horrible deed, he panicked, jumped out of the car and fled on foot. As he ran he cleaned himself up as much as possible. Finally, his feet slowed to a walk and headed towards home.

Making his way homeward he passed the house of Freddie Brown, the teenager who idolised him. The voices spoke to him again and, acquiescing to their demands, he went to the house and invited Freddie to come home with him. Thrilled, the unsuspecting sixteen-year-old followed him. The pair went straight to Marc's basement where, when Freddie's back was turned, Sappington pulled the shotgun from its hiding place in the corner and shot the boy in the back. The roar of the gun was terrific as its deadly pellets splattered a cloud of pink gore all over the walls and ceiling. Even with his ears ringing, Marc could hear the voices inside his head. 'Do it!' they told him. 'Do it now.' In a frenzy, Marc grabbed the axe and began hacking Freddie's small body into six huge, blood-covered pieces. When the body of his friend was dismembered, he grabbed a steak knife and hacked a large chunk from his thigh. He cut off smaller pieces, jamming one after another into his mouth, chewing and swallowing them as fast as he could. Then, picking up the dripping slab of meat, Marc wandered upstairs to the kitchen where he fried and ate slices of Freddie Brown. The rest of the meat was shoved into the freezer for a later time.

Returning to the basement, Marc stuffed the remaining pieces of Freddie into several garbage bags but decided to leave the bags open, along with the horrible smears of gore and bits of flesh that were scattered everywhere. Then, calmly, he walked out of the house for an afternoon stroll through the north side of Kansas City.

A few hours later, just after 6pm, Clarice Sappington came home from work as usual, but became frightened when she saw the droplets and smears of blood on the kitchen floor. Afraid that something terrible had happened to her boy, she followed the trail of blood down the steps and into the basement, even though it was Marc's private domain. Somehow, by sheer force of will, Clarice fumbled her way back upstairs to the telephone where she called 911 for the emergency services. Nearing hysterics she described what she had seen protruding from the trash bags in the basement. By the time the police and ambulance arrived, Clarice had descended into another of her occasional psychotic states. This time, she would remain in hospital for a very long time.

Even without Clarice's help the police knew their first order of business was to find her son. Witnesses who had seen Armando Gaitan enter the garage of David Mashak had described Gaitan's companion, and the description sounded very much like Marc Sappington. Up to now the police did not have enough evidence to link Sappington to the Mashak killing, but the mess in the basement made it clear that Marc was involved in something very, very bad. An APB (all points bulletin) was immediately put out for the arrest of Marc Sappington, aged twenty-one.

It was only a short time later that a local police cruiser spotted the suspect walking along one of the busy business streets of the north side. They jumped out of the car and hailed him to halt, but Sappington panicked and fled. When a nearby car pulled up to stop at a red light, he jerked open the driver's door, shoved the woman across the seat, jumped in and tore off through the heavy traffic. Minutes later police cars closed in from all sides, forcing Sappington to a halt. He was arrested on suspicion of murder and taken to police headquarters. His terrified hostage was released uninjured.

The interrogation of Marc Sappington was turned over to Detective Lieutenant Vince Davenport and two plain-clothes officers. For more than two hours that evening they tried one ploy after another to get Marc to tell them something about what had happened in his basement that day. By now, Sappington had not only been tentatively connected with the Mashak killing but also with the killing of Terry Green, whose body had been found in the back seat of a car in Kansas City, Missouri. Davenport was an expert at getting suspects to talk. He knew that sometimes it was best to use the good-cop–bad-cop routine and sometimes it was better to use gentle persuasion. One way or another he always got results, at least until tonight. No matter what he said, Marc Sappington refused to utter a syllable. Finally, tired and frustrated, Davenport decided to go home and sleep on it. Maybe by tomorrow he would think of a new ploy. Getting up from the chair, he started to put on his coat when he thought he heard Sappington mumble something. 'What? What did you say, son?'

'Vampirism.' He muttered so quietly Davenport could hardly hear him. 'Vampirism. Cannibalism.' Davenport took his coat off and sat down again. It was going to be a long night.

Once Marc began talking the words came tumbling out faster and faster. He described all four killings. He talked about the drugs and he talked about the voices in his head that were threatening to kill him if he didn't comply with their demands. At one point he looked Davenport straight in the eye and asked him if he would mind if he took a few bites out of the detective's leg. Davenport thought it was Marc's way of trying to break the tension, but later FBI profiler Candice DeLong said she believed Sappington was being completely serious.

While Sappington's statement and formal confession were still being typed up, detectives went to the juvenile detention centre where Armando Gaitan was being held and questioned him again. When they told him everything Sappington had confessed to, he finally broke down. Yes, it was Marc who had wielded the AK-47 that had killed David Mashak. Now connected with more than three murders, Marc Sappington was officially listed as a serial killer and once the news hit the papers and television it didn't take long for him to be dubbed 'The Kansas City Cannibal'.

The nature of Sappington's crimes, and his claims to have heard voices in his head, made it obvious to police, the court and the prosecutor's office that they were dealing with a very disturbed young man. Consequently, when he was not being held at the Wyandotte County Jail he was undergoing psychiatric evaluation. The psychiatrists prescribed drugs for his psychotic condition, but unless he was in hospital and under constant supervision he refused to take them, complaining that they made him feel tired. Dodging his medication whenever possible, his mental state fluctuated wildly from nearly normal to severely delusional. Under such conditions, an effective evaluation was well-nigh impossible. About the only thing the psychiatrists and prosecutor's office had agreed upon by the time Sappington's preliminary hearing came up in January 2002 was that he was not responsible enough for his actions to be given the death penalty. In the meantime, a sanity hearing was set for 13 September. When the appointed day arrived the only thing the judge and doctors could decide was that another sanity hearing would have to be held after further evaluations and testing.

The problem was that Marc Sappington's psychological profile flew in the face of almost every known fact about serial killers and cannibals. With one single exception, that of Wayne Williams, every known serial killer in American history had been white; Sappington was black. Serial killers almost never begin their killing until they are in their thirties and there was almost always a history of violence, usually sexual violence, before their killing spree began; Sappington was only twenty-one, had no history of sexual violence and, with one or two minor, drug-related exceptions, had never even been in trouble with the law. Finally, those serial killers who practise cannibalism and drink human blood invariably do so for sexual gratification. Despite repeated, in-depth psychological examinations, Sappington gave no indication that he received any form of sexual gratification from his vampiristic and cannibalistic acts; he insisted that he did what he did only because he was terrified of disobeying the voices. Marc Sappington was, in fact, unique in the annals of criminal psychology.

Faced with this conundrum, the prosecutors' office insisted that Sappington's acts were not the result of a psychosis but of his drug use, a factor which he could have controlled – through professional help – had he wanted to. With this in mind, even though they knew they were barred from requesting the death penalty, they sought four consecutive life terms without the possibility of parole.

At the second sanity hearing, psychiatrist William Logan testified that so long as Sappington refused his medication he would remain a danger to himself and to others. Even

Sappington's attorney, Patricia Kalb, admitted that her client frequently refused his medication. Based on Logan's opinion and the supporting evidence of doctors and Ms Kalb, Judge Dexter Burdette issued a ruling, based on a recent decision by the US Supreme Court, instructing the Wyandotte County Sheriff's Department to forcibly medicate Sappington. It was to be one of the first times in the history of American jurisprudence that a person would stand trial while being forcibly medicated.

The trial itself was rather anti-climactic. The physical evidence and the accused's confession spoke for themselves. There was no doubt that Marc Sappington had done the horrible things he was accused of doing. On 26 July 2004, Marc Sappington was found guilty on four counts of murder as well as kidnapping and aggravated burglary in connection with the car he had hijacked when fleeing from the police. Six weeks later, on 2 September, he was sentenced to life in prison with no hope of parole. Although Marc Sappington is safely locked up, he leaves us with a gnawing question. Why? What was it that turned this sweet, friendly kid into a vicious killer and a cannibal? Tens of thousands of people suffer from psychosis and never even contemplate such crimes. Millions of people are trapped in the self-defeating spiral of drugs and crime, but they don't eat people. So what really happened to Marc Sappington? We may never know.

Twenty

A Rising Tide of Flesh Eaters? The Future of Cannibalism

H aving looked at cannibalism in the distant past, as well as recounting fifteen specific instances of cannibalism that have taken place over the past six hundred years, it seems both fitting and necessary to project the future of how we perceive – and, in some cases, indulge in – mankind's ultimate taboo.

Readers may have noticed that the incidence of individual cases covered in this book has occurred at ever-shortening intervals of time. This is due to several factors. First, because many early cases may have gone unreported and, until the twentieth century, some may have been considered simply too horrible to become public knowledge. It is equally true that we wanted to keep the book as current as possible and space constraints simply made it impossible to cover every historical case we found. Indeed, we have accumulated sufficient data to write a second volume on case histories of cannibalism. But over and above these factors there would appear to be a frightening amount of evidence indicating that the phenomenon of cannibalism is on the rise. Is this, in fact, the case or does it only seem so?

For a variety of reasons, some known, some only speculated at, the republics of the former Soviet Union seem to be experiencing an unprecedented plague of cannibalism. At the end of the chapter on André Chikatilo we mentioned that since Chikatilo's capture the city of Rostov-on-Don has become the world's capital of serial killing, but the problem is much more pervasive than that. Russia and its near neighbours have a long and continuing history of people eating.

The rampant cannibalism that took place during the Ukrainian famine of the 1930s was mentioned in chapter one and the chapter on André Chikatilo, but this was not the first famine leading to cannibalism in that part of the world. It was not even the first such incident in the twentieth century. A decade and a half earlier, as the Russian Civil War continued to rage between Lenin's Red Army and the republican forces of the White Army, the Volga region experienced a similar disastrous famine that led to almost identical results. Reduced to mass starvation, the people had no choice but to eat their own dead or watch their children perish. Later, during the Second World War, Nazi Germany laid siege to Leningrad (now St Petersburg) and Stalingrad (now Volgograd) with such ferocity that millions died over the course of the onslaught, which lasted for nearly three years. Again, the living had no choice but to eat their dead or die themselves. Even faced with this awful option, in Leningrad alone well over a million people perished. Still, other nations have suffered unspeakably in wars and famines and not succumbed to cannibalism. Why the Russian states? And more to the immediate point, why is it still happening now?

Certainly, since the break-up of the Soviet Union the social, political and economic structure of the former Soviet states has all but collapsed. The resulting economic crisis has made meat, and, in many cases, any decent food, a luxury that few can afford. In consequence, large segments of the population have sought to drown their sorrows and hunger pangs in a sea of cheap vodka. As it has always done, drinking breaks down the inhibitions and chronic drinking breaks down the cognitive reasoning ability of the brain. When alcohol damage is great enough, and the hunger is severe enough, social and moral strictures collapse.

Russian criminologists admit that the wave of serial killings and cannibalism is directly connected to the economic and social trauma of the area and recognise the severity of the problem. 'We have information about cases where human flesh is sold in street markets; also when homeless people kill each other and sell the flesh. Every month we find corpses with missing body parts,' says one Russian criminologist who prefers not to be identified. But can a starvation economy account for the fact that more than thirty cases of cannibalism were prosecuted in the former Soviet states in 1996 alone? A few examples, listed chronologically, may serve to illustrate the extent of the problem:

1996

Until he was caught in St Petersburg, Ilshat Kuzikov marinated choice cuts of human flesh with onions, which he hung in a plastic bag outside his window. When police forced their way into his home, he offered them some of the meat and vodka if they would let him go. Ilshat, thirty-seven, said he became a cannibal because he couldn't buy enough to eat on his $20 a month pension.

A man in the Siberian coal-mining town of Kemerovo was arrested after killing and cutting up a friend, and using his flesh as the filling for pelmeni – a Russian version of ravioli. Any pelmeni he did not eat himself he sold in the local street market.

In March 1996 police in Sebastopol found the butchered remains of three members of the same family. In the kitchen of the apartment they discovered the internal organs of two victims in saucepans and, nearby on a plate, a freshly roasted piece of human meat.

During the winter of 1996/7, Vladimir Nikolayev, thirty-eight, was arrested for eating two people in the town of Novocheboksary. Nikolayev, a known criminal, was being arrested on an unrelated charge when police found a pan of roasted human meat on the stove and another in the oven. More body parts were found frozen in the snow on Nikolayev's balcony.

1998

In a supposed effort to rid Russia of the decadence of democracy, Sasha Spesivtsev, twenty-seven, killed and devoured at least 19 street children. Luring the starving children home with him, Spesivtsev killed and butchered them with the help of his mother.

1999

A man from the town of Perm Oblast took a package of meat he had purchased at the local street market to the police when his wife found remnants of human skin clinging to the flesh. The police traced the meat to two men who admitted killing and butchering their drinking partner. Before selling the meat on the street, they carved off the best cuts for themselves. One of the men's mothers cooked it up and shared it with the lads. The men insisted they only did it because of the high cost of normal meat.

In the semi-autonomous state of Kyargystan, Nikoli Dzhurmongaliev was captured after having killed as many as 100 women, serving many of them to dinner guests. When arrested, Dzhurmongaliev pointed out that two women could provide enough good cuts to feed him for a week.

On New Year's Eve, 1999/2000, Alexander Zapiantsev from the industrial city of Chelabinsk, in the Ural Mountains, invited the entire population of his apartment building to a feast. The meat at the dinner came from Valdemar Suzik, one of Zapiantsev's drinking buddies.

2000

Anatoly Dolbyshev, from the Ural town of Berezniki, was arrested for having murdered a friend of his mother and sold the meat at a local street market.

2002

In the town of Manturovo, on the Volga, Valentina Dolbilina, a 36-year-old mother, and Vitaly Bezrodnov, a 26-year-old factory worker, were arrested for killing and eating one of their drinking partners. Dolbilina, Bezrodnov and three others had become nearly comatose when Bezrodnov decided he was hungry. Together, he and Dolbilina chose among their unconscious friends. After dispatching the tastiest-looking one with an axe, they hacked off 15lb of choice cuts and started frying them up. One of their companions, who had wandered off to bed, was aroused by the smell and came to join them, little realising that he was eating his own brother.

Police in the Ukrainian town of Zhytomyr arrested two men and a woman for killing and eating a suspected six people as part of a series of satanic rituals. They were caught while trying to extort a ransom from the family of one of their victims.

2003

On two separate occasions convicts in Russia's overcrowded prisons were caught killing and eating fellow inmates.

Andrei Maslich, twenty-four, held at a local prison in Barnual, was caught twice committing acts of cannibalism, later claiming he was just bored and wanted to visit Moscow, where he thought he would be sent for psychiatric examination if he ate someone.

In the Semipalatinsk prison in Kazakhstan, four convicts decided to eat the next new prisoner to come into their cell block. Later, they claimed they were motivated by newspaper articles describing cannibalism in prisons.

If the current spate of cannibalism in Russia results from the stress of economic and social collapse, does similar social stress produce the same phenomenon elsewhere, or are the Russian people particularly susceptible to eating each other? Certainly, Germany has undergone tremendous economic and social upheaval since the incorporation of East and West Germany into a single, political unit in the early 1990s. Has this experience caused a similar rise in cannibalism? According to German criminologist Rudolf Egg, who testified at the Armin Meiwes trial, 'There are several hundred people with cannibalistic tendencies in Germany alone, and many thousands around the world.' Obviously, this is only one man's opinion – but should it frighten us?

Before attempting to make sense of the apparently increasing rate of cannibalism in the world, the authors feel it necessary to point out that we are neither criminal psychologists nor psychiatrists; for those opinions we have drawn on the work of experts. We are, however, historians who are experienced in recognising general trends in society over a long period of time, and it is from this standpoint that we draw the conclusions below.

It should be evident from the case histories presented in the chapters of this book dealing with individual cannibals that certain, similar factors might have influenced the behaviour of some of our subjects. Certainly, the vast majority of those who lived recently enough to have undergone psychological examination would appear to have suffered from severe psychoses. It is equally evident that the majority of them had difficult relationships with their parents, particularly in the lack of a mother with whom they could bond properly. Even in the case of Issei Sagawa, who seemed to have a stable home life, many of his earliest years were spent in hospital, thus depriving him of the early bonding experience necessary to establish the ability to socialise properly.

It is frightening to note that even while this book was being written there were no fewer than two cases of cannibalism reported in England alone. On Wednesday, 16 March 2005 the *Sun* newspaper reported on the case of Peter Bryan, thirty-five, a violent substance abuser, convicted murderer and diagnosed schizophrenic who had recently been given leave to come and go as he pleased from the mental health ward at London's Newham General Hospital. In February, Bryan pleased to go. Hours later he murdered 43-year-old Brian Cherry with a hammer and screwdriver, chopped up his victim's body and cooked and ate his brain. When police arrived at Bryan's flat, he was still covered in Cherry's blood, calmly cooking up a second helping of his victim's brain. His only comment to police was, 'I ate his brain with butter. It was really nice. I would have done someone else if you hadn't come along. I wanted their souls.' Even when placed in custody, Bryan killed another inmate stating that he had wanted to eat him raw. Bryan's statements would later make it clear that there was a distinctly sexual element to the murders.

Only thirty-three days after the Bryant case hit the papers, on 19 April, the *Daily Mirror*'s cover story related the case of serial killer Mark Hobson, also thirty-five. Hobson, a drug-using alcoholic, who reportedly averaged 36 pints of lager a day, murdered his girlfriend, Claire Sanderson, with seventeen hammer blows to the head before luring her twin sister to a similar fate. The twin, Diane, was violently sexually assaulted as Hobson tore, and ate, numerous pieces of her flesh, mostly from her breasts. Before his capture, Hobson also murdered a couple in their eighties. Both of these cases make it clear that the perpetrators, while committing acts of cannibalism, were primarily violent psychotics with severe alcohol and drug problems. Whether or not they ever ate another human being, they are obviously dangerous individuals.

If, indeed, there is a rising tide of cannibalism – along with other severe forms of anti-social behaviour – at work in our world, is it possible that the increasing crush of overpopulation is playing a part in the phenomenon of social degeneration? Certainly laboratory experiments with mice have shown that when a rodent population, kept in a confined space, reaches critical mass, the creatures turn on each other exhibiting behavioural patterns not only of violence, but also of cannibalism. In addition to, and in conjunction with, the sheer crush of humanity is the breakdown of community, religious and family structures that traditionally helped keep anti-social behaviour in check. The censure of family, friends, neighbours and clergy has nearly disappeared in a society where job-related moves, excessive political correctness and mass migration of the economically deprived have permanently altered the make-up of cities and towns everywhere.

Whatever the cause of the increased awareness of cannibalism, it is inescapable that the nature of cannibalism itself is also changing. Thanks to the internet people like Armin Meiwes can locate their victims without exposing themselves to the danger of being caught while abducting an innocent passer-by. Using pseudonyms and phoney identities prospective internet cannibals can converse freely with like-minded people all over the world at the touch of a button. Where once such topics as eating human flesh would have made a social pariah of anyone who even suggested such a thing, the internet allows those with cannibalistic tendencies to create their own little world far from the censorious eyes of society, and nearly beyond the reach of the law.

Criminologist Rudolf Egg believes there are thousands of cannibals and cannibal wannabes out there looking for a way to put their desires, urges and fantasies into practice. 'Cannibalism', says Egg, 'has always been around, but the internet reinforces the phenomenon. You can be in contact with the whole world and do it anonymously.'

In addition to this new means for the deranged, including cannibals, to find one another, and their willing victims, while hiding from society in general, there seems to be a change in both the physical and mental make-up of cannibals. The only known historical female cannibal (with the exception of the semi-legendary female members of the Sawney Beane clan) is Margery Lovett, whose story appears in chapter six of this book. Recently, however, some women have adopted the ways of the flesh eater. In addition to the four Russian women mentioned in the brief accounts given above, there is the case of Anna Zimmerman, a 26-year-old German mother of two. In 1981 Anna killed and butchered her boyfriend, froze the human cutlets and slowly shared them with her children. One is forced to wonder whether these instances are simply aberrations in an aberrant trend, or if women are staking a claim to equality among cannibals?

The case of Marc Sappington also presents new and disturbing trends in the make-up of the cannibal. Sappington's psychological profile seems to bear no resemblance to any known guideline which psychiatrists, criminal psychologists and police profilers traditionally relied on to build up a psychological picture of suspected cannibals. Again we are forced to ask, is this a trend or simply a one-off aberration?

It would be comforting to be able to present a tidy summation at this point, but the fact is, there is nothing tidy about cannibalism. What we can conclude is that in a world where every nasty act, every abominable crime, is pounced on by a gloating news media and trumpeted instantly around the world, things which were once swept conveniently under the carpet as socially unacceptable have become the daily diet of every scaremonger, opportunistic politician and paparazzo on the planet. But as to whether or not there really are more cannibals among us than there used to be, we are forced to conclude that the answer is 'yes'.

What leads us to this conclusion? Simple. There are more people on the planet than there used to be. In 1900 the population of the USA was 75 million; it now stands at 270 million. In 1950 the global population was about 4 billion people, now it is over 6 billion. If, as it appears, there really are more people eating their neighbours, it is probably only true because there are more people and we are more aware of world events than ever before. Still, the incidence of dangerous psychotics and dangerous criminals in society is worthy of our concern. If there is a lesson to be learned from all this, we have not been able to determine what it might be. What we do know is that, like so many sad trends that have carried over into the twenty-first century, man's inhumanity to man in general, and cannibalism specifically, are both very real and very frightening.

Notes on Sources

Chapter One

A debt of gratitude to all the authors who have recorded the legendary cannibals of the past, present and future, including Herodotus, Homer, Jonathan Swift, Daniel Defoe, E.A. Poe and the greatest chronicler of classical mythology, Thomas Bulfinch. Thanks too to the entire Monty Python troupe.

Chapter Two

We are endlessly grateful for the scholarly work and published articles concerning the Anasazi and other early cultures carried out by Christy Turner, Paola Villa, Douglas Preston, Brian Billman and others.

Chapter Three

A debt of gratitude beyond measure is due to the intrepid explorers and missionaries whose bravery and concise records and diaries made this chapter possible. They include – but are not limited to: H.W. Walker, Jens Bjerre, Alfred St Johnston, A.H. Keane, Russell Wallace, H.W. Bates, Algot Lange and Prof. A.P. Elkin.

Chapter Four

A special thanks to Dr Maynard Felix and Alexandre Dumas for their accounts of disasters at sea, and to Mick Angelo for his concise chronicles of Japanese atrocities during World War II.

Chapter Five

We acknowledge Sabine Baring-Gould and Ronald Holmes, for information provided in their books *The Book of Werewolves* and

Legend of Sawney Bean (respectively) for background information on the Beane legend. Also to R.H.J. Urquhart at http://ayrshirehistory.org for dispelling the myth.

Chapter Six

We are indebted to author Peter Haining for *Sweeney Todd: The Real Story*, the most in-depth study of Todd yet undertaken.

Chapter Seven

For his compelling work on Alfred Packer, to R.W. Fenwick, author of *Alfred Packer: The True Story of the Man-Eater*, we acknowledge a debt of gratitude. Our thanks also to the governments of the State of Colorado and the town of Littleton, Colorado for providing access to historical documents and photos of Alf Packer. We also appreciate the insights of Jeff Hoskin at www.concours.org.

Chapter Eight

For information on Karl Denke, we acknowledge Daniel Korn, Mark Radice and Charlie Hawes found in their book *Cannibal: The History of the People Eaters*. For information on Georg Grossman, we also acknowledge Brian Mariner and his work *Cannibalism: The Last Taboo*. Our thanks also to Alan Denke for his translation of articles from the *Warsaw Gazette*.

Chapter Nine

We are indebted to Harold Schechter for his thorough and insightful book *Deranged*, and also to Marilyn Bardsley for her in-depth articles on Albert Fish at www.crimelibrary.

Chapter Ten

For the general story of Ottis Toole and Henry Lucas we drew heavily on the work of Dr Joel Norris, entitled simply *Henry Lee Lucas*. Additional material was provided by Patrick Bellamy in his articles at www.crimelibrary. Additional information on Ottis Toole came from information found at www.mayhem.net.

Chapter Eleven

Our primary source for information on Ed Gein was *The Shocking Story of Ed Gein, The Original Psycho*, by Harlod Schechter. A special thanks to bbqshackowner, the webmaster of www.geocities for his archive of now rare 'Geiner' jokes.

Chapter Twelve

We acknowledge our primary sources of information on André Chikatilo as Richard Lourie's *Hunting the Devil* and Brian Marriner's *Cannibalism: The Last Taboo*. Additional important information was provided by www.crimelibrary.

Chapter Thirteen

The main facts on Jeffrey Dahmer were gleaned from Edward Baumann's book, *Step into My Parlor*. Quotations and insights from Dahmer's father, Lionel Dahmer, came from Mr Dahmer's book *A Father's Story*. Police record details came from the database at www.nndb.com and extracts from Jeffrey Dahmer's confession came from www.tornadohills.com.

Chapter Fourteen

We gratefully acknowledge Daniel Korn, Mark Radice and Charlie Hawes' book *Cannibal: The History of the People Eaters* and www.crimelibrary as providing essential information on Iessei Sagawa. English translations of excerpts from Sagawa's book, *In the Fog*, came from www.answers.com (a part of Wikipedia) and Nicolas Claux's website nicoclaux.free.fr.

Chapter Fifteen

Our thanks to Adrian Havill for his book on Hadden Clark, *Born Evil*, and to Paul Duggan and Veronica Jennings for their series of articles on Clark written for the *Washington Post* and archived on the *Post*'s website.

Chapter Sixteen

Gratitude is owed to author Jack Apsche for his biography of Gary Heidnik, *Probing the Mind of a Serial Killer*, to the *Pittsburgh Post Gazette*'s online morgue and their coverage of the Heidnik story, and to www.crimelibrary for additional information.

Chapter Seventeen

Thanks to David Lohr and his series of articles on Nico Claux at www.crimelibrary, and to www.mansonfamily picnic for Claux's recipies and to www.francesfarmersrevenge for the interview with Claux. Thanks, too, to Mr Claux for his co-operation.

Chapter Eighteen

Primary souces of information on the Armin Meiwes case were the series of articles found at www.gmax with additional background information from www.wikipedia.

Chapter Nineteen

For information on Marc Sappington, we acknowledge the articles which appeared in the *Kansas City Star* and are archived on their website. Additional important background information came from www.crimelibrary.com

Chapter Twenty

Special thanks for information on trends in cannibalism go to www.crimelibrary.com, and to the University of Texas conferences website. Thanks too, to the *Sun* and the *Daily Mirror* for coverage of current cases of cannibalism in the UK.

Bibliography

1: A Word of Warning

Bulfinch, Thomas, *Bulfinch's Mythology*, Laurel Classics, 1959

Chapman, Graham, Cleese, John, Gilliam, Terry, Idle, Eric, Jones, Terry, Palin, Michael, *The Complete Monty Python Scripts*, Methuen, London, 1989

Defoe, Daniel, *Robinson Crusoe*, Dover, New York, 1998

Harris, Thomas, *Silence of the Lambs*, St Martins Press, New York, 1991

Herodotus, *The Histories*, Norton, 1992

Holy Bible, World Syndicate Publishing, Cleveland, Ohio, 1938

Homer, *The Odyssey*, Penguin Classics, London, 2003

Murphy, E.M. and Mallory, J.P., 'Herodotus and the Cannibals', *Antiquity*, vol. 74, June 2000

Swift, Jonathan, *A Modest Proposal and Other Satirical Works*, Dover, New York, 1996

2: Ancient Origins

Billman, Brian, et al., 'Cannibalism, Warfare and Drought in the Mesa Verde Region during the Twelfth Century AD', *American Antiquity*, vol. 65, no. 1, 2000

Dallas Morning News, 1 June 2001

Diamond, Jared, 'Archaeology: Talk of Cannibalism', *Nature*, 7 September 2000

Fernandez-Jalvo, Yolanda, 'Human Cannibalism in the early Pleistocene of Europe', *Journal of Human Evolution*, no. 37, 1999

James, E.O., *Origins of Sacrifice*, John Murray, 1933

Japan Times, 13 July 1999, Cart, Juli, 'Did Cannibalism Kill Anasazi Civilization?'

Korn, Daniel, Radice, Mark and Hawes, Charlie, *Cannibal: The History of the People Eaters*, Channel 4 Books/Pan Macmillan, 2002

Preston, Douglas, 'Cannibals of the Canyon', *New Yorker*, 30 November 1998

Tannahill, Reay, *Flesh and Blood*, Abacus Books, London, 1976

Turner, Christy G., 'Cannibalism in Chaco Canyon', *American Journal of Physical Anthropology*, no. 91, 1993

Verrengia, Joseph B., 'Evidence Shows Cannibalism by Ancient Indians', *Nature*, September 2000

Villa, Paola, 'Cannibalism in the Neolithic', *Science*, vol. 233, 23 July 1986

Villa, Paola, 'Cannibalism in Prehistoric Europe', *Evolutionary Anthropology*, vol. 1, no. 3, 1992

http://nandotimes.com

http://sipapu.ucsb.edu/html/faq.html

3: Institutionalised Cannibalism

Angelo, Mick, *Man Eats Man: The Story of Cannibalism*, Jupiter, London, 1979

Baker, John R., *Race*, Oxford University Press, 1974

Bates, H.W., *The Naturalist on the Amazon*, John Murray, 1863

Bentley, Revd W. Holman (Baptist Missionary Society), *Pioneering on the Congo*, TRS, 1900 (2 vols)

Bjerre, Jens, *The Last Cannibals*, Michael Joseph, London, 1956

Chalmers, Revd James, *Life and Work in New Guinea*, RTS, 1895

Diaz, Bernal, *The Conquest of New Spain*, Harmondsworth, 1963

Elkin, Prof. A.P., *The Australian Aborigines*, Angus & Robertson, 1938

Gwyther, J., *Captain Cook and the South Pacific*, Houghton Mifflin, Boston, 1954

Harris, Marvin, *Cannibals and Kings: The Origins of Cultures*, Glasgow, 1978

Hitt, Russell T., *Cannibal Valley*, Hodder & Stoughton, New York, 1963

Horne, G. and Aiston, G., *Savage Life in Central Australia*, Macmillan, London, 1924

James, E.O., *Origins of Sacrifice*, John Murray, 1933

Keane, A.H. FRGS, *South America*, no pub, London, 1909

Korn, Daniel, Radice, Mark and Hawes, Charlie, *Cannibal: The History of the People Eaters*, Channel 4 Books/Pan Macmillan, London, 2002

Lange, Algot, *In the Amazon Jungle*, Putnam, New York, 1912

Langford-Hinde, Sidney, *The Fall of the Congo Arabs*, Methuen, 1897

Marriner, Brian, *Cannibalism: The Last Taboo!*, Senate, Teddington, Middlesex, 1997

Maynard, Dr Felix and Dumas, Alexandre, *The Whalers*, Hutchinson, 1937

Murray, Lt Gov. J.H.P., *Papua, or British New Guinea*, Faber Unwin, London, 1912

Rice, A.P., in *The American Antiquarian*, vol. XXXII, 1910

Roscoe, John, *The Bagesu and Other Tribes of the Uganda Protectorate*, The Royal Society, London, 1924

St Johnston, Alfred, *Traveller in the Fiji Islands: Camping among Cannibals*, Macmillan, London, 1883

Seligmann, C.G., *The Melanesians of British New Guinea*, Cambridge University Press, 1910

Spence, Basil, in *Sudan Notes and Records*, vol. III, no. 4, December 1920

Tacitus, *The Annals of Imperial Rome*, Penguin Classics, London, 1951

Tannahill, Reay, *Flesh and Blood*, Abacus Books, London, 1976

Walker, H.W., FRGS, *Wanderings among South Sea Savages*, Witherby, 1909

Wallace, A. Russell, *Travels on the Amazon*, Ward Lock, 1853

Watsford, Revd John, *Ono Fiji*, private diary, unpublished, 6 November 1846

Williams, F.E., *Orikaiva Society*, Clarendon Press, Oxford, 1930

http://www.skeptics.com.au/journal/canib-aborig.htm

http://wwwmcc.murdoch.edu.au/ReadingRoom/impi/articles/can_is
   m.html
http://www.convictcreations.com/history/escapes.htm

4: Cannibalism in extremis

Angelo, Mick, *Man Eats Man: The Story of Cannibalism*, Jupiter
   Books, London, 1979
Baker, John R., *Race*, Oxford University Press, 1974
Marriner, Brian, *Cannibalism: The Last Taboo!*, Senate, Teddington,
   Middlesex, 1997
Maynard, Dr Felix and Dumas, Alexandre, *The Whalers*, Hutchinson,
   1937
Read, Piers Paul, *Alive: The Story of the Andes Survivors*, Secker &
   Warburg, 1974

5: Sawney Beane

Baring-Gould, Sabine, *The Book of Werewolves*, Senate, Teddington,
   Middlesex, 1995
Holmes, Ronald, *Legend of Sawney Bean*, Frederick Muller, London,
   1975
Johnson, Capt. Charles, *A General and True History of the Lives and
   Sections of the Most Famous Highwaymen, Murderers, Street-
   Robbers, &c.*, London, 1734
Nicholson, John, *Historical and Traditional Tales Connected with the
   South of Scotland*, London, 1843
Tannahill, Reay, *Flesh and Blood*, Abacus Books, London, 1976

http://www.ayrshirehistory.org.uk/sawney/myth.htm
http://www.geo.ed.ac.uk/scotgaz/people/famousfirst1131.html
http://www.tartans.com/articles/famscots/sawneybean.html
http://www.seanachaidh.org/sawney.htm

6: Margery Lovett and Sweeney Todd

Haining, Peter, *Sweeney Todd: The Real Story*, Barnes & Noble, New
   York, 1993

Marriner, Brian, *Cannibalism: The Last Taboo!*, Senate, Teddington, Middlesex, 1997

Prest, Thomas Peckett, *The Story of Pearls: The Barber of Fleet Street, A Domestic Romance*, no pub., London, 1850

http://www.crimezzz.net/serialkiller_index/serienkiller_t.htm

http://www.crimelibrary.com/serial_killers/weird/todd/todd_9.html?sect=3

7: Alfred Packer

Fenwick, R.W., *Alfred Packer – the True Story of the Man-eater*, Denver Post, Denver, 1963

Gantt, Paul H., *The Case of Alfred Packer, the Man-eater*, University of Denver Press, Denver, 1952

Kushner, Ervan F., *Alfred G. Packer, Cannibal! Victim?*, Platte'n Press, Frederick, Colorado, 1980

Marriner, Brian, *Cannibalism: The Last Taboo!*, Senate, Teddington, Middlesex, 1997

Scientific Sleuthing Inc., *Alfred G. Packer Exhumation Project, Lake City, Colorado, 17 July 1989*, George Washington University Press, Washington, DC, 1989

Stimson, George P., *The Strange Case of Alfred Packer*, Literary Club, Cincinatti, Ohio, 1945

http://www.concours.org/rtd-color.html

http://www.colorado.gov/dpa/doit/archives/pen/packer/index.htm#chrono

http://www.littletongov.org/history/biographies/packer.asp

8: Karl Denke and Georg Grossman

Angelo, Mick, *Man Eats Man: The Story of Cannibalism*, Jupiter Books, London, 1979

Korn, Daniel, Radice, Mark and Hawes, Charlie, *Cannibal: The History of the People Eaters*, Channel Four Books/Pan Macmillan, London, 2001

Marriner, Brian, *Cannibalism: The Last Taboo!*, Senate, Teddington, Middlesex, 1997

Polish Word, 2 August 1999

Warsaw Gazette, 30 July 1999

http://www.denke.org/forum/_articles/00000011.htm

http://lynxstarquette.tripod.com/id10.html

http://www.denke.org/stowoe.htm

http://www.denke.org/karldenke.htm

9: Albert Fish

Heimer, Mel, *The Cannibal*, Pinnacle Books, New York, 1971

Korn, Daniel, Radice, Mark and Hawes, Charlie, *Cannibal: The History of the People Eaters*, Channel Four Books/Pan Macmillan, London, 2001

Marriner, Brian, *Cannibalism: The Last Taboo!*, Senate, Teddington, Middlesex, 1997

Martingale, Moria, *Cannibal Killers*, St Martins Paperbacks, New York, 1993

Schechter, Harold, *Deranged*, Pocket Books, New York, 1990

Schechter, Harold and Everitt, David, *The A–Z Encyclopedia of Serial Killers*, Pocket Books, New York, 1996

Wertham, Dr Fredric, *The Show of Violence*, Doubleday, New York, 1949

http://www.crimelibrary.com/serial_killers/notorious/fish/gracie_1.html

10: Ottis Toole and Henry Lee Lucas

Call, Max, *Hand of Death*, Prescott Press, 1985

Norris, Dr Joel, *Henry Lee Lucas*, Kennsington Publishing, New York, 1991

Wilson, Colin, *The Giant Book of Serial Killers*, The Book Company, 1996

http://members.tripod.com/ahrens/serial/lucas.htm
http://www.crimelibrary.com/serial_killers/predators/lucas/confess_
    1.html
http://www.mayhem.net/Crime/lucas.html
http://www.arminm.com/ottis_otoole.htm
http://www.carpenoctem.tv/killers/lucas.html
http://crimemagazine.com/lucas.htm
http://www.whale.to/b/toole.html

11: Ed Gein

Marriner, Brian, *Cannibalism: The Last Taboo!*, Senate, Teddington,
    Middlesex, 1997
Schechter, Harold, *Deviant: The Shocking True Story of Ed Gein, the
    Original Psycho*, Pocket Books, New York, 1998
Woods, Paul Anthony, *Ed Gein: Psycho*, St Martins/Griffin, New
    York, 1995

http://www.crimelibrary.com/gein/geinmain.htm
http://www.houseofhorrors.com/gein.htm
http://www.geocities.com//bbqshackowner/LBS-EdGein.html
http://www.prairieghosts.com/ed_gein.html

12: André Chikatilo

Cullen, Robert, *The Killer Department: Detective Viktor Burakov's Eight-
    year Hunt for the Most Savage Serial Killer in Russian History*,
    Pantheon Books, New York, 1993
Korn, Daniel, Radice, Mark and Hawes, Charlie, *Cannibal: The
    History of the People Eaters*, Channel 4/Pan Macmillan, London,
    2002
Krivich, Mikhail and Ol'gin, Ol'gert, *Comrade Chikatilo: The
    Psychopathology of Russia's Notorious Serial Killer*, Barricade
    Books, Fort Lee, New Jersey, 1993
Lourie, Richard, *Hunting the Devil: The Pursuit, Capture and Confession
    of the Most Savage Serial Killer in History*, HarperCollins, New
    York, 1993

Marriner, Brian, *Cannibalism: The Last Taboo!*, Senate, Teddington, Middlesex, 1997

Martingale, Moira, *Cannibal Killers: The History of Impossible Murders*, Carroll & Graf, New York, 1993

Matthews, Owen, *Newsweek*, 25 January 1999

Tannahill, Reay, *Flesh and Blood*, Abacus Books, London, 1976

http://www.crimelibrary.com/serial_killers/notorious/chikatilo/coat_1.html

http://www.anoca.org/he/police/andrei_chikatilo.html

13: Jeffrey Dahmer

Baumann, Edward, *Step into My Parlor: The Chilling Story of Serial Killer Jeffrey Dahmer*, Bonus Books, Santa Monica, California, 1991

Dahmer, Lionel, *A Father's Story*, William Morrow & Co., New York, 1994

Davis, Don, *Milwaukee Murders, Nightmare in Apartment 213: The True Story*, St Martins Paperbacks, New York, 1995

Korn, Daniel, Radice, Mark and Hawes, Charlie, *Cannibal: The History of the People Eaters*, Channel 4/Pan Macmillan, London, 2002

Martingale, Moira, *Cannibal Killers*, St Martins Paperbacks, New York, 1993

Schwartz, Anne E., *The Man Who Could Not Kill Enough; The Secret Murders of Milwaukee's Jeffrey Dahmer*, Book Club Associates/Birch Lane Press, New York, 1992

Tannahill, Reay, *Flesh and Blood*, Abacus Books, London, 1976

Tithecott, Richard, *Of Men and Monsters: Jeffrey Dahmer and the Construction of the Serial Killer*, University of Wisconsin, 1999

http://www.nndb.com/people/959/000031866/

http://www.rotten.com/library/bio/crime/serial-killers/jeffrey-dahmer/

http://www.bbc.co.uk/crime/caseclosed/dahmer1.shtml

http://www.tornadohills.com/dahmer/life.htm

http://en.wikipedia.org/wiki/Jeffrey_Dahmer
http://www.crimelibrary.com/serial_killers/notorious/dahmer/train_3.html
http://serial-killers.virtualave.net/dahmer.htm

14: Issei Sagawa

Korn, Daniel, Radice, Mark and Hawes, Charlie, *Cannibal: The History of the People Eaters*, Channel 4/Pan Macmillan, London, 2002

Marriner, Brian, *Cannibalism: The Last Taboo!*, Senate, Teddington, Middlesex, 1997

Tannahill, Reay, *Flesh and Blood*, Abacus Books, London, 1976

http://iml.jou.ufl.edu/projects/Spring03/Rawlins/sagarrest.htm
http://www.answers.com/topic/issei-sagawa
http://nicoclaux.free.fr/sagawa/sagawaconf.htm
http://nicoclaux.free.fr/sagawa/sagawamain.htm
http://www.shotsmag.co.uk/SHOTS%2016/Cannibal/cannibal.htm
http://www.crimelibrary.com/serial_killers/weird/sagawa/1.html
http://www.arminm.com/issei_sagawa.htm

15: Hadden and Bradfield Clark

Havill, Adrian, *Born Evil: A True Story of Cannibalism and Serial Murder*, St Martins True Crime, New York, 2001

Washington Times, 1992, courtesy American Cybercasting Corporation

http://www.washingtonpost.com/wp-srv/local/longterm/library/dorr/dorr111592.htm
http://www.crimelibrary.com/serial_killers/weird/clark/index_1.html
http://www.mayhem.net/Crime/haddenclark.html

16: Gary Heidnik

Apsche, Jack, *Probing the Mind of a Serial Killer*, International Information Association, Oak Ridge, Tennessee, 1993

Cyriax, Oliver, *Crime – An Encyclopedia*, Trafalgar Square Publishing, London, 1996

Douglas, John E. and Olshaker, Mark, *Obsession*, Pocket Books, New York, 1998

Englade, Ken, *Cellar of Horror*, St Martins Press, New York, 1992

Heidnik, Gary M., In the Court of Common Pleas, First Judicial District of Pennyslvania, Criminal Trial Division: Commonwealth vs. Gary Heidnik., court of Common Pleas: Pennsylvania, 1988

Pittsburgh Post Gazette, News website – www.postgazette.com

http://www.arminm.com/gary_michael_heidnic.htm
http://www.crimelibrary.com/serial_killers/weird/heidnik/index_1.html
http://www.missstrict.net/heidnik.html
http://www.rotten.com/library/bio/crime/serial-killers/gary-heidnik
http://www.geocities.com/schoolgirlsadist/heidnik.html
http://www.bizarremag.com/true_crime.php?id=264

17: Nicolas Claux

http://www.mansonfamilypicnic.com/cook.htm
http://www.francesfarmersrevenge.com/stuff/serialkillers/nicint.htm
http://www.crimelibrary.com/serial_killers/weird/nico_claux/index.html

18: Armin Meiwes

http://www.cbc.ca/stories/2004/01/30/cannibal040130
http://www.guardian.co.uk/germany/article/0,2763,1099477,00.html
http://www.theage.com.au/articles/2004/01/14/1073877901829.html?oneclick+true
http://www.4law.co.il/cann19104.htm
http://www.gmax.co.za/look04/01/19-germany.html
http://www.horror-report.com/february04/cannibal.html
http://en.wikipedia.org/wiki/S/b/Armin_Meiwes
http://www.crimelibrary.com/criminal_mind/psychology/cannibalism/9.html?sect=29

http://www.francesfarmersrevenge.com/stuff/serialkillers/meiwes.
htm

http://news.bbc.co.uk/2/hi/europe/3286721.stm

19: Marc Sappington

http://www.onemissingperson.org/news/KS-SEP-03-2004-0653e-
Kansas-man-gets-life-for-murder--cannibalism.html

http://www.crimelibrary.com/serial_killers/weird/sappington/1.html

http://www.stuffmagazine.com/articles/index.aspx?id=799

http://www.kansascity.com/mld/kansascity/4069230.htm

http://www.theage.com.au/articles/2003/08/06/1060064226437.
html?oneclick=true

20: Rising Tide

Daily Mirror (north-west edition), Tuesday, 19 April 2005

Korn, Daniel, Radice, Mark and Hawes, Charlie, *Cannibal: The History of the People Eaters*, Channel 4/Pan Macmillan, London, 2002

Marriner, Brian, *Cannibalism: The Last Taboo!*, Senate, Teddington, Middlesex, 1997

Rykovtseva, Yelena, 'Cannibals Return to Russia: Human Flesh Being Sold on Streets', *Moscow News*, no. 34, 25 August–1 September 1996

Sun, Wednesday, 16 March 2005

http://www.crimelibrary.com/criminal_mind/psychology/cannibalis
m/6.html?sect=19

http://www.utexas.edu/conferences/africa/ads/804.html

Index